Performing Gender, Place, and Emotion in Music

Eastman/Rochester Studies in Ethnomusicology

Ellen Koskoff, Series Editor
Eastman School of Music
(ISSN: 2161-0290)

Burma's Pop Music Industry:
Creators, Distributors, Censors
Heather MacLachlan

Yorùbá Music in the Twentieth Century:
Identity, Agency and Performance Practice
Bode Omojola

Javanese Gamelan and the West
Sumarsam

Gender in Chinese Music
Edited by Rachel Harris, Rowan Pease, and Shzr Ee Tan

Performing Gender, Place, and Emotion in Music:
Global Perspectives
Edited by Fiona Magowan and Louise Wrazen

Performing Gender, Place, and Emotion in Music

Global Perspectives

Edited by Fiona Magowan
and Louise Wrazen

UNIVERSITY OF ROCHESTER PRESS

Copyright © 2013 by the Editors and Contributors

All Rights Reserved. Except as permitted under current legislation, no part of this work may be photocopied, stored in a retrieval system, published, performed in public, adapted, broadcast, transmitted, recorded, or reproduced in any form or by any means, without the prior permission of the copyright owner.

First published 2013
Transferred to digital printing and reprinted in paperback 2015

University of Rochester Press
668 Mt. Hope Avenue, Rochester, NY 14620, USA
www.urpress.com
and Boydell & Brewer Limited
PO Box 9, Woodbridge, Suffolk IP12 3DF, UK
www.boydellandbrewer.com

hardcover ISBN-13: 978-1-58046-464-2
paperback ISBN-13: 978-1-58046-543-4
ISSN: 2161-0290

Library of Congress Cataloging-in-Publication Data

Performing gender, place, and emotion in music : global perspectives / edited by Fiona Magowan and Louise Wrazen.
    pages cm — (Eastman/Rochester studies in ethnomusicology, ISSN 2161-0290 ; v. 5)
   Includes bibliographical references and index.
   ISBN 978-1-58046-464-2 (hardcover : alkaline paper) 1. Music—Performance—Psychological aspects. 2. Gender identity in music. 3. Emotions in music. I. Magowan, Fiona, editor. II. Wrazen, Louise Josepha, 1956– editor. III. Series: Eastman/Rochester studies in ethnomusicology ; v. 5.
   ML3830.P373 2013
   780.9—dc23

2013024098

A catalogue record for this title is available from the British Library.

This publication is printed on acid-free paper.
Printed in the United States of America

Contents

Acknowledgments   vii

Introduction: Musical Intersections, Embodiments, and Emplacements   1
   Fiona Magowan and Louise Wrazen

Part One: Landscape and Emotion

1. Engendering Emotion and the Environment in Vietnamese Music and Ritual   17
   Barley Norton

2. Gendering Emotional Connections to the Balinese Landscape: Exploring Children's Roles in a Barong Performance   38
   Jonathan McIntosh

3. Performing Emotion, Embodying Country in Australian Aboriginal Ritual   63
   Fiona Magowan

Part Two: Memory and Attachment

4. Christian Choral Singing in Aboriginal Australia: Gendered Absence, Emotion, and Place   85
   Muriel Swijghuisen Reigersberg

5. Transforming the Singing Body: Exploring Musical Narratives of Gender and Place in East Bavaria   109
   Sara R. Walmsley-Pledl

6. A Place of Her Own: Gendered Singing in Poland's Tatras   127
   Louise Wrazen

Part Three: Nationalism and Indigeneity

7. Singing the Contentions of Place: Korean Singers of the Heart and Soul of Japan   147
   Christine R. Yano

| 8 | "In Our Foremothers' Arms": Goddesses, Feminism, and the Politics of Emotion in Sámi Songs
Tina K. Ramnarine | 162 |

Afterword   185
Beverley Diamond

Selected Bibliography   195

List of Contributors   201

Index   203

Acknowledgments

This volume has had a long gestation period since its conception. It was originally inspired by suggestions for a gender and music study group conference panel at the 2007 International Council of Traditional Music (ICTM) in Vienna. This evolved into a plenary at this Thirty-Ninth ICTM World Conference. Contributors to the volume were asked to take up some of the issues raised in the ensuing conference debate. Since then, these issues have also been enhanced by complementary perspectives from anthropology, gender studies, musicology, cultural geography, music psychology, and philosophy. Thus, the diversity and richness of the contributions illustrate multiple ways in which debates around these themes cross over and diverge within and between disciplines.

As editors, we would like to thank the contributors for their enthusiasm and lively engagement with the issues, as well as for their patience in the revising and publishing stages of the volume. Their willingness to stay with the project across the time frame is testament to the significance of the issues they raise for ethnomusicology, which speak to changing perspectives around these contemporary concerns.

We are very grateful to two anonymous reviewers for their perceptive comments and to Ellen Koskoff, series editor, and Ryan Peterson, managing editor, for their support and assistance in the preparation of this volume. We would like to thank Monique Giroux, Sija Tsai, and Jennifer Taylor for assistance with editorial details. We also thank Angela Snieder for the preparation of maps, and Lillian Heinson and James Davis for the conversion of photographs. The index was compiled by Dave Prout. The cover design was prepared by David Drummond.

Introduction

Musical Intersections, Embodiments, and Emplacements

Fiona Magowan and Louise Wrazen

The following ethnographic accounts of music and dance from Europe, Southeast Asia, and Australasia examine how performances of gender, place, and emotion intersect. Ethnomusicology and anthropology have long recognized the connections between these aspects of performance, yet they are seldom analyzed together. Most recent studies have examined music in relation to either gender, place, or emotion. Instead of addressing each field of inquiry as an individual lens through which to understand musical practices, our aim is to explore the ways in which the three elements overlap. Our volume proposes that the intersections of gender, place, and emotion generate an interplay of performative issues, rather than discrete, bounded areas of inquiry.

The studies presented here reveal how the gendered practices of music making are intimately shaped by performers' emotional engagements with place. In addition, because places feed into performers' imaginations, affecting gendered musical meanings and experiences, contributors to this volume show how these elements of performance—gender, place, and emotion—intertwine in a "relationship of circularity."[1] "Circularity" in this sense refers to a multilayered approach in which each element implicates the others in a coconstitutive relationship. The process is examined from different regions around the globe, as contributors address two key questions: How are aesthetic, emotional, and imagined relations between performers and places embodied musically? And in what ways is the performance of emotion gendered across quotidian, ritual, and staged events?

The book is divided into three parts, each elaborating on gender, place, and emotion as interrelated facets of music making. The first part addresses how gender influences performers' emotional engagements with landscapes; the second part considers how emotional attachments to place are variously affirmed or contested through singing; and the third part reveals how these attachments to place provide catalysts for national performances of solidarity and cultural revival. Together the three sections develop themes related to gender as musical performance, emotional resonance in performance, and the dynamics of performative environments, which we discuss here before turning to an overview of the chapters themselves.

Gender as Musical Performance

Through the study of gender, place, and emotion in music, our contributors marshal a new generation or wave of scholarship built on the histories and diverse theoretical foundations of the well-established domain of gender research.[2] In their landmark volume, Pirkko Moisala and Beverley Diamond observe that the publications of the 1990s reveal "how difficult it has been to articulate a theoretical agenda" around music and gender.[3] More recently, Ellen Koskoff notes that "we in ethnomusicology have not crystallized our gendered stories into a 'grand' or 'field' theory," and she has articulated a general skepticism toward the potential effectiveness of making any "grand theories about anything for all musical cultures."[4] As the contributors to this volume reflect on the dynamics of gender performativity, their theoretical contributions also avoid "a homogeneous approach to gender studies," preferring instead a "range of positioning."[5] Thus, it is not our intention to create an overarching theory of gender in relation to music, place, and emotion per se but to address (as Marcia Herndon argues) the ongoing need for "the inclusion of gender as an essential aspect of all ethnomusicological research."[6] The authors of these essays develop a thematic agenda for the cross-cultural comparison of gendered values in music making, through ways of being masculine and feminine as organizing principles of performative action.

Regarding this first theoretical strand of the volume, our contributors examine how the gendered dynamics of performance influence performers' emotional engagements with their natural and social environments. In doing so, they provide new perspectives on how to "situate gender in its proper place as a major factor in musical exegesis and analysis."[7] They illustrate how gendered experiences are mediated between performers and listeners as men and women engage emotionally in the real and imagined worlds in which they perform. Music making is thus not just about being male or female but it is also about becoming men or women and understanding their spheres of participation and senses of belonging in the world. By singing and dancing, performers evoke different kinds of emotional bonds among themselves and with their audiences, creating varied senses of interdependency, intimacy, and reciprocity. Some contributors, for example, show how singers' repertoires enable audiences to relate to the sentiments and politics of belonging to a place. Singers invite listeners to participate in a sense of musical intimacy through the affective power of songs, lyrics, and meanings which, in turn, gives rise to sentiments of identity, place, and nation. This kind of musical intimacy is generated by four processes: mutuality (in terms of a shared sense of interdependency), belonging (as an affiliation to people and places), meaning making (through gendered, ethnic, political, national, and other identifications), and performative competency (as expressed through musical relations, skills, and insights achieved through the course of performing).[8] Musical intimacy can also extend beyond a particular performance context, influencing the wider popularity of a musical genre and its political impact upon public life. As mass audiences come to relate to the politics and personae of particular male and female performers, these singers may become catalysts of a broader "cultural intimacy" as they shape audiences' views about a nation or region through their popular appeal.[9] Issues of musical and cultural intimacy in performance, therefore, speak to changing ideas of gender and embodiment in current music scholarship.

Emotional Resonance in Performance

The second key strand in our volume is the analysis of emotion in shaping men's and women's roles in and experiences of music making. Authors explore how the gender dimensions of musical intimacy arise as learned and intensely emotional practices of intersubjectivity.[10] Thus, they analyze how music making is a means of disciplining mind and body through gendered experiences, representations, and significations. A key problem in the neuroscientific study of emotion, however, is that the experience of music (i.e., how performers or audiences feel) and the emotions that are intended to be generated by musical production may not correspond, since these are two different kinds of processes.[11] Feelings have generally been distinguished from emotions on the basis that the latter entail conscious judgments as a result of having particular sensations.[12] Emotional meaning for an individual thus arises, in part, from the analysis of sensations or feelings. This creates a dilemma for analysts who wish to understand how feelings are shared with others within particular performance contexts. Recognizing that a key conundrum for scholars working in cross-cultural contexts has been how to approach "the translation of emotion concepts and the social processes surrounding their use," authors examine the evocation of emotion as a dialectical relationship among music making, gender, and environment.[13] They avoid trying to pin down certain emotions to cultural terms that describe what others say about how they feel. Instead, they address Ruth Finnegan's call for "in-depth research exploring the complex and subtle intertwining of cultural expectation, specific setting, and individually embodied practice."[14] Indeed, as Ramon Pelinski has argued, even if the feelings evoked by a performer seem to mirror those of a listener, one can never know if the experience is shared between the two.[15]

Some scholars have shown how discourses of "emotion-talk" might bridge interpretive problems between meaning and feeling. They have asserted that emotions (derived from bodily feelings) pertain to cultural categories, and can therefore be performed and analyzed in culturally informed, gender-specific ways.[16] As Denis Dutton notes, emotional expression in performance is a matter of "technical mastery and of feeling—of 'meaning it.'"[17] Whether performing informally or formally, onstage or in ritual, participants and audiences can variously perpetuate or contest meanings and feelings.[18] Emotional efficacy, thus, resides in the ways in which sounds and movements are cognitively and affectively integrated in what Feld has identified as a "felt iconic wholeness."[19]

Music psychologists have further recognized that a music-body-memory nexus is shaped by environmental factors that modulate emotion and mood states.[20] Patrik N. Juslin outlines a series of seven mechanisms that induce musical emotion in addition to cognitive assessment, abbreviated as the BRECVEM model. This music-body-memory nexus involves "*Brain stem reflexes, Rhythmic entrainment, Evaluative conditioning, Contagion, Visual imagery, Episodic memory,* and *Musical expectancy.*"[21] Music psychologists have shown how musical practices have physiological effects on the body and voice in performance, on mood associations, on race and gender bias, and on perceptions of self-identity.[22] Dieter Lohmar argues that emotional effects occur because "'mirror neurons' secure the empathetic opening of the individual to the lived experience of the other."[23] Bringing together issues of gender and emotion in performance through a phenomenological framework, contributors to this volume consider why there is "remarkable consistency in the constructions different individuals make of essential aspects of the environment (textures, sounds, shapes, colours, space)."[24] Thus, they address our final mediating influence, that of relationships to place and the performative environment, to examine how shared experiences might be best interpreted in performance.

Performative Environments

Place is a deeply contested notion that has become increasingly contingent in the twenty-first century. Edward L. Casey has suggested that we are "ineluctably place-bound," with the result that "we are not only in places but of them."[25] Insofar as this suggests that "we are never without emplaced experiences,"[26] this place-bound existence may be highly contested or unstable, providing the larger conceptual framework for the gender-performance dynamics explored in this volume. While the study of place-related components such as geography, landscape, environment, home, and country, among others, has inspired a rich academic discourse, these terms ultimately overlap to create potentially conflicting frames of reference and understandings of a place destabilized; place is both everywhere and nowhere.[27] To say that place is everywhere is self-evident: at its most fundamental, place is where we always are as much as it is contained within the "inner place," that is, the body as a context for understanding and perceiving the external situatedness of being. To suggest that place is nowhere and has lost its solidity is an oxymoron,[28] yet one becoming increasingly imaginable as human displacement, global communication systems, and environmental vulnerabilities redefine human relationships and destabilize once certain associations.[29]

Since the influential work of R. Murray Schafer on soundscapes focused on resonances of the landscape as modalities of performance, questions of what constitutes acoustemological fragmentation, or the dislocation of sounds from their ecological source (unsettled "senses of place"), have not dissipated but have become all the more important for understanding the musical complexities of performance.[30] Nevertheless, questions of globalization and musical change are at the forefront of identity politics and human rights, as communities address issues of deterritorialization that have generated fractures in deeply held cultural, social, and geographical relations. While deterritorialization may be considered to have negative consequences for communities because it operates at the expense of stable cultural identities, it also invites cultural transformation as a positive response to global influences. In this mode, rather than seeking to sustain previous cultural practices, the imagination becomes the tool for the creation of alternative identities and experiences, which in turn demand more sophisticated analyses of the contested relationships of attachment and belonging. Political conflict and bloodshed, a globally driven economic marketplace, environmental degradation, and expanding virtual worlds all contribute to sensual fragmentation and emotional insecurity. Inevitably, analyzing the effects of performance in such shape-shifting environments poses particular challenges for scholars. As Zygmunt Bauman has noted, "fluid modernity" is not easy to capture, for its malleability "requires a lot of attention, constant vigilance and perpetual effort—and even then the success of the effort is anything but a foregone conclusion."[31]

Problems of how to grapple with such complexities of place have gathered clarity and momentum through their interrogation by philosophers who have discussed the interweaving of place with body and body with place, as well as through the work of cultural geographers, ecologists, and anthropologists who have variously shown how engagements with landscape are fluid and shifting.[32] Music research has responded in various ways to contested pluralities of place through reconceiving the local, recognizing a more expansive system of relationships, and, in general, a theoretical shift toward the global economy, which, according to Ellen Koskoff, has occurred at the expense of field research built on "real people and the truth of their musical lives."[33]

As the vessels through which gendered musical lives are constructed, musicians' bodies act as emotional conduits for performers' social relationships and their attachments to place. Although emotional meanings are not consistent between music practitioners, Ruth Finnegan has argued that performers' "habitual musical pathways" are based on "shared and purposive collective *actions*."[34] As performers' social networks and musical pathways meet and merge, so they come to generate new kinds of musical experiences out of their constructions and intimations of place.[35] Contributors argue that performance is to a large extent contingent on performers' imagined and emotional relationships with place, whether in terms of its ecological features or related nationalist sentiments. Some, for example, illustrate how the performance of cultural continuity can be a response to indigenous expectations around rights and relationships to the land as well as being an articulation of power and cultural critique. Others show how Western and indigenous performances cut across boundaries of time, place, and context and how their impacts are difficult to anticipate either on performers or on the cultures to which they belong. Indeed, they bring categories such as Western and indigenous into question, generating competing senses of identity that can transform musicians' senses of place. What constitutes indigenous performance is rendered problematic, destabilizing claims to nationalism, ethnicity, and land rights. By questioning how shared musical emotions are generated, our authors propose that gendered attachments to place are shaped through differentiated musical experiences. Thus the embodiment of place is arguably among the most and least stable aspects of lived experience today: on the one hand, it is ideologically rooted, fixed, and stable; while, on the other hand, it is imagined, moveable, and dependent upon human desire. Thus, contributors debate how places are ever-changing performative resources for music making.

Chapter Organization

While the common objective of exploring the performative interplay among gender, place, and emotion unifies the geocultural diversity of chapters, the volume is organized into three parts to foreground distinctive themes: Landscape and Emotion, Memory and Attachment, and Nationalism and Indigeneity. Each of these sections explores its own thematic focus while also integrating the chapters around ideas of embodiment and experience, performing emotion, and gendered sentiments.

Part 1: Landscape and Emotion

The first three chapters ask how we should understand musical tensions between ideas of ecology, emotional belonging, and spirituality. These authors develop theoretical insights into what Keith H. Basso terms "interanimation," as performers attend to particularities of the landscape that evoke images of place-making as personally and communally affecting. They variously discuss how singers and dancers enliven the topography through a "vigorous conflation of attentive subject and geographical object," creating fields of meanings.[36] These fields of emotional meanings are not confined to performers, however, since places also hold memories for others listening. This is particularly evident in many instances of indigenous performativity, which require that performers and listeners attend to the sensuous and sentimental aspects of their natural environment.

As Barley Norton (Vietnam), Jonathan McIntosh (Bali), and Fiona Magowan (Aboriginal Australia) show, locally produced musics interact with the "local structure of feeling" to create gendered senses of difference.[37] They illustrate how rituals from Southeast Asia to Australia derive their power in part from the mediational forces of their particular environments that conjoin noumenal with phenomenal realms. Central to their arguments are the ways in which sentient landscapes shape musical senses of belonging through an indigenous hermeneutics of performance. They consider what kinds of emotions can be generated by sounds within landscapes and analyze how spiritual and emotional engagements are evoked through male and female song and dance performances that tie participants to places. Each author takes up the question of how to understand musical experiences of place and environment in shaping collective "emotional labor."[38]

Drawing on field research in northern Vietnam, Barley Norton explores how the performances of spirit mediums embody geocultural associations that connect gender and emotion to the environment, while in Bali Jonathan McIntosh shows how geographic orientation is related to the noumenal effects of dance, influencing how boys and girls learn about their environment and access social and spiritual power. In the last chapter of this section, Fiona Magowan examines how the sentient environment in the Northern Territory of Australia is the basis of men's and women's performances in Aboriginal ritual, where noumenal power is directed toward the ancestral law—as "the music of nature becomes the nature of [not only] music" but also art and dance.[39] Men's and women's ritual singing is shown to be a means of emplacing performers politically in the landscape through the evocation of ancestral rights to land. As singing facilitates the recollection of past experiences, so it affords performers and listeners the opportunity to reestablish connections with a landscape that may have been "rendered absent," legitimizing memories of the past for the purposes of asserting their rights in the present.[40]

Each of these chapters illustrates how the performance of emotions is powerful for participants and audiences. As the effects of trance influence performers' emotional relationships with the spirit world in Vietnam, so too in Bali do children come to appreciate the complex spiritual and emotional dynamics evoked by the masculine and feminine characters performed in the Barong. In Aboriginal Australia the sounds and contours of sea and land are spiritual essences that animate the activities of singing, dancing, and painting. In each case emotions extend outward from performers through their representations of the landscape, in turn bringing the spiritual effects of the land into their and others' bodies. This is an important process in indigenous performance and provides a basis for understanding the role of the environment in illness and well-being, as also evidenced elsewhere. In an Amerindian context, for example, Henry Stobart has captured a rich relationship between the healing powers of sound and their presence in the landscape to speak of "landscapes of music."[41] For many indigenous groups today, performing emotions and memories of places and ancestors in ritual continues to be key to intergenerational continuity, environmental sustainability, and personal well-being.

Part 2: Memory and Attachment

The following three chapters consider how singing can evoke emotions through musical memories and the musical imagination. Contributors each illustrate how the immediacy of the performing voice resonates within the singing body as a musical instrument, eliciting powerful emotions in listeners. They argue that singing can inspire place memories by generating links with places remembered while affecting listeners through their associations with the locations in which songs are performed. Thus, they explore the effects that places have on male and female performers and show how emotions experienced in singing not only affect the constitution of social relations but also influence the nature of gender identity through performance. Authors further demonstrate how performers' voices "inhabit an intersubjective acoustic space."[42] In doing so, they contribute to a culturally delimited vocality within which "meanings cannot be recovered without reconstructing the contexts of their hearing."[43]

Muriel Swijghuisen Reigersberg (Aboriginal Australia), Sara R. Walmsley-Pledl (Germany), and Louise Wrazen (Poland) examine singing as a context in which music has come to shape affective movements of the inner self, memory, and imagination. How places enter into men's and women's emotions and imaginations in the present draws our attention to place as contingent of time. These chapters resonate with Casey's notion of being "*of* a place" even while not necessarily *in* it.[44] The first two of these chapters, by Muriel Swijghuisen Reigersberg and Sara R. Walmsley-Pledl, refocus the performative lens toward feelings of well-being (or, alternatively, trauma) in vocal performances. In Queensland, Australia, Swijghuisen Reigersberg contends that choral singing performed for young male offenders in a detention center evokes senses of home, history, and longing. Other feelings of nostalgia, transcendence, and self-revelation infuse choral singing as a site of memory in East Bavaria, as recounted by Walmsley-Pledl. In this context, choral singing is seen as a liberating experience because it has the potential to rewrite scarred memories of unhappy musical experiences from childhood. In the third chapter, Wrazen extends the impact of musical influences on the inner self to suggest that voice can connect the "inner and outer" worlds through performance and lifelong attachments to the landscape in the Podhale region of southern Poland. She shows how one woman's voice has led her to new places in the world while simultaneously reinforcing strong associations with those landscapes most familiar to her. Tied to a sensory experience of place, singing has here become essential to processes of memory, even when moved to the recording studio or concert hall.

Each of these chapters elaborates on individual music experience as constituted in relation to the specifics of a local setting. While chapters 4 and 5 examine how narrating musical events and singing about experiences of local environments influence performers' senses of well-being in choral settings, Wrazen focuses, in chapter 6, on one woman (in a polyphonic singing tradition) to consider women's experience of singing in, and of, the landscape as a way of creating a personal intimacy with place. All three contributors explore how singing can create resilience and transform negative emotions, such as loss or hurt, to feelings of harmony and empowerment through gendered senses of spatial and temporal belonging. In each case, contributors show how managing emotions is important for performers to ensure an appropriate social order is maintained around "feeling rules," either to create continuity with the past or to reenvision it.[45] As these chapters show, singing can thus offer an emotional catharsis that also transforms the singer into an active agent through the possibility of reimagining current realities. As an aspect of the "audible voice," singing becomes "an instrument of empowerment."[46] Through singing, processes of remembering can span a gamut of emotions, ultimately reaching an accord and empathy with and through the landscape.

Part 3: Nationalism and Indigeneity

The recording studio and public stage are the key dimensions of the third section of the volume. Contributors elaborate on how the performance of emotions within and across regions and borders is an essential part of the construction of nationalism and indigenous personhood. Music is often used as a means of engaging political concerns to critique or transcend nationalist sentiment, producing a transnational consciousness about the politics of identity. Contributors show how performativity can be influential in expressing contested identities across different domains: from politicized responses in theatrical dramatization to emotional performances of life-changing events that have socially transformative outcomes for the nation. As nations come together to assert their rights, these authors ask, what are the homogenizing effects of pan-indigenous mobilization, and how do these play out emotively at local levels?

Christine R. Yano (Korea and Japan) and Tina K. Ramnarine (Norway, Sweden, Finland, and Russia) consider how transnationalism generates a particular sensitivity and disposition toward topography, as disparate locales vie for political recognition. Understanding performance in transnational arenas means attending to multiple expressions of an extroverted sense of place, which includes an awareness of its links with the wider world.[47] Each of the authors in this section variously examines how singing in the concert hall, the recording studio, or in festivals operates as a commodifying practice, connecting traditional performance with modernity and generating contested discourses of nationalism and indigeneity in the process. In different ways, they show how the emotional terrains of performance operate in the production and contestation of racial meanings and question how musical materials might challenge local, national, and global boundaries.[48] Despite the strong emotional flow between disparate performance contexts, they demonstrate how the structural elements of performativity enable performers to cope with the circumstances and contexts of daily life, while critiquing various transnational domains of engagement.

Christine R. Yano explores the issue of how music can be used to mediate private encounters, public disclosures, and national sentiment within the context of the commercial *enka* stage in Japan. Yano examines how the Korean singer Kim Yonja becomes racialized and feminized in her performance of the sentimental song genre of Japanese enka, which is said to embody the "heart and soul of Japan." She shows how tears become symbolic capital in the commodification of emotion, as audience responses reflect the ironies of rancorous colonial relations between Korea and Japan, the ill-treatment of Koreans by Japanese in World War II, and the continuing discrimination of the ethnic minority *zainichi Kankokujin* (living-in-Japan Koreans). Indigenous performance also mediates national sentiment in an Arctic context as Tina K. Ramnarine argues that in transnational, pan-indigenous Sámi agendas, the reclamation of the past in song is an effective tool for reviving awareness of indigenous environmental relations over time. Two female singers, Ulla Pirttijärvi and Tiina Sanila, highlight the different ways in which singing evokes notions of Sáminess, the historical processes that shape women's vocal expression, and the connections between traditional and modern musical practices. Ultimately, contributors in this section problematize how identities are imagined and embodied in performance as "sites of contention over which memories to evoke" within and beyond the nation.[49]

In her afterword, Beverley Diamond asserts the broader significance of the volume by identifying several issues that emerge, suggesting that the "contingencies" of musical ability, age-related social roles, and historical change thread their way through the chapters and anticipate future directions in research. Diamond concludes by drawing our attention to the inevitability of massive environmental change that now inflects any ontological consideration of "place."

Repositioning Performative Encounters

Rather than analyzing the performance of emotions as some kind of disembodied construct, all the authors have sought to consider emotional responses as observable phenomena of musical experience. Thus, this volume proceeds from a methodological consensus built around fieldwork, albeit recognizing that the field can no longer be considered to be a homogeneous domain. While contributors' deep engagement with musicians and thick descriptions of musicking show complex cultural specificity and variation across the different regions, they also point to some commonalities around indigenous intentions and the gendered dimensions of musical embodiment. In each case, we see how performing emotions across different places inscribes them with feelings and meanings that can be mobilized for political, national, or spiritual purposes. The integration of gender, place, and emotion in performance further exposes many questions around cultural heritage, nationalism, and the reclaiming of an environmental ethic. It brings to light how the growing industries of music technology, along with innovative recording methods, contribute to what are often highly emotional processes of identity formation, cultural resistance, and revival.

Our volume outlines a shift in music studies toward an integrated consideration of factors such as gender and place among other variables of musically embodied expression such as emotion. By teasing out this experiential density in performance, complex issues and desires for social change are revealed about music politics and nationhood, power and equality among performers, and environmental sustainability. Taken together, the chapters in this volume illustrate that

- gendered emotions in performance contribute to contestations over (as well as the regeneration of) ecological and spiritual life in a fast-paced global world;
- performances of place challenge and legitimize national discourses of pan-indigeneity as well as intergenerational belonging; and
- emotional performances and the performance of emotion can be powerful forces in many domains, shaping collective identification and the rebranding of a nation in processes of repatriation.

As our authors show, there is no singular mode of defining the nexus between music, gender, and emotion, because each informs the other to produce culture-specific transformations in manifold performative encounters.

Notes

1. Lucy Green, *Music, Gender, and Education* (Cambridge: Cambridge University Press, 1997), 16.

2. The ethnographic analyses of our volume builds on the "three waves" of historical and theoretical scholarship identified within feminist and music studies: (1) the need to redress the virtual absence of women as subjects of music research, (2) an emphasis upon "gender-centric" approaches to gender relations in performance, and (3) a postmodern concern with social structure as musical difference (Ellen Koskoff, foreword to Moisala and Diamond, *Music and Gender*, x). Works in the domain of gender research include Marcia Herndon and Susanne Ziegler, eds., *Music, Gender, and Culture* (Wilhelmshaven: Florian Noetzel Verlag, 1990); Susan McClary, *Feminine Endings: Music, Gender and Sexuality* (Minneapolis: University of Minnesota Press, 1991); Philip Brett, Elizabeth Wood, and Gary C. Thomas, eds., *Queering the Pitch: The Gay and Lesbian Musicology* (New York: Routledge, 1994); Susan C. Cook and Judy S. Tsou, eds., *Cecilia Reclaimed: Feminist Perspectives on Gender and Music* (Urbana: University of Illinois Press, 1994); Elaine Barkin and Lydia Hamessley, eds., *Audible Traces: Gender, Identity, and Music* (Zurich: Carciogoli Verlagshaus, 1999); Tullia Magrini, ed., *Music and Gender: Perspectives from the Mediterranean* (Chicago: University of Chicago Press, 2003); and Eileen M. Hayes and Linda F. Williams, eds., *Black Women and Music: More Than the Blues* (Urbana: University of Illinois Press, 2007).

3. Pirkko Moisala and Beverley Diamond, eds., *Music and Gender* (Urbana: University of Illinois Press, 2000), 1

4. Ellen Koskoff, "Response to Rice: A Recall of Arms," *Ethnomusicology* 43, no. 2 (2010): 330.

5. Moisala and Diamond, *Music and Gender*, 3.

6. Marcia Herndon, "Epilogue: The Place of Gender within Complex, Dynamic Musical Systems," in Moisala and Diamond, *Music and Gender*, 357.

7. Ibid., 348.

8. See Ellen Dissanayake, *Art and Intimacy: How the Arts Began* (Seattle: University of Washington Press, 2000), 8.

9. Martin Stokes, *The Republic of Love: Cultural Intimacy in Turkish Popular Music*. Chicago: Chicago University Press.

10. See Maurice Merleau-Ponty, *The Phenomenology of Perception*, trans. Colin Smith (London: Routledge and Kegan, 1962).

11. See Philip N. Johnson-Laird and Keith Oatley, "Emotions, Music and Literature," in *Handbook of Emotions*, ed. Michael Lewis, Jeannette M. Haviland-Jones and Lisa Feldman Barrett (London: Guildford, 2008), 102–13.

12. Jesse Prinz, "Are Emotions Feelings?" *Journal of Consciousness Studies* 12, nos. 8–10 (2005): 10.

13. Catherine Lutz and Geoffrey M. White, "The Anthropology of Emotions," *Annual Review of Anthropology* 15 (1986): 407–8.

14. Ruth Finnegan, "Music, Experience, and the Anthropology of Emotion," in *The Cultural Study of Music: A Critical Introduction*, ed. Martin Clayton, Trevor Herbert, and Richard Middleton (New York: Routledge, 2003), 187.

15. Ramón Pelinski, "Embodiment and Musical Experience," *Transcultural Music Review* 9 (2005) http://www.sibetrans.com/trans/trans9/pelinski-en.htm.

16. See, for instance, Peta Tait, *Performing Emotions: Gender, Bodies, Spaces, in Chekhov's Drama and Stanislavski's Theatre* (Aldershot: Ashgate, 2003).

17. Denis Dutton, "Authenticity in the Art of Traditional Societies," *Pacific Arts* 9–10 (1994): 217.

18. There are difficulties both in understanding how music effects emotional transference from one person to another cross-culturally, and also in articulating (through language) the experiences of music making. Building on the position of Charles Seeger (*Studies in Musicology 1935–75* [Berkeley: University of California Press, 1977]), Steven Feld (in "Communication, Music, and Speech about Music," *Yearbook for Traditional Music* 16 [1984]: 13) has also pointed to this disjuncture between language and musical experience. Although one's experience of music can be put into words and therefore communicated, music's "generality and multiplicity of possible messages and interpretations" suggests an ineffable quality of musical experience that brings "a special kind of feelingful activity and engagement on the part of the listener."

19. For "felt iconic wholeness," see Steven Feld, "Aesthetics as Iconicity of Style, or 'Lift-up-over-Sounding': Getting into the Kaluli Groove," *Yearbook of Traditional Music* 20 (1988): 107. See also John Leavitt, "Meaning and Feeling in the Anthropology of Emotions," *American Ethnologist* 23, no. 3 (1996): 514–39; and Michelle Rosaldo, "Toward an Anthropology of Self and Feeling," in *Culture Theory: Essays on Mind, Self, and Emotion*, ed. Richard A. Shweder and Robert A. LeVine (Cambridge: Cambridge University Press, 1984), 137–58.

20. John A. Sloboda and Susan A. O'Neil, "Emotions in Everyday Listening to Music," in *Music and Emotion: Theory and Research*, ed. Patrik N. Juslin and John A. Sloboda (Oxford: Oxford University Press, 2001), 413–29.

21. Juslin, Patrik N. "Music and emotion: Seven questions, seven answers," in *Music and the mind: Investigating the functions and processes of music*, eds I. Deliège & J. Davidson (New York: Oxford University Press, in press).

22. See Elizabeth Hallam, Ian Cross, and Michael Thaut, eds., *The Oxford Handbook of Music Psychology* (Oxford: Oxford University Press, 2009).

23. Dieter Lohmar, "On the Function of Weak Phantasmata in Perception: Phenomenological, Psychological and Neurological Clues for the Transcendental Function of Imagination in Perception," *Phenomenology and Cognitive Sciences* 4 (2005): 155–67.

24. Antonio R. Damasio, *Descartes' Error: Emotion, Reason, and the Human Brain* (New York: Putnam and Sons, 1994), 97.

25. Edward L. Casey, "How to Get from Space to Place in a Fairly Short Stretch of Time: Phenomenological Prolegomena," in Feld and Basso, *Senses of Place*, 19.

26. Ibid.

27. See, for example, Dennis Cosgrove, *Social Formation and Symbolic Landscape*. (Wisconsin: The University of Wisconsin Press, 1998).

28. Zygmunt Baumann, *Liquid Modernity*. (Oxford: Blackwell, 2000), 58.

29. See, for example, Marc Auge, *Non-places: Introduction to an Anthropology of Supermodernity*, trans. John Howe (London: Verso, 1995).

30. R. Murray Schafer, *The Tuning of the World* (Rochester, VT: Destiny Books, 1977). For the landscape as modalities of performance, see, in particular, Feld's elaboration of acoustemology, "Waterfalls of Song: An Acoustemology of Place Resounding in Bosavi, Papua New Guinea," in *Senses of Place*, ed. Steven Feld and Keith H. Basso (Santa Fe, NM: School of American Research Press, 1996), 91–136; and Theodore Levin, *Where Rivers and Mountains Sing: Sound, Music and Nomadism in Tuva and Beyond*, with Valentina Süzükei (Bloomington: University of Indiana Press, 2006). For acoustemological fragmentation, see Feld and Basso, *Senses of Place*.

31. Bauman, *Liquid Modernity*, 8.

32. Philosophers include Merleau-Ponty, *Phenomenology of Perception*; Yi-Fu Tuan, *Space and Place: The Perspective of Experience* (Minneapolis: University of Minnesota Press, 1977); and Casey, "Space to Place," 13–52. Cultural geographers, ecologists, and anthropologists include Irwin Altman and Setha Low, eds., *Place Attachment* (New York: Plenum, 1992); and Barbara Bender, ed., *Landscape: Politics and Perspectives* (Oxford: Berg, 1993).

33. For reconceiving the local, see, for example, Levin, *Rivers and Mountains Sing*; and Richard K. Wolf, ed., *Theorizing the Local: Music, Practice, and Experience in South Asia and Beyond* (Oxford: Oxford University Press, 2009). For different systems of relationships, see Arjun Appadurai, *Modernity at Large: Cultural Dimensions of Globalization* (Minneapolis: University of Minnesota Press, 1996). For the global economy, see Ellen Koskoff, "(Left Out in) Left (the Field): The Effects of Post-postmodern Scholarship on Feminist and Gender Studies in Musicology and Ethnomusicology, 1990–2000," *Women and Music* 9 (2005): 97–98.

34. Ruth Finnegan, *The Hidden Musicians* (Middletown, Connecticut: Wesleyan University Press, 2007), 305 (italics in original).

35. By intimations of place, we seek to draw attention to the ways in which place not only exists physically but as a concept that brings together ideas of movement and change between geographical locations with notions of modernity, transcendence or other-worldliness. For a discussion of "intimations of community" see Ruth Finnegan *Tales of the City*, Cambridge: Cambridge University Press, 1998), 153.

36. Keith H. Basso, "Wisdom Sits in Places," in Feld and Basso, *Senses of Place*, 56.

37. Sheila Whiteley, Andy Bennett, and Stan Hawkins, *Music, Space and Place: Popular Music and Cultural Identity* (Aldershot: Ashgate, 2005), 3.

38. Arlie Hochschild, *The Managed Heart: Commercialization of Human Feelings* (Berkeley: University of California Press, 1983).

39. Feld, "Aesthetics as Iconicity," 102.

40. Suzanne Kuchler, "The Place of Memory," in *The Art of Forgetting*, ed. Adrian Forty and Suzanne Kuchler (Oxford: Berg, 1999), 54.

41. Henry Stobart, "Bodies of Sound and Landscapes of Music: A View from the Bolivian Andes," in *Musical Healing in Cultural Contexts*, ed. Penelope Gouk (Aldershot: Ashgate, 2000), 26–45.

42. Leslie C. Dunn and Nancy A. Jones, introduction to *Embodied Voices: Representing Female Vocality in Western Culture*, ed. Leslie C. Dunn and Nancy A. Jones (Cambridge: Cambridge University Press, 1994), 2.

43. Ibid.

44. Casey, "Space to Place." See also Louise Wrazen, "Relocating the Tatras: Place and Music in Górale Identity and Imagination," *Ethnomusicology* 51, no. 2 (2007): 185–204.

45. Arlie Hochschild, *The Managed Heart: The Commercialization of Feeling* (Berkeley: University of California Press, 1983), 18.

46. Dunn and Jones, introduction to *Embodied Voices*, 1.

47. See Doreen Massey, *Space, Place and Gender* (Cambridge: Polity, 1994), 154.

48. For example, see Regula Qureshi, "The Indian Sarangi: Sound of Affect, Site of Contest," *Yearbook for Traditional Music* 29 (1997): 1–38; and Deborah Wong, "Taiko and the Asian/American Body: Drums, Rising Sun and the Question of Gender," *World of Music* 42, no. 3 (2000): 67–78. See also Martin Stokes, ed., *Ethnicity, Identity and Music: The Musical Construction of Place* (Oxford: Berg, 1994); and John Connell and Chris Gibson, *Sound Tracks: Popular Music, Identity, and Place* (New York: Routledge, 2003).

49. Tim Cresswell, *Place: A Short Introduction* (Oxford: Blackwell, 2004), 90.

Part One

Landscape and Emotion

Chapter One

Engendering Emotion and the Environment in Vietnamese Music and Ritual

Barley Norton

This chapter examines how musical performance is bound up with displays and exchanges of sentiment in Vietnamese spirit possession rituals, known as *len dong*. It aims to show how the expression of emotion is culturally mediated through ritual practice and musical performance by exploring the affective modalities of mediumship from new perspectives.[1] I also consider the ways in which emotional expressions in ritual practices are inflected by gender relations to the environment and discuss how the exchange of sentimental relations (*tinh cam*) among musicians and between musicians and their audience is a highly prized ideal during mediumship rituals and many other traditional contexts for musical performance.

Deeply felt sentiments are mediated, shared, and expressed in mediumship practices in numerous ways. The process of coming out as a medium, the special relationships mediums develop with certain spirits, the bodily experience of spirit possession, the enactment of ritual acts, divine utterances, and the music and dance performed during rituals are all invested with emotional associations and meanings.[2] To explore these affective meanings, I examine the symbolic, bodily, and social aspects of ritual experience and performance and consider the religious framework of mediumship as a complex system of affect.[3] In this system, linkages between emotion, the environment, gender, and ethnicity are encoded in the sonic and mythical identities of the spirits. Through expressive musical performance and ritual practice, a range of emotions and particular environments in the natural world are related to the ethnicity and gendered characteristics of incarnated spirits. I begin with a symbolic analysis of the expressive potential of the religious system and consider how spirit possession embodies emotional differences according to the types of spirits being manifest and the gender identity of the performer. I then discuss how the call to mediumship for women and men relates to gender identity, emotional temperament, and a background of personal crises. The combination of these elements shapes how music is intertwined with the bodily feeling and emotional arousal of possession. Finally, I investigate how the affective dimensions of mediumship music, known as *chau van*, along with others genres of Vietnamese traditional music such as the southern chamber music *don ca tai tu*, extend through the musicians and listeners to facilitate the development of sentimental relations.

Introduction to Mediumship Rituals

Len dong rituals hold a central place in the system of religious beliefs known as the Four Palace religion (Dao Tu Phu) or Mother religion (Dao Mau). The pantheon of spirits, which forms the backbone of the religious system, consists of a hierarchy of ranks of spirits: the mother spirits (*mau*), General Tran Hung Dao (and some of his family members), mandarins (*quan*), ladies (*chau*), princes (*ong hoang*), princesses (*co*), and young princes (*cau*). Within each rank, spirits are numbered as first, second, and third, and so on, with the exception of some regional spirits, which are not always named with an ordinal number. During len dong a medium usually incarnates several spirits from each rank in sequence according to the hierarchy of the pantheon. When a spirit is about to be incarnated, a red cloth is placed over the medium's head by assistants (usually two or four) who surround the medium. Following the onset of possession, the assistants remove the head cloth and dress the medium in the special clothes of the spirit incarnated. The medium then performs a conventional sequence of ritual acts and dances.

Although some individual spirits carry out distinctive acts and have their own dances, the ritual sequence for each spirit rank exhibits some similarities. Prestigious male spirits such as the mandarins, for instance, offer incense to the altar and wave incense to ward off evil spirits before performing vigorous military dances with swords (see fig. 1.1). After the military dances, the medium sits down in front of the temple altar and then drinks rice wine, smokes cigarettes, and interacts with ritual participants. In contrast to the typical ritual sequence for the mandarins, the lady spirits do not perform the ritual acts with incense, and their dances utilize objects such as fans and small ropes set on fire rather than swords. When the incarnation of each spirit draws to a close, the assistants throw the red cloth over the medium's head once again.

Mediums usually arrange at least two len dong a year—either in public temples (*den*) or their own private temples or shrines in their homes (*dien*)—on auspicious dates, such as the death anniversaries of spirits, *ngay gio*, or on dates around the beginning and end of the year or the changing of seasons.[4] Len dong are held to serve (*hau*) the spirits, and they are a vehicle through which divine advice and healing are sought for issues or difficulties mediums and

ENGENDERING EMOTION AND THE ENVIRONMENT 19

Figure 1.1. A female medium called Phuong waves incense while possessed by the Second Mandarin at Hao Nam temple in Hanoi in 2008. Photograph by Jamie Maxtone-Graham.

their disciples face in their everyday lives.[5] When possessed, the medium transmits (*truyen*)—through ritual acts and divine words—the advice and blessing of the spirits. At certain stages of the ritual progression disciples approach the possessed medium to consult the spirits incarnated on a wide range of issues such as bad health, work, financial matters, or difficulties in interpersonal relations with friends and family.

Chau van music, which is played continuously throughout len dong, is known for its vibrant, catchy melodies and infectious dance rhythms.[6] Chau van songs are strophic, and a short instrumental section known as *luu khong* (lit. "flowing without [words]") is played between each verse. Chau van bands typically consist of two to five male musicians who usually both sing and play instruments. All bands in northern Vietnam include a player of the two-stringed moon lute (*dan nguyet*) and a percussionist who plays a set of percussion instruments, including the clappers (*phach*), drum (*trong*), a small cymbal (*canh*), and a small gong (*thanh la*) (see fig. 1.2). To this core band, other instruments such as the *dan tranh* zither and various bamboo flutes (e.g., *tieu* and *sao*) may be added. Some temples have their own resident bands, but most musicians travel around to perform at different temples at the request of mediums.

Chau van bands perform distinctive sequences of songs, which I refer to as "songscapes," for each spirit incarnated.[7] The songscapes performed by

Figure 1.2. A chau van band performing at Hao Nam temple in Hanoi in 2008. The band is led by the moon-lute player Pham Van Ty, accompanied by two musicians playing a set of percussion instruments and bamboo flutes. Photograph by Jamie Maxtone-Graham.

bands during rituals are codified by the chau van musical system, as certain songs must be performed for particular ritual actions and spirits. Some songs are performed for several spirits and ranks of spirits, but others are reserved for specific spirits (or ranks of spirits), depending on the spirit's identity. Understood as a musical entity narrating the progression of each possession, songscapes tend to be unique for each spirit. There is also some flexibility, at certain points during possession, for musicians to choose different songs to suit the moment and the preferences of ritual participants.

It is the medium holding the len dong who organizes all aspects of the event, including inviting friends and disciples and paying for the musicians. The number of people who attend depends on the size of the temple and the popularity and renown of the medium, but usually about thirty to forty people participate in rituals. The majority of mediums and disciples are female, although there is a significant minority of male mediums and religious devotees. Potentially any religious adept may be initiated as a medium, but to become a medium he or she must be recognized as having a destined aptitude or spirit root (*can*) by an experienced master medium (*dong truong*) or a spirit priest (*thay cung*).[8] Mediums are numerous in cities, towns, and villages throughout Vietnam, but they are especially prevalent in northern Vietnam. Drawing on field research I conducted between 1996 and 2005, in this chapter I discuss mediumship practices in northern Vietnam.[9]

The Affective System of Mediumship: Music, Gender, and the Environment

The religious framework that modulates mediums' emotional relations with spirits might be thought of as an "affective system," a term used by John Leavitt to refer to "collective symbolic productions," which "may be observed to provoke typical reactions in a group of people" who share the system.[10] By employing the term "affective system," I mean to suggest that the religious system of mediumship, primarily constituted through the practice of spirit possession, affords a certain repertoire of emotional possibilities for religious followers. These emotional possibilities are, to a great extent, delineated by the typical attributes of the spirits, but they are not defined by them. The affective system is formed by religious followers' knowledge and understanding of the spirits' characters, temperaments, and powers, yet the symbolic identities of spirits are sufficiently ambiguous and multivalent to enable mediums to forge their own pathways through the system. Ritual participants become sensitized to the emotional propensities of spirits and become inculcated to the affective system of mediumship through listening to chau van songs and through interactions with embodied spirits, such as verbal exchange and offering and receiving blessed gifts (*loc*).

Associations with particular emotions are an important aspect of the identity of spirits incarnated during len dong.[11] The identities of spirits are influenced by various factors, including gender, place, ethnicity, status, and age, as well as the individual histories and myths of the spirits recounted in the poems used as song texts. The emotional associations accorded to spirits are quite broad and are often understood and enacted by mediums in different ways. Particular spirits do not represent a single, fixed emotion; rather, they are known for having a propensity for certain types of emotional expression. Although there is insufficient space in this chapter to discuss all the spirits incarnated during rituals, in this section I examine some of the interconnections between music, gender, emotion, and the environment in the religious system of mediumship. I illustrate how the "process of 'engendering'" during ritual performance—a process by which shared understandings about gender become naturalized—relates to emotional expression and environment.[12]

The emotional associations and behavior of spirits are connected to their place and environment both in the "yin" other world (*coi am*) and the "yang" human world (*duong tran*). In the religious system of mediumship, most of the spirits incarnated during rituals belong to one of four palaces (*phu*) or domains in the celestial world (fig. 1.3). These four palaces may be represented as follows.

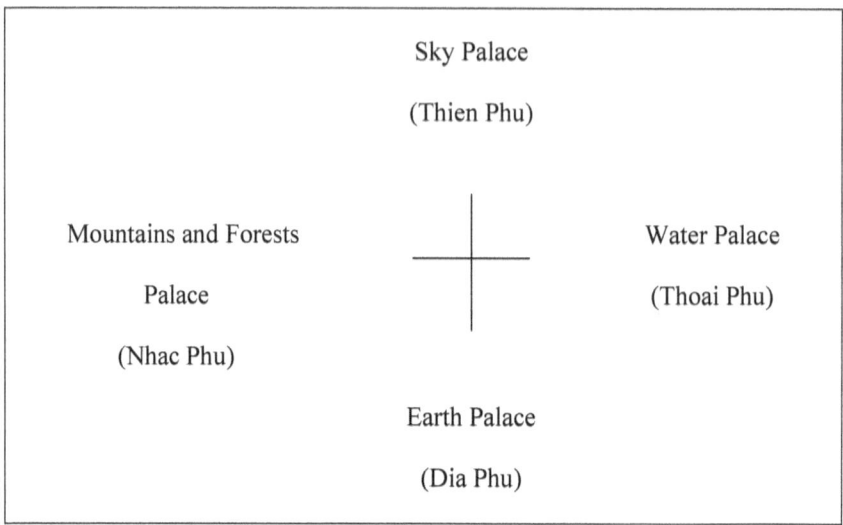

Figure 1.3. Cosmological orientation of the Four Spirit Palaces.

In the cosmological scheme of the Four Palace religion, there are correspondences between the palaces where the spirits reside in the yin other world and the natural landscape of Vietnam in the yang human world. These correspondences are especially prominent in relation to the yin dyad between the Mountains and Forests Palace and the Water Palace, which has parallels with the yang pairing in the human world between the lowlands, or downstream (*mien xuoi*), and the mountainous regions (*mien nui*) upstream. This yang polarity is prominent in conceptualizations of the Vietnamese nation and its geography. One of the Vietnamese terms for nation, *nui song* (lit. "mountains and rivers"), for instance, points to the contrast between the mountains in the north and center of Vietnam and the country's delta regions, that is, the Red River Delta in the north and the Mekong Delta in the south (map 1.1). In the cosmology of the Four Palace religion, this geographic polarity has gendered ethnic and affective dimensions, which relate to conceptions of the environment and ethnicity in Vietnam.

Many of the most popular spirits belonging to the Mountains and Forests Palace are female, and some are categorized as ethnic minority spirits. Several of the ladies, for example, are identified with ethnic minority groups who live in mountainous regions in Vietnam; these include the First Lady (Dao ethnicity), the Sixth Lady (Nung ethnicity), the Tenth Lady (Tay ethnicity), and the Lady Thac Bo (Muong ethnicity).[13] The affective associations of female mountain spirits—in both the lady and princess ranks—are predominantly happiness and cheerfulness, although these are mixed with flashes of tempestuousness and truculence. These associations are enacted performatively through

Map 1.1. Vietnamese regions and capital cities. Map by Angela Snieder.

vivacious dancing and lively songs belonging to the Xa group of melodies. The otherness of the ethnic minorities and the naturalness of the mountains are evoked when mountain spirits are incarnated. For instance, mediums dress up in clothes that imitate the ethnic dress of minority groups and distribute natural products such as betel nuts and fruit. Sonically, the otherness of mountain spirits is constructed through the use of the Xa group of songs, which participants said evoke the atmosphere (*khong khi*) of the mountains. The lively Xa songs have distinctive melodic phrasing, rhythms, and instrumentation (such as the inclusion of the Hmong flute [*sao Hmong*] and the use of an inverted small gong with keys placed inside).

In the song texts for mountain spirits, remote forests in mountainous areas are depicted as abundant with produce and teaming with wildlife, and this feeds into the representation of the mountain spirits as ebullient and wild. The following song text for the Second Lady (Chau De Nhi), which refers to her tempestuous character, is typical of the poems dedicated to mountain spirits:

> The lovely spirit from the magnificent forest,
> Her character is tempestuous.
> The light of the candles flicker on the mountain shack,
> The Second Lady dances with two lit-ropes for the mother spirits.
> She has power over the forests.
> On the horizon, the clouds and river valleys meet,
> The Lady frolicking among the cinnamon and peach trees.
> The moon and stars flicker in the dispersing clouds,
> She wears a conical hat and a basket of flowers is slung over her shoulder.
> When going to Tuan Quan one must cross the Gium mountain,
> Return to Pho Vi and Suoi Ngang waterfall [in Northeast Vietnam]
> When it is peaceful and the sky is calm,
> She sits on the mountain peak teasing the moon.
> She stops playing musical instruments and begins to sing,
> She talks clearly in the Man and Muong languages and in Vietnamese.

This song text describes the natural environment and refers to historical, sacred places in Vietnam that are sites of pilgrimage. The Tuan Quan temple and the Suoi Ngang waterfall, for instance, are in the northern mountainous provinces of Yen Bai and Lang Son, respectively. Through the "textual poesis of placename paths," chau van songs take ritual participants on sacred journeys through the Vietnamese landscape.[14] The references to the Man and Muong languages in the song text connect the Second Lady to those minority groups who live in the northern mountainous regions, and during possession mediums sometimes imitate the style of speech and the languages of ethnic minority groups living in Vietnam. At one ritual, for instance, the medium spoke Vietnamese with a regional ethnic minority accent when possessed by the Second Lady. On this occasion, the spirit's divine utterances were lighthearted and joyous: the medium asked for strong Laotian tobacco to smoke and teased the musicians by criticizing their performance of the Xa songs.

The mountainous regions, then, are largely the domain of female spirits, who are associated with ethnic minority groups.[15] By contrast, male spirits who belong to the Viet (or Kinh) ethnic majority feature more prominently in the spiritual geography of lowland areas. For instance, some of the most revered and frequently incarnated spirits in the mandarin and prince ranks, such as the Third and Fifth Mandarin and the Third Prince, belong to the Water Palace. These warrior-scholar (*van vo*) spirits are renowned for their military prowess and scholarly and artistic talents. As powerful figures of authority, they are typically stern and serious, and when incarnated they usually perform military dances with swords and spears. Musically, the seriousness and prestige of warrior-scholar spirits are depicted through performance of the Phu group of songs. This group is distinguished from other chau van song groups, such as the Xa and Con, through the use of long, melismatic, rhythmically fluid, and high-syncopated vocal phrases. The poems used as lyrics for Phu songs also employ unusual poetic meters and are typically sung with a more serious (*nghiem tuc*), more intense vocal quality when compared with other chau van songs. In general, the behavior of prestigious male spirits tends to be more restrained compared with the vivacious conviviality of female mountain spirits. Some of the warrior spirits, such as the Fifth Mandarin, are known for having short tempers, although the anger of mandarins is typically thought to be more frightening and severe than expressions of petulance by female mountain spirits.

The Water Palace is not exclusively the domain of male spirits, but female lowland spirits, like their male counterparts, are Viet rather than ethnic minority spirits, and they have a different array of emotional associations than female mountain spirits. The Third Princess (Co Bo), for example, the most renowned female spirit of the Water Palace, is known for her compassion for the suffering of humanity and is reputed to be one of the saddest spirits in the pantheon. One medium remarked, "whoever has difficulty in love and is sad [*buon*] serves the Third Princess.... If someone hasn't married a wife or husband then they have a destined affinity for the Third Princess (*can* Co Bo), because she doesn't live with anyone. She is alone." In keeping with the Third Princess's character, some of the songs performed for her, such as "Van" and "Con Oan," are sung in a slow tempo with a soft singing style, and religious devotees said these songs evoked feelings of sadness.

Notably, female spirits, both lowland and mountain, are more closely associated with the natural world and the environment than male spirits. In general, the natural world is anthropomorphized most strongly in the female form, and this is evident in the frequent use of honorific titles for female spirits that connect them to the environment. For example, the Third Princess and Little Princess spirits are often referred to as the "Third Princess of the Water" (Co

Bo Thoai) and the "Little Princess of the Mountains" (Co Be Thuong). In a comparable way to the female mountain spirits, the ritual actions of the Third Princess connect her to the environment. When incarnated, she performs a rowing dance with oars for which the musicians sing a special song called "Cheo Do" (Boat Rowing). As the following extracts illustrate, the song texts for the Third Princess depict her drifting around the country in a rowing boat, and they describe her power to alleviate human suffering:

> The Third Princess carries the mother deities across the river in a boat,
> She saves all mortals from hardship and danger.
> Traveling everywhere,
> The Third Princess is drifting, heave ho, in all four directions.
> The wind in the pine trees and the clouds,
> The Princess rescues the mortals.
> Who is in the boat, heave ho, that drifts on the edge of the river?
> The boat of the Third Princess of the Water Palace, heave ho, rowing to the temple.

Once the rowing dance is finished, the medium sits in front of the altar and interacts with religious devotees. Shortly after the rowing dance at one ritual I attended, in December 1996 in Ha Tay Province about fifty kilometers from Hanoi, the Third Princess showed discontent and unhappiness by making the possessed medium feel cold. The medium called out, "The Third Princess is freezing! I'm frozen to the core; please burn an incense stick. I can't stand it any more. Dead people are always cold, cold in and cold out. I can cause death straight away if you do not make things better. Why die? People in the human world are blind and deaf." Shortly after these words, the possession ended abruptly, and the medium left the temple, leaving the ritual participants to wonder what was going to happen next. After a break of about ten minutes, the medium came back into the temple and consulted the spirits as to whether or not she should continue the ritual. She did this by tossing old yin yang coins, and on the second throw the coins gave a positive response, so she continued the ritual and was then possessed by the Seventh, Ninth, and Little Princess, and the Third Young Prince.

When the Seventh Princess (Co Bay) was incarnated, the spirit explained why the Third Princess had made the medium's body cold. The utterances of the Seventh Princess included the following:

> The Third Princess scolded, but I have returned to rescue. You didn't make any offerings at all! Offer the Third Princess these clothes!
>
> Today I transmit and then you can tell the future.... Your husband said that "tongues have no bones and there are many twisty roads," so the Third Princess scolded and punished [you].
>
> Why was nothing given to the Third Princess, yet [votive offerings] are presented to me? For several days I have told everyone to concentrate "with one

gut" [i.e., completely] on the spirits. Don't imitate stupid people of the mortal world, otherwise the Third Princess will scold and punish.

These words make clear that the Third Princess "scolded" and "punished" because she was unhappy with the devotion and offerings of the religious devotees. In discussions with the medium several days after the ritual, the medium also said that her husband had criticized her religious activities because he did not believe (*tin*) in the spirits. The phrase "the tongue has no bones and there are many twisty roads" is a reference to his criticisms.[16] Incidents such as this one demonstrate the Third Princess's tendency to express negative sentiments when she is incarnated.

In addition to sadness, rituals also often involve humor. Outbursts of laughter among ritual participants most commonly occur when female mountain spirits and child spirits are incarnated. The most frequently incarnated child spirits are the Little Lady (Chau Be), the Little Princess (Co Be), and the Little Young Prince (Cau Be), all of whom belong to the Mountains and Forests Palace. Like other mountain spirits, these spirits tend to have a cheerful disposition, but because of their young age they are often emotionally changeable in a similar way to a child. They may joke and tease one moment and be stubborn and have tantrums the next.[17] One medium I spoke to said that her two daughters, who were soon to be initiated, had the destined aptitude for the Little Princess (*can* Co Be) because they often sulked (*hon doi*) and had tantrums.

During a possession by the Little Young Prince that I witnessed, the medium playfully joked around with ritual objects. Using a baby voice and mispronouncing the consonants of words as a child might, the possessed medium commented that the headscarf she was wearing was ugly and out of shape. She then jokingly compared a bent incense stick, which had been presented as an offering by one of the disciples, to the shape of an old lady. She declared, "This incense stick is shrewish and bent like an old lady! Coddling me, hey!" provoking much laughter among other ritual participants. There was also amusement when the medium turned to me and challenged me to guess how many bills of Vietnamese currency she was holding. If I guessed correctly, I would be given the money as a blessed gift; I said sixteen bills when in fact there were only fourteen, so the money was distributed to the medium's disciples instead.

This section has provided a sketch of the affective system of mediumship and changing emotional flow or emotional texture of rituals. In his writing on Kota funerals in South India, Richard Wolf has used the term "emotional texture" to describe the way in which the affective character of funerals changes as the ceremony unfolds. In Wolf's words, "Emotional texture is a way of talking about the changing configurations of affective meanings that Kotas . . . assign to rituals."[18] The emotional texture of len dong changes as spirits with different emotional associations are incarnated, and each ritual occasion is unique. In general terms, however, rituals usually start in a controlled and reserved manner during the possessions by mandarin spirits, and the liveliness and happiness of rituals usually reaches a peak when the mountain lady spirits are incarnated. After the ladies, when the medium is possessed by princes and princesses, the emotional texture is often more mixed, and sad sentiments are sometimes expressed. The end of rituals is usually lighthearted and jokey, as mediums are possessed by cheeky child spirits. Throughout rituals, musical performance plays an important role in modulating the emotional texture of rituals and engendering ritual participants. Chau van songs are associated with particular sentiments, and different songs are performed at each stage of possession to match the flux of ritualized emotion.

Initiation, Gender, and Somatic Expressions of Emotion

In interviews I conducted with mediums, it was striking how often they referred to their emotional temperament or disposition when discussing the reasons why they were initiated. Most female mediums said they were hot tempered (*nong ruot/nong tinh*) and difficult (*kho chiu*), which meant they were prone to turbulent moods and emotional outbursts in their everyday lives. Within mediumship circles, hot temperedness is understood as a typical character trait that predisposes certain women to become mediums. Such women are often drawn to spirits who share their emotional subjectivity, such as tempestuous lady spirits or angry mandarins, because these spirits are sympathetic to mortals who are emotionally volatile. When possessed, mediums may express anger or impatience through impetuous ritual acts and divine utterances, and many said they felt more at ease and calm after "serving the spirits." Some male mediums also said they were hot tempered, but for men their calling to mediumship was more commonly explained in terms of their effeminate gender identity. Male mediums are referred to as effeminate (*dong co*), and because of their strong femininity (*nang ve nu tinh*) they were usually recognized as having the spirit root of one of the female spirits.

Emotional volatility, hot temperedness, and effeminacy predispose individuals to become mediums, but the calling to mediumship is typically marked by a traumatic event or crisis. If the crisis is diagnosed by a master medium or spirit priest as an affliction caused by the spirits, then initiation is prescribed to satisfy the spirits and alleviate the affliction. The crises mediums experience often take the form of an illness or a bout of madness (*dien*). In interviews mediums said they experienced illnesses such as severe tiredness, weakness, headaches, and backaches, which could not be alleviated through Western biomedicine. They typically described their madness in terms of an involuntary possession by malevolent spirits that resulted in the loss of bodily control, erratic behavior, and a breakdown in core relationships with family and friends.

In her study of health and family planning in a Vietnamese rural community, Tine Gammeltoft argues that one of the ways Vietnamese women communicate distress to others is through "somatic expressions."[19] Gammeltoft develops a persuasive argument that women's somatic complaints are closely bound up with social and emotional distress and that physical suffering may be one of the most effective means available for women to draw attention to and alleviate stressful social circumstances. In a similar way, the physical symptoms mediums experienced often seemed to be related to emotional disturbance and social suffering. When talking about their afflictions, many mediums referred to difficult circumstances or a tragic event in their lives, which meant they were "forced" to "come out" as mediums. For example, some described how terrible working conditions had made them ill, while others related their initiation into mediumship to tragic events such as the death of one of their children or to a bout of madness that made them neglect their children. Afflictions such as these were cited as evidence of "punishment" by the spirits that could be alleviated only through initiation.

The emotional turbulence of the crises mediums experienced prior to initiation reveals the gendered nature of emotional expression and mediumship. More women than men are drawn into mediumship because of emotional turmoil in their lives, and the men who experience such turbulence and become mediums are understood to be effeminate. Heightened emotional arousal is central to possession, and the crises mediums experience might be understood as a kind of preparation for the performance of sentiment during rituals.

"Having Heart": The Body, Possession, and Music

The sensory presence of spirits is grounded in the body. During rituals mediums adopt a particular "somatic mode of attention," which facilitates bodily engagement with the spirits.[20] Spirits enter the body (*nhap than*), and mediums experience somatic changes when they embody spirits. During interviews mediums made clear that the primary site of embodiment is the heart (*tam*). There is a dialectical relationship between the heart and spiritual forces. For possession to occur, mediums said that they must have heart (*co tam*) or have a true heart (*thuc tam*) and that they must be devoted with one heart (*nhat tam*) to the spirits. They said that the spirits "entered" or "inscribed" the heart and affected the "innermost feelings" of the heart. In return, the spirits witness the hearts (*chung tam*) of followers, and premonitions (*linh cam*) and miraculous responses (*linh ung*) guided by the spirits are felt in the heart. In a similar way to the heart, the heart-soul (*tam hon*) is also affected by the presence of spirits: mediums said that their heart-soul felt different than normal; one medium remarked that her heart-soul "floated up" when possessed.

While the heart featured most prominently in mediums' descriptions of the feeling of possession, the heart and the stomach or gut were used interchangeably in some expressions. For example, true gutted (*thuc long*) and one gutted (*mot long*) were used synonymously with "true heart" and "one heart," respectively. In Vietnam the heart and guts are understood as seats of emotion, and this is evident in numerous Vietnamese emotion terms that refer to the stomach and heart.[21] Singers may also say that they sing in the stomach (*hat trong bung*) when referring to the vocal expression of emotion.[22] But the heart and the guts are not just connected to feeling; they are also closely intertwined with cognition. A medium, for instance, remarked that her heart thought (*nghi*) about the spirits. In Vietnamese it is also possible to say that one thinks in the stomach (*nghi trong bung*).[23] When I asked mediums how they felt during possession, it was hard to find an appropriate way to phrase the question, and in everyday Vietnamese speech it is more usual to inquire about somebody's feelings by asking what they think rather than what they feel. From a Vietnamese perspective, then, feeling involves thinking and thinking involves feeling, and the body is implicated in the expression of both thought and emotion.

Musical performance stimulates the heartfelt emotion-thought necessary for the embodiment of spirits through making mediums animated (*boc*) and impulsive (*boc dong*). The term *boc* literally means to rise up or emanate (e.g., smoke, vapor), but it is also used metaphorically to express excess, heat, or animation regarding a person's behavior or character. *Boc* then may be used to describe a person's fiery or tumultuous character (*tinh hay boc*) or the rising up (*boc len*) of emotion. The compound word *boc dong*—which I have rendered as impulsive—is commonly used to refer to the impetuous character of mediums and their behavior when possessed. Mediums also refer to having a "heavy energy" (*nang luong manh*) and say they receive this abundance of energy from the spirits.[24]

Numerous mediums I spoke to linked their impulsive behavior during possession and the rising up of emotion to listening to songs. According to mediums, chau van songs induce high energy, euphoric emotions such as happiness (*vui*), joy (*sung suong*), elation (*phan khoi*), and intoxicating passion (*say me*). For example, one medium remarked that "listening to chau van is profoundly moving, it makes me joyous," and another said, "when I listen to chau van I find that I am charmed, my heart-soul is charmed, then the spirits enter me." Prior to the onset of each spirit possession, the musicians perform "Thinh Bong" (lit. "Inviting the Spirits"). The soaring vocal phrases of 'Thinh Bong" invite the spirit to descend to the human world and are accompanied by loud percussion rhythms and fast instrumental phrases on the moon lute and other instruments. Reflecting on listening to "Thinh Bong," one medium said, "when I hear the invitation to the spirits before the spirit enters, my heart-soul flies. I feel elated." This comment gives an indication of how music intensifies the euphoric emotions felt in the heart and heart-soul, which are necessary to facilitate the onset of possession. Such states of emotional arousal are commonly experienced in numerous spirit possession rituals around the world, and Judith Becker has argued that high-energy, high-arousal emotions are "fundamental to the triggering of trancing."[25]

Following the onset of possession, music continues to shape ritual action and modulate the emotional texture of rituals, as different songs with different affective associations are performed. In some cases, songs are directly linked to specific ritual actions. For example, the "Sai" melody, which is known as a strong and serious melody, is always performed when prestigious male spirits like the mandarins and princes wave incense in front of the altar. An example of a text that is often used when "Sai" is performed for the Tenth Prince is as follows:

> The bunch of incense is a powerful pen,
> It makes the army generals return to protect,
> It orders the ministries of war.

Through such song texts, the ritual actions of the medium are described, and the efficacy and power of the incarnated spirit is affirmed.

In addition to the interconnections between songs and specific ritual actions, religious devotees used a specific term to describe the effect of music on dance: they said the rhythm of songs incites (*kich dong*) dance. Female spirits dance to the heavily accented and lively (*soi noi*) one-beat rhythm (*nhip mot*), whereas male spirits usually dance to the stately or majestic (*oai nghiem*) three-beat rhythm (*nhip ba*). In their most basic versions, the one-beat rhythm consists of a quarter note followed by an eighth-note rest and a heavily accented eighth-note "up beat," and the three-beat rhythm consists of a quarter note, a quarter-note rest, and two more quarter notes. When performing the dances of female spirits, mediums invariably follow the beat of the one-beat rhythm. A core movement of many of these dances is a jogging step, which consists of bouncing from one foot to the other in time with the pulse of the rhythm played on the set of percussion instruments. The dances for male spirits, however, do not necessarily follow the pulse of the three-beat rhythm. During the military dances of mandarin spirits, for example, mediums usually wield swords while bobbing up and down in a vertical plane, by bending their knees without lifting their feet completely off the ground. This vertical movement is not usually linked to the pulse of the music: it usually slips in and out of phase with the percussion rhythms.

At different stages of possession, then, musical performance contributes to the affective system of mediumship. The music performed by chau van bands helps stimulate the emotional arousal of possession, narrates the progression of ritual action, and incites dance. Through performing a songscape that evolves as each possession unfolds, musicians aim to create a spiritual atmosphere (*khong khi tam linh*) for ritual participants.

Drawing on Pierre Bourdieu's concept of habitus, Judith Becker has coined the term "habitus of listening" to emphasize the culturally diverse ways in which listeners develop tendencies to experience and respond to music in particular ways. In Becker's words, "A '*habitus of listening*' suggests, not a necessity nor a rule, but an inclination, a disposition to listen with a particular kind of focus, to expect to experience particular kinds of emotion, to move with certain stylized gestures, and to interpret the meaning of sounds and one's emotional responses to the musical event in somewhat (never totally) predictable ways."[26] During len dong mediums exhibit a habitus of listening, which predisposes them to listen and respond to chau van songs in particular ways. Mediums are culturally expected to experience emotional arousal during rituals and to listen to chau van in a way that increases the rising up of emotion. The inclination to respond to music and the presence of spirits in this way would seem to be strongly influenced by the crises mediums experience prior to initiation. Other ritual participants are not expected to be animated by ritual music in the same way as mediums, but the performance of chau van helps focus attention on the embodied spirits and ritual activity. As is discussed in the following section, music performance also assists in establishing sentimental relations among musicians and between musicians and listeners.

Music Performance and Sentimental Relations

The concept of *tinh cam*, which may be glossed as sentiment or sentimental relations, refers to the sharing of feelings between people and is a highly prized ideal that lies at the heart of many aspects of social life in Vietnam. Shaun Malarney, for instance, demonstrates how sentimental or tinh cam relationships, developed through morally charged exchanges, are central to Vietnamese funerals. Importantly, tinh cam is relational and inherently social as it depends on interaction and exchange between people. As Gammeltoft notes, "the term *tinh cam* has slightly different connotations than 'feelings'; it usually refers either to feelings between people or to the capacity to feel for others rather than to an individual's inner emotional life."[27]

Although funeral ceremonies are quite distinct from mediumship and do not involve mediums, len dong is also a site where tinh cam relationships flourish. Through the interactions that occur at rituals—the intimate muttering of wishes and prayers when disciples approach the possessee, the fun and jocularity of receiving the gifts of the spirits, the sharing of thoughts and gossip with friends—participants are able to show solidarity and sympathy for one another. Listening to chau van music together, and at times clapping along to the beat when mediums are dancing, also encourages the ritualized performance of sentiments to be shared by all religious devotees.

Sentimental relations between musicians are required for a performance to have meaning and feeling. The members of chau van bands must have respect and understanding for one another; otherwise musicians said the music would not have heart (*khong co tam*) and would not have soul (*khong co hon*). The importance of sentimental relations between musicians applies to traditional music ensembles beyond chau van bands. As Lauren Meeker observes in relation to the music theater form *cheo* and the folk song tradition *quan ho*: "Today, sentiment [tinh cam] is seen as an essential element of the spirit of Vietnamese culture. Sentiment is, for instance, the social glue which is said to bind singers to their music and to each other. . . . This deep sentiment is said to enable the true expression of the song and it allows one to sing with 'all one's heart' (*het long*)."[28]

The notion that music expresses emotion is also a fundamental principle of Vietnamese music performance. Probably the most detailed theories concerning the expressivity of Vietnamese music have been espoused by renowned performers of the southern Vietnamese music genre *don ca tai tu* or *nhac tai tu*. Paul Trainor's thesis on this genre provides a detailed comparison of Tran Van Khe's and Nguyen Vinh Bao's understandings of modality in don ca tai tu and the ethos of different modes.[29] Although Trainor's analysis reveals differences in their categorization of modes and their emotional associations, both of these master musicians tie emotional expression to the modal characteristics of pieces. According to these theories, emotional associations are understood to be hardwired in the musical characteristics of modes. In other words, expressivity is embedded in don ca tai tu music through a formalized code. To cite a specific example, when I spoke to Nguyen Vinh Bao in the summer of 2008, he said that the Dao mode—and the piece "Dao Ngu Cung," which uses the Dao mode—expressed feelings of heroism (*anh hung*), majesty (*uy nghi*), and power (*oai hung*).[30] He also remarked that images such as a fighting cock (*ga da*) and a military general (*ong tuong*), which embodied the sentiments of the mode, came into his mind. For a performance to convey the emotions of its pieces, Nguyen Vinh Bao stressed the importance of having an appropriate performance context, which included ensuring that the musicians have tinh cam so they would be inspired (*ngau hung*) to improvise interesting phrases and that the performance was for a small audience in a relaxed setting conducive to fostering sentimental relations between the performers and audience.

Chau van musicians did not articulate musical theories that connect emotions to modal characteristics such as scale and ornament in the same way as don ca tai tu musicians. However, they did discuss the emotional associations of chau van songs and stressed the importance of sentimental relations in performance. For example, the master chau van musician Le Ba Cao discussed the sentiment of three of the main Phu songs—"Phu Dau," "Phu Noi," and "Phu Binh"—in the following terms: "All the Phu songs manifest our sincere emotions [*the hien len chan tinh cua nguoi ta*]. For example the "Phu Dau" melody manifests sadness.... 'Phu Noi' expresses a sincere feeling in the guts, for example, tinh cam between people, and 'Phu Binh' is fresh and bright and manifests happiness in people's guts."[31] To convey such sentiments, Le Ba Cao emphasized the importance of having a genuine and sincere emotional disposition. He said that because chau van music was a manifestation of the heart-soul (*the hien cho tam linh*), musicians should not perform if they were irritated, sad, or worried about something.[32] Rather, they must "have heart" when they perform at rituals, just as mediums must devote their hearts to the spirits.

Conclusion

This chapter has discussed Vietnamese mediumship as a forum in which sentiments are felt, performed, and shared through ritual practice and music. I have suggested that mediumship may be understood as an affective system in which emotions are embedded in a spiritual and human landscape, which relates to the ethnicity, gender, and place of spirits. Mountain spirits mark out a territory that is feminine, ethnic, natural, lively, wild, happy, humorous, and tempestuous. In both the yang human and the yin spirit world, the environment of the mountains and forests is opposed to the lowlands and rivers, the latter being represented as more masculine, controlled, powerful, and prestigious than remote mountainous regions. Spirits associated with the lowlands may exhibit a range of emotions ranging from sadness to anger. In this way, the process of engendering during rituals is based on interconnections between gender, emotion, and the environment.

The emotional terrain laid out by the religious system of mediumship is navigated by possessed mediums and is performed in song by chau van bands. When mediums embody a sequence of spirits during rituals, they engage in a multisensory conceptualization and embodiment of place, evoked sonically and visually through bodily practice. Possession rituals provide mediums with scope to perform emotions associated with spirits through a range of ritual practices, including dancing and listening to music, distributing blessed gifts, and uttering divine messages. The emotional texture of rituals changes as the sequence of spirit possessions progresses, and mediums draw on and enact the emotional associations of spirits in different ways.

The emotional arousal of possession is felt in the body, and listening to music with a sensibility, a particular habitus of listening, which animates emotion. Mediums develop a propensity to experience the heightened emotions of possession through the crises and suffering they experience prior to initiation. Notably, women rather than men are culturally expected to become mediums, and this is related to dominant conceptions of women being emotionally volatile and hot tempered. The few men who become mediums are known for having feminine characteristics, for being effeminate. This suggests that emotionality is related to femaleness and that the display of affect is strongly gendered.

In Vietnamese conceptions the heart and guts are the seat of the emotions, and emotions are both felt and thought. Mediums embody spirits through a particular somatic mode of attention, a bodily process of feeling and thinking about the spirits. Both music and the spirits stimulate emotion-thought, felt in the heart, gut, and heart-soul, to effect the transformation of possession. Through the sung narration of ritual action, chau van performance draws ritual participants into the sacred script of possession, and it also aids in the fostering of tinh cam or sentimental relations. Although rituals encourage a highly emotive way of listening, the notion that music performance fosters tinh cam among musicians, and between musicians and listeners, is central to Vietnamese musical expression in general. For a musical performance to have heart, that is, to have meaning and feeling, it must be inspired and must help foster enduring, sentimental relationships.

Notes

1. My previous writing on Vietnamese mediumship has addressed some of the emotional dimensions of spirit possession. See Barley Norton, *Songs for the Spirits: Music and Mediums in Modern Vietnam* (Urbana: University of Illinois Press, 2009).

2. In this chapter I do not adopt the distinctions that some theorists have made between sentiment, emotion, affect, and feeling. I use them interchangeably, following everyday English understandings. When referring to Vietnamese concepts relating to sentiment, such as having heart (*co tam*) and sentiment or sentimental relations (*tinh cam*), I make this clear by retaining the Vietnamese phrasing.

3. Other ethnomusicological studies that explore various issues relating to symbolic, bodily, and social aspects of musical affect include Steven Feld, *Sound and Sentiment: Birds, Weeping, Poetics, and Song in Kaluli Expression* (Philadelphia: University of Pennsylvania Press, 1990); Elizabeth Tolbert, "Women Cry with Words: Symbolization of Affect in the Karelian Lament," *Yearbook for Traditional Music* 22 (1990): 80–105; Thomas Turino, "Signs of Imagination, Identity, and Experience: A Peircian Semiotic Theory for Music," *Ethnomusicology* 43, no. 2 (1999): 221–55; David Henderson, "Emotion and Devotion, Lingering and Longing in Some Nepali Songs," *Ethnomusicology* 40, no. 3 (1996): 440–68; Richard K. Wolf, "Emotional Dimensions of Ritual Music among the Kotas, a South Indian Tribe," *Ethnomusicology* 45, no. 3 (2001): 379–422; Judith Becker, *Deep Listeners: Music, Emotion, and Trancing* (Bloomington: Indiana University Press, 2004); and Fiona Magowan, *Melodies of Mourning: Music and Emotion in Northern Australia* (Perth: University of Western Australia Press, 2007).

4. Many mediums also hold len dong during large festivals such as the Phu Giay festival in Nam Dinh province, about one hundred kilometers south of Hanoi, which is held annually in the third lunar month.

5. The therapeutic aspects of mediumship as a form of folk healing have been explored by several scholars, including Kirsten W. Endres, *Performing the Divine: Mediums, Markets and Modernity in Vietnam* (Copenhagen: NIAS Press, 2011); Nguyen Thi Hien, "Yin Illness: Its Diagnosis and Healing within Lên Đồng (Spirit Possession) Rituals of

the Việt," *Asian Ethnology* 67, no. 2 (2008): 305–21; and Nguyen Kim Hien, "*Len dong:* Mot Sinh Hoat Tam Linh Mang Tinh Tri Lieu?" [*Len dong:* A Spiritual Practice Bearing Therapy Features?], *Van Hoa Dan Gian* 76, no. 4 (2001): 69–78. In this paper I concentrate on the emotional dimensions of rituals, which I consider to be key to the efficacy of rituals and their therapeutic role.

6. Recordings of some chau van songs can be heard on the CD *Northern Vietnam: Possession Songs*, released on Buda Records in 1997. Chau van songs and video extracts of len dong rituals are also included on the DVD that accompanies my book *Songs for the Spirits*.

7. See Norton, *Songs for the Spirits*.

8. Spirit priests are usually chau van musicians skilled in a wide range of spirit invocations and other forms of spirit worship (*cung*).

9. There are differences in the music and ritual practices of mediumship in northern, central, and southern Vietnam. Field research on len dong and chau van in Hanoi and other parts of northern Vietnam in 1996–97, 1998, and 2004–5 was funded by scholarships and grants awarded by the British Academy, the School of Oriental and African Studies, the Central Research Fund of the University of London, and the Arts and Humanities Research Council.

10. John Leavitt, "Meaning and Feeling in the Anthropology of Emotions," *American Ethnologist* 23, no. 3 (1996): 532.

11. See also Karen Fjelstad and Lisa Maiffret, "Gifts from the Spirits: Spirit Possession and Personal Transformation among Silicon Valley Spirit Mediums," in *Possessed by the Spirits: Mediumship in Contemporary Vietnamese Communities*, ed. Karen Fjelstad and Nguyen Thi Hien (Ithaca, NY: Cornell Southeast Asia Program, 2006), 111–26.

12. Jane C. Sugarman, *Engendering Song: Singing and Subjectivity at Prespa Albanian Weddings* (Chicago: University of Chicago Press, 1997), 253.

13. According to official classifications, there are "fifty-three ethnic minority nationalities in Vietnam making up about 14 percent of the population." Philip Taylor, "Minorities at Large: New Approaches to Minority Ethnicity in Vietnam," *Journal of Vietnamese Studies* 3, no. 3 (2008): 3. For further information on issues relating to ethnic minority groups in Vietnam and relations with the "Viet" majority and the state, see the rest of the articles in this issue of *Journal of Vietnamese Studies*.

14. Steven Feld, "Waterfalls of Song: An Acoustemology of Place Resounding in Bosavi, Papua New Guinea," in *Senses of Place*, ed. Steven Feld and Keith H. Basso (Santa Fe, NM: School of American Research Press, 1996), 114.

15. Some male spirits belong to the Mountains and Forests Palace, such as the Second Mandarin (Quan De Nhi), The Seventh Prince (Ong Hoang Bay), and the Little Young Prince (Cau Be). However, they are not as closely connected to the environment as female mountain spirits, and the Xa group of songs that musically evoke the atmosphere of the mountain are not performed for these male spirits.

16. Writings on Vietnamese mediumship from the late colonial period, such as Long Chuong, *Hau Thanh* [Serving the Spirits] (Ha Noi: Nha Xuat Ban Ha Noi, 1990 [1942]), suggest that antagonism between female mediums and disapproving husbands has been a recurring issue in the history of mediumship, and some female mediums today hide their ritual activities from their husbands. For further discussion, see Norton, *Songs for the Spirits*.

17. Based on their research with Vietnamese mediums in the Silicon Valley in the United States, Karen Fjelstad and Lisa Maiffret similarly note that the Little Young Prince, one of the most popular spirits among mediums in the Silicon Valley, is an

especially expressive spirit who "often acts like a two year old, laughing one moment and crying the next." "Gifts from the Spirits," 119.

18. Wolf, "Emotional Dimensions," 382.

19. Tine Gammeltoft, *Women's Bodies, Women's Worries: Health and Family Planning in a Vietnamese Rural Community* (Richmond: Curzon, 1999), 227.

20. See Thomas J. Csordas, *Body/Meaning/Healing* (Basingstoke: Palgrave MacMillan, 2002).

21. For example, one of the terms for guts (*long*) appears in expressions such as "to fall in love" (*phai long*) and "to hurt someone's feelings" (*mech long*), and the heart appears in compound words such as *tam tu*, which refers to somebody's innermost feelings or thoughts.

22. See also Fiona Magowan, this volume.

23. Gammeltoft, *Women's Bodies, Women's Worries*, 211. The merging of heart with mind, feeling, and cognition is also evident in Vietnamese translations for English words such as intellect (*tam tri*), psyche (*tam nao*), psychology (*tam ly*), and mental illness (*tam than*), which all include the term Vietnamese term for heart (*tam*).

24. Pham Quynh Phuong, *Hero and Deity: Tran Hung Dao and the Resurgence of Popular Religion in Vietnam* (Singapore: Silkworm Books, 2009), 109.

25. Becker, *Deep Listeners*, 52.

26. Ibid., 71.

27. Shaun Kingsley Malarney, *Culture, Ritual and Revolution in Vietnam* (London: Routledge Curzon, 2002); Gammeltoft, *Women's Bodies, Women's Worries*, 206.

28. Lauren Meeker, "Musical Transmissions: Folk Music, Mediation and Modernity in Northern Vietnam" (PhD diss., Columbia University, 2007), 12.

29. John Paul Trainor, "Modality in the Nhac Tai Tu of South Vietnam" (PhD diss., University of Washington, 1977). See also Tran Van Khe, *La Musique Vietnamienne Traditionnelle* (Paris: Presses Universitaires de France, 1962); and Le Tuan Hung, *Dan Tranh Music in Vietnam: Traditions and Innovations* (Melbourne: Australian Asia Foundation, 1998).

30. In Trainor's discussion of Nguyen Vinh Bao's thoughts on the ethos of *don ca tai tu* modes, he reports that Vinh Bao "made no judgment on the dao nuance" ("Modality," 183). However, this was not the case when I discussed the Dao mode with Nguyen Vinh Bao more than thirty years after Trainor conducted his research.

31. Le Ba Cao, personal communication, Hanoi, 2004.

32. In an interview in 2004 Le Ba Cao discussed emotional expression in music performance as follows: "Playing and singing must be 'grasped thoroughly' (*quan triet*).... There are times when naturally one finds one is happy, the sound of the instrument blossoms, and the playing is excellent. But there are times when naturally the 'guts are not relaxed' (*trong long khong duoc thoai mai*). Sometimes when one plays all the notes it has 'no feeling' (*khong cam thay*), it is 'not interesting' (*khong hay*).... In the old days to play music you had to observe three 'taboos' (*kieng ky*). You couldn't play if you were 'irritated and sad in your guts' (*trong long dang co su buon buc*) or if you hadn't washed your hands or clothes, or if you didn't have a clean mind, that is, if you were worrying about something. This is because the sound of the instrument is an expression of the 'heart-soul' (*tam linh*) of the people."

Chapter Two

Gendering Emotional Connections to the Balinese Landscape

Exploring Children's Roles in a Barong Performance

Jonathan McIntosh

In Bali the spiritual world is mapped onto the physical landscape of the island, connecting specific emotional reactions to places based on spiritual understandings about them that begin at a very early age. One of the ways in which children learn about their world and how to perceive and react to their island is through theatrical performance. In this chapter I describe how children express this connection to the landscape through the performance of Barong (a traditional dance performance that depicts a mythical, masked creature). The performance embodies a complex interrelationship among emotions associated with the Balinese spirit world, their physical surroundings, and their gendered participation in Balinese society (map 2.1).

The term "Barong" generally refers to a male deity within the Bali-Hindu religion, represented as a mythical beast animated by two male dancers. Barong has three manifestations: a mask, a creature, and a dance.[1] The formidable mask represents an animal, and the dancers perform inside a shell covered with various layers of fur and cloth that forms his elongated body. Every 210 days, during the Balinese New Year celebrations (Galungan and Kuningan), two dancers who make up the four-legged Barong perform in villages.[2] Accompanied by a troupe of musicians performing in a gamelan ensemble, Barong roams the streets until he is invited by someone to dance outside their house or business to ward off evil spirits at this auspicious time of the new year. This performance with dancers, musicians, and Barong is referred to as *ngelawang*. As a collective, the ngelawang then moves from house to house, where Barong dances at the gate (*lawang*) of a family compound or in the street just outside it. Traditionally, these activities are organized and performed by men, and it is also a time when boys and male adolescents make their own Barong and take them on the road.

Map 2.1. Indonesia and the island of Bali. Map by Angela Snieder.

Although a number of notable scholars have written about this area of Balinese studies, they refer only to Barong performances by adults.[3] Other authors, in particular Michel Picard and Annette Sanger, have written about commercial Barong performances organized for tourists.[4] Ethnographic material relating to children's performances, however, is limited. Apart from references by Colin McPhee and Margaret Mead, and a passing mention by I Wayan Dibia and Rucina Ballinger, the topic remains largely unexplored by ethnomusicologists.[5] I examine how children learn to perform Barong and why their involvement is critical not only to the continuity of the tradition but also to reaffirming emotional connections to the Balinese landscape and delineating gender differences between boys and girls.[6]

I begin by outlining the role of Barong in Balinese society, tracing its historical origins, and discussing the various types of Barong to be found across the island.[7] This background is important to understand the central roles played by two key characters in Balinese cosmology: Barong and his witchlike counterpart, Rangda.[8] I argue that the ways in which children and adults react to the appearances of Barong and Rangda during a popular dance-drama called Calonarang enable children to learn about the spiritual world as aspects of spatial and, in particular, vertical orientation.[9] By noting children's different reactions to the two characters, I discuss how the theatrical confrontation between Barong and Rangda relates to fear and anxiety and serves as a metaphor for parent-children relations in Bali.[10] In the second part of the chapter, I focus on a children's Barong performance that occurred in August 2004, in the villages of Keramas and Medahan, in the administrative district of Gianyar. I do this to draw attention to the ways in which the children's Barong serves to counterbalance emotions of fear and anxiety associated with Rangda. Finally, by comparing my research with similar work carried out in the 1930s, I analyze continuities and changes in contributions made by boys and girls in the children's ngelawang to demonstrate that the activity serves not only to reaffirm emotional connections to the Balinese landscape but also to reinforce traditional modes of gendered activity.[11] Thus, and as found elsewhere in this volume, the chapter furthers our understanding of the ways in which music and dance performance reaffirms important links between age and generation, gender, place, and emotion.

Barong

The exact origins of the Barong are vague. The word "Barong" derives from the Sanskrit word *bahrwang*, which literally means "bear," and refers to a mythological animal.[12] I Madé Bandem claims that Barong originates from pre-Hindu society and, because of its similarities to the Chinese dragon, is thought to have arrived in Bali from Buddhist mainland Asia.[13] Dibia and Ballinger provide a possible explanation for the arrival of Barong in Bali.[14] The authors write that a Chinese dragon was seen dancing at a beach in the south of the island in the thirteenth century A.D. It is said to have come from a Chinese boat that hit the rocks that surround the southern coastline. It then followed that the Balinese created their own version of this Chinese dragon and called it Barong Ketet, or Ket.[15]

As the spiritual protector of a village, a Barong dances to ward off evil spirits and to prevent illness. The Balinese believe that this practice brings good luck, since the performance achieves balance between positive spirits largely represented by Barong and negative spirits mainly represented by the witch Rangda. The word "Rangda" means "widow" and, according to Balinese cosmology, the character represents the destructive side of humankind. Her appearance is more frightening than that of Barong: she has a long, spiky tongue; pendulous breasts; and, hair down to her knees. Some Barong and Rangda masks are considered to have sacred qualities and possess spiritual power (*sakti*). The majority of Barong masks, however, are for dancing and ngelawang. These masks, which are not considered to be sacred per se, are often attached to cloth bodies and used for entertainment purposes.[16] Despite lacking sakti, secular Barong masks are often appropriated to fulfill sacred and spiritual functions, such as in the context of children's ngelawang.

Children's Barong in Balinese Society

In Bali Barong is not just a form of entertainment; he is the spiritual protector and guardian of a village. Considered from an adult's perspective, Barong performance is a serious and integral part of the Bali-Hindu religion, but from a child's point of view it has a somewhat different meaning. For boys and girls Barong performance is considered a fun, social activity filled with laughter and enjoyment. It is through this community entertainment that children come together in a social activity primarily religious in practice.[17]

Barong is one of the most popular children's ceremonial dances performed in a variety of public contexts. These most notably include the collective ngelawang that moves from house to house during the New Year period (as described in detail in the second half of this chapter), as well as children's play activities. Upon hearing the distinctive metallic timbres emanating from the traveling gamelan ensemble that accompanies a ngelawang, villagers immediately enter the street in anticipation of the thrilling spectacle that is to unfold before them. As loud, colorful, animated, and extremely charismatic events, Barong performances elicit highly emotive socioreligious experiences through the responses of spectators, dancers, and musicians, which in turn delineate particular gender roles.

The socioemotive religious experiences associated with Barong performance can be attributed in part to the sonic world created by the gamelan ensemble that accompanies the ngelawang. R. Anderson Sutton defines a gamelan ensemble as a "set of instruments unified by their tuning and often decorated with carving and painting."[18] Consisting mainly of percussion instruments, including metallophones (large glockenspiel-like instruments), gongs, and drums, gamelan orchestras are synonymous with Indonesia but are particular to the islands of Java and Bali. Through the interaction of players and instruments within an ensemble, gamelan music stresses notions of unity, community, and totality.[19] Furthermore, within Balinese ceremonial contexts, such as that of the ngelawang, gamelan music contributes to the noisy (*ramê*) aesthetic required to ward off malevolent spiritual beings.

Masks are always used for Barong performances, and they are an important component of the way in which children learn to relate to Balinese society and their island.[20] The most common type of mask is called Barong Ketet, or Ket for short. He does not correspond to any real animal but is easily recognizable because of his large, shaggy, doglike body, made from shredded leaves (*peraksok*). Barong Ketet is most commonly inferred when discussing the term "Barong"; however, this is only one type of mask. Other masks take the form of a lion (Barong Singa), tiger (Barong Macan), boar (Barong Bangkal), dog (Barong Asu), serpent

(Barong Naga), cow (Barong Lembu), and even an elephant (Barong Gadja). Parents sometimes purchase small Barong masks for boys as toys and choose the type of mask to be worn by their sons. The type of mask bought for the child is often commensurate with the financial status of the parents. For example, a small lion mask is more expensive than a child's boar or tiger mask.

Barong animal masks have distorted facial features and clacking jaws, the latter representing power and anger, as well as presenting a visual and audible threat to invisible harmful deities. Barong comprises two male dancers—the first forms the front legs and operates the mask to imitate an animal's facial expressions, while the other forms the hind legs and operates the tail of the animal. In performance, the dancers move in a highly stylized manner, mimicking the actions of the animal being portrayed. For example, the shaggy Barong Ketet tends to waddle, whereas the tiger Barong (Barong Macan) moves with a smooth swagger.

Throughout Bali various Barong masks are thought to embody characteristics of particular Bali-Hindu gods. For example, Angela Hobart notes that the Barong Ketet mask embodies the god Siwa (the divine teacher and educator) as well as the goddess Durga (who is also associated with Rangda).[21] In contrast, the tiger mask (Barong Macan) embodies the god Brahma (the creator and procreator). The characteristics portrayed by each mask in performance instill emotions associated with different animals, in turn reinforcing the necessary reverence to be shown for each religious figure. Although children's Barong masks are not imbued with such mystical powers, their performances are considered to contribute to the rebalancing of the cosmos during New Year celebrations.

Despite deliberate parental choices of Barong mask and their associated meanings, it is the act of playing with or performing Barong that creates distinct gender differences in Balinese society. For instance, girls generally do not wear Barong masks—only boys tend to play or perform Barong. Indeed, the verb *mabarong-barongan* refers to the act of young boys playing Barong. Therefore, Barong dancing is a "male prerogative," and this could be the reason why only boys are given "play" masks.[22] Additionally, some of my female informants stated that women would not be able to dance Barong due to the weight of the mask and costume. Despite this, girls sometimes participate in ngelawang activities. Venerated with monetary offerings and welcomed with warmth and excitement through the emotional response of the audience, the tangible figure of Barong is celebrated by boys and girls, men and women, communicating the important social and religious precepts that underpin Balinese society to children.

Barong and Rangda

The main role of a Barong performance is to reestablish spiritual balance in Balinese cosmology. Generally, Barong represents spiritual protection and order, whereas Rangda represents negativity and destruction. If the two characters appear together in a theatrical performance, there is inevitably a confrontation between them, but neither character emerges victorious. Instead, the confrontation serves to strike a balance between the spiritual powers of the two. This balance is necessary because the Balinese believe that negativity exists in all humans and is manifested in the spirits of chaos (*bhuta kala*), whose queen is Rangda. Such spirits, they believe, are able to transform themselves into witches (*leyak*) associated with female sorcery and danger; these witches reside in the village graveyard (*sema*), which is a spiritually dangerous place because of its association with Rangda and her followers.[23] This sense of balance is further conveyed through the emotional responses displayed by adults and children to the two characters: Barong tends to be greeted with warmth and affection, whereas Rangda instills fear and anxiety. The Balinese believe that such a cosmological equilibrium can be achieved only if individuals have an equally emphatic emotional response toward Barong and Rangda. This suggests a form of respect ultimately due to both deities, for if one character were not given adequate attention, cosmological chaos would then ensue.

Such reactions to the appearance of Barong and Rangda could be clearly observed during a Calonarang theatrical performance (a dance-drama based on semihistorical events from Java in the eleventh century A.D.) that I observed in 2004. The play is always performed at night when spiritual influences are at their strongest—and often at times of illness or on certain auspicious days. The performance usually takes place near the graveyard or outside the village death temple (*pura dalem*), both the domains of Rangda. During the New Year celebrations in August, I accompanied several of the boys and teenagers from the privately run dance studio (*sanggar tari*) in the village of Keramas to a Calonarang performance.[24] The performance took place in the outer courtyard (*jaba*) of the death temple in the ward of Biya (Banjar Biya) in the west of the village. As the Calonarang incorporated a comic opera (Arja) by a visiting troupe of actors, large crowds had gathered to watch the performance.

The atmosphere in the temple was relaxed until the crowd heard that Barong was about to appear. As soon as these whispers reached us, Barong Bangkal, which takes the form of a boar, suddenly emerged from the innermost part of the temple (*jeroan*). As he approached, the audience parted to each side, creating a pathway to the stage. The mask had a large snout and narrow eyes, and his body was made of black-and-white cloth. When he began to dance in time with the musical accompaniment provided by the gamelan ensemble, he moved with heavy, deliberate footsteps.[25] Notably, the children sitting at the front of the audience did not seem scared in his presence, and from time to time some of them even tried to reach out and touch him. If he came too close, however, even the brave children quickly withdrew their hands so they would not be caught in the clacking jaws of the mask. When this happened, the audience laughed with delight at the startled reactions of the children.

By contrast, the appearance of Rangda was met with screams and much commotion from the audience. Like Barong, Rangda also entered the outer courtyard from the inner courtyard. The shouts and the melancholic roaring from inside Rangda's mask quickly prompted the children whom I had accompanied to fearfully congregate behind me, huddling together and using my body as a shield while the drama continued to unfold. All of a sudden, Rangda rushed forward through the audience to confront Barong; he simultaneously jumped down from the stage to meet her. After five minutes of confrontation accompanied by loud playing from the village gamelan ensemble, the two characters simply stopped their fighting and retired back to the inner courtyard of the temple, where offerings were made to each of the masks and the dancers were blessed with holy water (*tirta*).[26] Soon afterward, at three o'clock in the morning, the audience dispersed and, tired, went home to sleep.

Children's Reactions to Barong and Rangda

To understand the different emotional reactions to the appearances of Barong and Rangda, it is first of all necessary to understand how children learn about the importance of spatial awareness in relation to Balinese cosmology and Balinese geography.[27] These connections among people, landscape, and the spirit world are integral to the way in which the Balinese conduct their everyday activities and also infuse parent-child relationships. In particular, the term *kaja*, meaning "upstream," "inward," or "toward the mountain," refers to Bali's highest mountain, Mount Agung (Gunung Agung, literally meaning "Great Mountain"), which is considered to be the spiritual center of the Bali-Hindu religion. Thus, kaja is associated with positive deities, including Barong, and ancestral spirits who, during Balinese New Year celebrations, descend from heaven via Mount Agung. Conversely, *kelod*, meaning "downstream," "outward," or "toward the sea," is associated with Rangda and other destructive spirits believed to reside at lower levels and in the sea.[28] *Kangin* denotes to the right and *kauh* to the left when one faces kaja. Kangin is closely associated with kaja and thus positive spirits, whereas kauh is aligned with kelod and is therefore linked with negative spirits.[29] And so, Barong, whose numerous constituent characters are largely depicted by various animal masks, is associated with kaja, which represents well-being, positivity, and spiritual protection.

Children, from an early age, learn about the kaja-kelod system of spatial orientation at home. All family compounds are built with the family shrine (*sanggah*) toward kaja or kangin; the kitchen (*paon*) and bathroom (if there is one) are situated toward kelod or kauh and are regarded as dirty and unclean. At the same time, children become aware of vertical hierarchies of sacredness through the body. The Balinese believe that the head of a person is the most sacred part of the body and should generally not be touched by other people.[30]

In addition, this notion is reinforced in practice as the Balinese sleep with their heads toward either kaja or kangin. Thus, experiencing the cosmological significance of spatial and vertical hierarchies of spirit activity and sacredness enables Balinese children to learn about the world that surrounds them. This process occurs gradually as children are exposed to various Balinese activities and theatrical performances.

The theatrical confrontation between Barong and Rangda also serves as a metaphor for Balinese parent-child relations, according to Gregory Bateson and Margaret Mead.[31] Not only does this confrontation express "the residue in adults of what they experienced as children," but it also "shapes [children's] reading of the experiences to which they become subjected daily." Mead explains that these experiences, connected to the spiritual and spatial significance associated with Barong and Rangda, occur as a result of the relationship a child has with its parents during the early stages of enculturation.[32] As newborns, babies are always carried by adults and older siblings, but when a child first learns to walk, "its ventures away from support and parents are controlled by the mother or child nurse mimicking terror and calling it back with threats that are random in content—'Tiger!' 'Police!' 'Snake!' 'Feces!'" Mead contends that the control exerted by these threats, and the theatrical manner in which they are performed, teach a child "that undefined space may at any moment be filled with unknown terror."[33] In this context, a child becomes anxious and quickly learns to associate undefined space with negative forces—forces that become notably manifested in a tangible form through the appearance of the witch Rangda.[34]

Bateson and Mead note that mothers evoke similar emotions in their children by picking up or passing round other mothers' babies. They do this to "tease and tantalize, while the child responds with mounting emotion which is invariably undercut before climax." A mother acts like this so that her son or daughter becomes aware of the concept of fear (*dengen*) in Balinese cosmology, a concept regarded as "a value as well as a threat."[35] The Balinese mother often does this by employing the phrase *sing bani* to encourage a small child "not to be brave or daring" by "not doing something that is potentially dangerous or harmful."[36] The aim of this command is to instill a sense of fear in children that serves to protect them from physical, as well as spiritual, harm. In contrast, a "Balinese father attends very little to children except his own," and, generally, the relationship is regarded as "gentle, playful [and] satisfying."[37] During fieldwork, I witnessed the kind of parent-child interactions described by Bateson and Mead on a daily basis. Although a father also teases his son or daughter, his actions do not educe such strong emotional responses as those of a Balinese mother. Therefore, the behavior of fathers is believed to give "security" to children, just like Barong.[38] This notion of security then counteracts the ideas of fear that a mother instills in her child—negative emotions manifested in the appearance of Rangda. This suggested homology could explain the continued social significance of the children's ngelawang during the auspicious time of the Balinese New Year, to which I now turn in the second part of this chapter.

Children's Barong

Like similar adult processions, children's performances of ngelawang serve to remind the community of the need to reestablish a sense of balance between positive and negative forces in the Balinese cosmos. It starts with members of the community inviting the children's Barong to dance. By observing the theatrical representation of the rebalancing of the cosmos, the audience witnesses and is reassured of the reconstitution of this cosmological harmony. Moreover, the journey of Barong, as a public ceremony through the village, is also necessary for the generational transference of Balinese-Hindu religious knowledge. Having described the role of Barong and Rangda in Balinese cosmology, and the responses of children and adults to these characters as defined by geoemotional relationships, I now move on to discuss children's Barong, with particular reference to a ngelawang from the villages of Keramas and Medahan in the administrative district of Gianyar.

Barong was originally incorporated into the play world of children as a means of imitating the activities of adults. Mead writes that only young boys are sometimes given "little" Barong masks and one of their mother's shawls to play with.[39] In children's play activities, these little masks are sometimes roughly treated and are not afforded the same reverence as those used in adult performances. As a result, they often become damaged, so much so that a mask can eventually fall apart. McPhee provides the first short account of a children's Barong from the 1930s in the village of Sayan, Gianyar.[40] Documenting the adventures of small boys who formed a music club to emulate the activities of older children and adults, the author demonstrates how music and dance performance enables boys to embody attributes essential to being a man in Balinese society.[41] In addition, McPhee notes several factors that differentiate children's Barong performances from those of adults.[42] Generally, children's Barong are fashioned from inexpensive materials—the masks and costumes tend not to be as good quality, or spiritually important, as those used by adults—and there tend to be fewer individuals in the accompanying entourage. Even though children's groups are smaller in size, however, the musical accompaniment is no less sophisticated than for adult performances.

In August 2004 a small *gamelan gaguntangan* ensemble, an orchestra primarily used to accompany comic opera (Arja) performances, accompanied the children's ngelawang in Keramas and in the neighboring village of Medahan. With the exception of the two drums (*kendang*) played by the male dance teacher from the sanggar and another male performer affiliated with the organization, young boys and teenagers from the sanggar played the various instruments in the gamelan gaguntangan ensemble. Colin McPhee and Lisa Gold both write that the *gamelan pelegongan* (a late nineteenth-century ensemble originally used to accompany the female *legong* dance) and the *gamelan gong gede* (a large ceremonial ensemble) tend to provide the musical accompaniment for Barong.[43] Michael Bakan, however, also notes that the *gamelan batel bebarongan* (a processional orchestra) accompanies sacred Barong performances.[44] Therefore, the use of a gamelan gaguntangan ensemble to accompany the children's ngelawang in Keramas and Medahan highlights an important musical point of difference between children's and adults' Barong performances.

This particular type of gamelan orchestra is inexpensive and usually features bamboo instruments, for example, a bamboo zither (*guntang*) and an end-blown bamboo flute (*suling*). Neither of these instruments nor metallophones were included in the ensemble that accompanied the children's Barong. Metallophones would have been too heavy for the children to carry during the procession, and their inclusion along with a guntang, as well as one or several suling, would have required a large amount of rehearsal time to learn the appropriate parts to accompany a Barong performance.[45] Instead, the children's gamelan ensemble consisted of various gongs, mounted cymbals (*ceng-ceng*) and drums light enough to be played and carried at the same time. The exceptions to this rule were the large slab-gong (*gong pulu*) and the mounted cymbals. The slab-gong consisted of two large bronze gamelan keys suspended over a wooden resonator. For two of the older boys to transport it, the wooden resonator was attached to two long bamboo poles with four pieces of material. The two boys then placed the poles over their shoulders, and as they walked the boy at the back played the gong pulu by striking both keys simultaneously with two large, padded beaters. Every time the children's Barong was invited to perform, the boys took a well-earned rest and placed the slab-gong on the ground. Similarly, during performances, the mounted cymbals were also placed on the ground.

Other instruments in the gamelan ensemble included a small handheld gong with a raised boss, used as the time keeper (*kempli*); a small gong with a raised boss (*klentong*); and a high-pitched chime-gong (*kelenang*) mounted on a small stand, similar in shape, but smaller than the kempli. The kempli and kelenang were struck with long wooden beaters wound with a chord at one end. The kempli was struck with a small, padded beater. The only other instrument used was a *krentengan*. Although similar in shape to the kempli, it produced a dull timbre, since the boss of the gong was raised only slightly from the face of the gong. The krentengan had two roles in the ensemble. During the procession and the slower parts of the performance, it usually played the beat with the kempli. But during faster, more dramatic sections in the children's performance, it played syncopated rhythms with the drum and cymbals.

To comprehend the "sonic landscape" of the children's Barong performance more fully, it is helpful to abstract and highlight two components from the polyphonic texture of the gamelan gaguntangan musical accompaniment: rhythmic patterns and the metric or colotomic structure. Rhythmic patterns played by the drums and cymbals serve to regulate musical time in the Barong performance (as in all other gamelan compositions). Such patterns often correspond to the steps of Barong and enable the front dancer and drummer to communicate during a performance. The fundamental cyclical organizing principle of gamelan music, the term "colotomic structure" refers to the order in which various gongs in a gamelan ensemble are struck, as well as the space between the striking of these gongs. The children's dance teacher uses a form of "mouth gamelan" to instruct the boys in how to perform the musical accompaniment for Barong. As a form of solfège, mouth gamelan relies on onomatopoeic syllables that signify the timbre produced by various gongs in a gamelan ensemble, and in this case a gamelan gaguntangan ensemble. For example, the gong pulu is vocalized as a low-pitched *sir* or *gir* (with a long rolled "r" at the end, for example, *sirrr*), and the klentong was shortened to a high-pitched *tong*. The kelenang is represented by the very high-pitched vocable *nang*, played in between the striking of the gong pulu and the klentong. Maintaining the pulse, and represented by the vocable *tuk*, the kempli demarcates each beat of the musical cycle.

Along with other associated aspects of Balinese theatrical performance, including makeup and costuming, the colotomic structure also denotes the character of a particular dance. As Gold points out, the restriking of the large gong in a gamelan ensemble (*gong ageng* or, in the case of the children's ngelawang, the gong pulu) and the spaces between the striking of the other gongs "affects the dramatic mood and degree of tension" of the music.[46] The children's ngelawang uses two basic gong structures, *batel* and *omang*, which are also found in adult Barong performances. Repeated for as long as deemed necessary to convey the drama and energy of a ngelawang performance, these gong structures tend to be played in a fast and loud manner. Batel, meaning "agitated," contains two beats per colotomic cycle. It is most often used to accompany fighting scenes in Balinese dance-drama and shadow puppet theater (*wayang kulit*) and to announce the arrival of an unrefined (*keras*) character in dance-dramas, such as comic opera (Arja) and mask dance-drama (Topeng) (see table 2.1).[47] Omang is commonly used to accompany a Barong dance and contains four beats per colotomic cycle (see table 2.2). Both of these colotomic structures also reinforce notions of balance in the musical accompaniment, with the klentong sounding the midpoint of each cycle and the gong pulu simultaneously marking the end of one cycle and the beginning of the next. As a result, the batel and omang colotomic structures further emphasize notions of spatial, spiritual, and physical balance encapsulated in Barong performance.

Table 2.1. Colotomic structure for batel

n	T	n	G
	t		t
	1		2

Table 2.2. Colotomic structure for omang

n	T	n	G
t	t	t	t
1	2	3	4

In table 2.1 the numbers 1 and 2 represent the two beats of the batel colotomic cycle, which in turn are signified by the striking of the kempli (t = tuk). The striking of the klentong (T = tong) coincides with beat one and the sounding of the gong pulu (G = sir or gir) corresponds with beat two. The high-pitched chime-gong kelenang (n = nang) is played on every offbeat. In table 2.2 the numbers 1 to 4 represent the four beats of the omang colotomic cycle, which in turn are signified by the striking of the kempli (t = tuk). The striking of the klentong (T = tong) coincides with beat two and the sounding of the gong pulu (G = sir or gir) corresponds with beat four. The high-pitched kelenang (n = nang) is played on beats one and three.

Having described some of the musical aspects relating to Barong performance, I now move on to provide an ethnographic account of the children's ngelawang in the villages of Keramas and Medahan. Throughout this section I analyze the appearance and movement styles of key characters within the children's performance to reveal particular aspects of positive and negative spiritual forces pertinent to Balinese society. The interactions between the various characters that appear in the children's Barong performance are, therefore, key to the balance of the cosmological and gendered world. Moreover, I also demonstrate how the ngelawang is a context in which children learn how to elicit from audience members the appropriate emotional responses associated with specific character types drawn from Balinese theatrical performance.

"On the Road" with a Children's Ngelawang

At the sanggar in the village of Keramas, a short ceremony was held to bless the children's tiger Barong (Barong Macan) before the start of the ngelawang. Mantras were recited by the children's male dance teacher; Barong was sprinkled with holy water (*matirta*) to reenergize the mask for performance; a simple rice and coconut offering (*canang*) was placed on top of the body of the animal. During the ceremony, two of the younger boys stood inside the shell of Barong before passing the mask and the attached body over to the older boys who would dance for the first part of the ngelawang. Although they never performed Barong during the ngelawang, standing inside the shell of Barong for the purpose of the ceremony allowed the young boys to feel the weight of the mask and costume, as well as try out certain dance moves and positions. As such, this opportunity provided the children with a valuable insight into what it means to dance Barong. Throughout the ceremony an umbrella (*pajeng*) was also held over Barong's head to shade him from the sun, its black-and-white checkered cloth (*kamben poleng*) a further indication of his holy status. All around, the smell of jasmine incense filled the air and, with the ceremony complete, it was the moment to take Barong outside the compound for the very first time (see fig. 2.1).

Barong moved cautiously, lifting his paws into the air before gingerly touching them down into the swirling dust of the road. As he did so, the gamelan gaguntangan ensemble performed the omang gong cycle. Played at a slow tempo, and combined with the sparse texture of the ensemble, it added to the sense of tension created by the performance. The movements of Barong were dependent on the cyclical structure of the music. Generally, the dancers lifted their feet when the klentong was struck. The klentong marked the midpoint of the colotomic cycle. When the same feet were placed on the ground, this movement coincided with the striking of the low-pitched slab-gong that marked the final beat of the cycle. In doing so, the movements of Barong mirrored the symmetry and balance of the musical structure.

The two boys coordinated their movements inside the shell of Barong, lifting and lowering their left and right feet in tandem. The dancer at the back always followed the lead of his partner in front. Their combined efforts meant that the movements of Barong resembled the smooth, prowling steps of a tiger. The mask, held slightly inside the shell of the body, moved slowly, with the large, bulging eyes gradually glaring from one person to the next as its body gently swayed from side to side. This air of uncertainty continued for some time until the drum broke the tension. A succession of quick, short drum rhythms indicated that the gamelan ensemble should play an *angsel*—a sudden rhythmic break indicating a specific dance movement.[48] On cue, the musicians and Barong reacted: the volume of the accompaniment increased, and Barong shook and quivered violently. With his jaws wide open, he executed a step sequence of left-right-left (*ngeseh*) before finishing in the basic right (male) position (*agem kanan*).[49] (In this position, each dancer transfers the weight of his body onto his right leg and places his left leg in front, the ball of the left foot touching the road with toes flexed upward.) Once the agem kanan was complete, the two boys inside Barong straightened their posture. This caused the body of Barong to rise higher into the air. All of a sudden, Barong had changed from a somewhat nervous creature into an animal with a more ferocious personality.

Figure 2.1. The children's Barong begins to dance. Photograph by the author.

This Barong dance combined basic male dance positions and other movements by improvising them within the stylistic parameters of the genre. This improvisation resulted from a continuous dialogue between Barong and the drum, the lead instrument in the gamelan ensemble. Sometimes, Barong indicated a change in the musical accompaniment through the placement of his front feet or the movement of the mask. Here Barong led the players in the gamelan. On other occasions, the drum played specific patterns to indicate to Barong, and those playing in the gamelan ensemble, to move on to a different position or movement. This form of communication occurred throughout the performance but was particularly important just before or during the angsel.

During the angsel the music got louder. This increase in dynamic indicated to the audience that Barong was about to complete a specific dance movement. Although the audience may not have been aware of the technicalities of the dancing, such as the names of specific dance positions, most Balinese know from similar performances which movements are associated with the various levels of dynamics in the musical accompaniment. After the completion of the angsel, the dynamic always returned to a medium level. Several angsel later, the drum signaled for the tempo to slow gradually. This change indicated to the audience that this part of the performance was coming to an end. Reacting to the accompaniment, Barong walked in a circle before finally sitting on the ground. The boys inside the costume stretched their legs out in front of them, the front dancer crossing his legs and placing the mask on his feet. Not letting the mask come into contact with the ground was a sign of respect toward

Barong. Once more, the character changed, reverting from a fierce and violent creature into something resembling a young tiger cub. Tired after his exertions, Barong was ready for sleep.

As soon as Barong sat down, the gamelan signaled the entrance of a new character by playing a fast and loud batel.[50] On cue, a boy, performing the role of a monkey (*bojog*), entered the performance space. Crouching on all fours and wearing a gray mask with bushy, black eyebrows and a protruding jaw, the monkey scrambled around until eventually it spotted the sleeping Barong. To indicate that Barong had fallen asleep, the front dancer held the mask slightly inside the shell of the body, with the jaws a little apart. By gently moving the mask up and down, it looked as if Barong was snoring. Inquisitively, the monkey crept up to Barong on all fours and waved its hand in front of Barong's eyes to make sure he was asleep. Suddenly, Barong woke up and looked around. Startled, the monkey scrambled to the side of the road without being seen. Barong looked around bemused, tossing his head from side to side, but not noticing anything out of the ordinary he once more settled down and fell fast asleep. Despite this, the monkey cheekily resumed waving his hand in front of Barong until, accompanied by strong strikes of the drum and cymbals, Barong woke up for a second time.[51] This time, Barong snapped his jaws several times at the monkey—each clack accompanied by yet more drum strikes and cymbal clashes (see fig. 2.2). Sometimes these musical accents matched the clacking of the jaws exactly, at other moments they did not. Each accent added to, and reinforced, the fast pace of the unfolding drama.

Following a few moments of uncertainty, the two characters began to communicate with each other through mime. Sudden reactions from each character were marked by yet more drum and cymbal strikes, just as in other theatrical genres, such as Arja and Topeng. The monkey also appeared to tease Barong with some invisible food before withdrawing it at the last possible moment. Upset at this, Barong turned his head to one side and sulked. There then followed a comical sequence in which the monkey scrambled to crouch in front of Barong's face, but each time he did so Barong simply ignored him, lifting his head in the air and placing it on the opposite side. This continued for a while until the monkey decided to try and make up for his actions by agreeing to pluck fleas from the paws and beard of Barong. Possibly alluding to the gentle and playful relationship between a child and his or her father, the movements of both characters were slowly executed and exaggerated to maximize audience reaction.[52]

This section was brought to a close by yet another loud burst of batel from the gamelan that signaled the arrival of the final two elderly male characters, known as *bondres*. The bondres—dance-drama characters associated with slapstick comedy as well as vulgar humor—wore masks that covered only the top half of the face, thereby enabling them to speak. The masks were each a different shade of brown, carved with deep wrinkled lines and crooked teeth. As

GENDERING EMOTIONAL CONNECTIONS   53

Figure 2.2. Encounter between Barong and the monkey. Photograph by the author.

the bondres entered the performance space, one character walked with a wide, lopsided gait and brandished a wooden mock knife (*tiuk*); the other, bent over, leaned on a spear (*tombak*) (see fig. 2.3). The boys performing the bondres hunched their shoulders and retracted their necks in toward their bodies. This made their bodies look old, which further helped them to become the characters portrayed by their masks. The audience roared with laughter at the bondres because the movements of the children's characters perfectly mimicked those executed by adult performers in Arja and Topeng dance-dramas.

When the children eventually stopped moving, they waited for the noise of the audience to subside before they continued. As the children waited for this to happen, and as a means of reinforcing how spatial orientation is manifest in the ngelawang performance, the bondres purposely positioned themselves to the kelod of the Barong and monkey. This spatial reference was significant for two reasons. First, it served to restate the Barong's association with the positive spiritual powers of kaja. Second, and as a dramatic technique regularly employed in Balinese performance in relation to the introduction of theatrical characters, it served to communicate to the members of the audience that the bondres characters embodied qualities very different from those of Barong. The establishment of such a dichotomy inferred that the bondres, through their physical positioning toward kelod, were in some way associated with the malevolent realm of Rangda. Since the character of Rangda does not appear in children's ngelawang performances, however, the spatial reference between Barong and the bondres is another way in which villagers are reminded of the

Figure 2.3. The entrance of the bondres. Photograph by the author.

need to reestablish cosmological balance between positive and negative spiritual forces during the auspicious occasion of the Balinese New Year.

Once the audience settled, and the music softened, the characters spoke to each other, addressing the audience at the same time. The boys conversed in colloquial Balinese with rough (*keras*), hoarse voices. By means of their conversation, and by the knife and spear they carried, the audience learned that the two characters were on a hunting expedition, although they had not yet spotted the monkey crouched quietly to the side, nor had they noticed the sleeping Barong. The boys' improvised conversation was loosely based around material devised by the children's male dance teacher during rehearsals for the ngelawang.[53] After a moment or two, the bondres characters walked around the performance area looking for something to hunt. During their search, they brought their hands up to shade their eyes as they pretended to peer into the distance. Eventually they came across the monkey and stood on either side of it. In vain, the bondres attempted to kill their intended prey with their weapons; however, the monkey was too quick for them. Each attempt was signaled by further loud accents played on the drums and cymbals. After dodging numerous machete and spear blows, the monkey woke Barong from his slumber. The performance then climaxed when Barong came to the rescue of the monkey and chased the bondres away. Here, Barong was playful and everyone delighted in the unchoreographed and unscripted action that unfolded at the end of each performance. The excitement of what became the inevitable chase was something that the children and adults in the audience anticipated.

By dramatizing the rescue of the monkey from the clutches of the bondres, the children's performance serves to reaffirm the role of Barong as the protector of the village. Therefore, by interacting with one another, the various characters (such as the tiger Barong, the monkey, and the bondres) perform a story illustrating the power of Barong and his role in Balinese society. The boys who perform these roles must accurately portray each character to elicit appropriate emotional responses from both their fellow performers and the spectators. The inclusion of such a storyline in the children's ngelawang not only highlights Balinese gender roles but also confirms Hobart's observation relating to the embedding of social and moral precepts in Galungan performances.[54] Such observations reinforce the earlier discussion regarding the way in which Barong is a fun and enjoyable activity for children, but nonetheless a performance that serves to underscore important moral boundaries and aspects central to the Bali-Hindu religion. Similarly, the skirmish between Barong and the bondres at the denouement of the ngelawang performance—a reference to the confrontation between Barong and Rangda—served to underline the interconnections concerning spatial orientation, the kaja-kelod axis, and spiritual, physical, and emotional well-being in Balinese cosmology.

Gendered Expectations of Participating in the Ngelawang

Approximately twenty boys from the sanggar, accompanied by two male musicians (including the children's dance teacher), took part in this event. The children were drawn mainly from the advanced dance level (*tingkat mahir*), but not all participated in the dance. Only the most experienced boys performed Barong. Less experienced boys took the parts of the other characters in the play or played in the gamelan ensemble. The very youngest boys were there simply to walk in the procession. Another reason why the more experienced boys danced Barong was because they were taller and stronger than the others. As a result, they were better able to execute dance movements and maneuver the body of Barong with considerable skill, while at the same time carry the weight of the frame. No girls from the sanggar danced the role of Barong or played in the accompanying gamelan. Nevertheless, four girls, aged six to fourteen, walked with the procession, collecting the monetary offerings presented to the group after each performance. Taking on and fulfilling such gendered tasks serves to reaffirm traditional female roles in Balinese society. For example, women are largely responsible for making numerous daily offerings to the Bali-Hindu deities both at home and in the village temple, and they also take charge of the household income and finances. Thus, the girls' participation in the ngelawang is consistent with the role that they will later take on as women.[55] As the girls neither danced nor took part in the gamelan ensemble,

Barong continues to be a male-only performance genre, and when asked why they did not participate in the theatrical performance, all the girls unequivocally told me that only boys danced Barong.

Referring to cultural expressions commonly defined as "male" or "boys' things" in Bali, Laura Noszlopy states that "although young women participate to a limited extent in the practice of these, they are not nearly as visible or active at the points of display as their male peers."[56] This was certainly true for the children's ngelawang, where the four girls tended to position themselves to the side of each Barong performance, away from the limelight. As the children's Barong processed through Keramas and Medahan, however, the girls often walked alongside and even in front of the Barong (see fig. 2.4). This development concerning girls' participation in the ngelawang and walking at the head of the procession contradicts Jane Belo's view that, although women are responsible for "preparation of the necessary offerings," only men participate in a Barong performance.[57] In contrast, Hobart observes, more than fifty years later, that women and girls do sometimes escort traveling Barong.[58] She admits, however, that they tend to take up positions toward the rear of the accompanying entourage. Returning to the children's ngelawang, it appears then that traditional Balinese gender roles prohibited the four girls from dancing Barong and even playing in the gamelan ensemble.[59] My observations of this children's Barong performance seem to indicate changes relating to the strict gender roles governing who may participate in ngelawang. Nevertheless the question still remains: why did the girls choose to participate with the boys from the sanggar in the event if they knew that their involvement in the activity would be limited to walking in the procession?

The disparity between boys' and girls' levels of participation, however, was not reflected in the amount of money each child received for his or her participation. The amount of money offered to Barong for a performance varied between one thousand and five thousand rupiah (approximately ten cents and fifty cents). Most people tended to give either one thousand or two thousand rupiah for a performance. This was considerably less than the amount given to adult groups, five thousand rupiah for a performance. A possible reason for this could be that adults' groups are perceived to be better than children's groups. Another reason could be the degree of spiritual power embodied in adult masks and the protection they offer to the village when used in performance. When compared with adult Barong masks, those used by children are not believed to possess the same level of supernatural power. Nevertheless, the money collected during the ngelawang was divided equally among the children. Wayan, the dance teacher, was happy for the children to retain this money and made no request for payment to contribute toward financing the construction of Barong.[60] Each child received eleven thousand rupiah, and this was spent mostly on sweets.

Figure 2.4. Girls from the sanggar carry offerings for Barong. Photograph by the author.

In her 1930s research on the enculturation of Balinese children, Belo writes that when a child is born "no special point is made as to whether it is a male or a female."[61] All children are considered to be "little gods," and it is not until the age of six or seven years that parents start to differentiate appropriate gender roles for boys and girls. At this stage, boys are gradually allowed to play away from home. Due to increasing domestic responsibilities, which include cooking, cleaning, looking after younger siblings, or helping to make numerous religious offerings for both daily and ceremonial use, girls tend to stay near to the family compound.[62] Bateson and Mead also note that when girls gradually stop participating in play activities with boys, the situation eventually results in girls becoming "torn between two systems of behavior, that of the grown woman [in the domestic realm] and that of the boys who are their playmates."[63] The fact that the girls from the sanggar participated in the ngelawang could possibly indicate that they still wanted to be included with the boys—their former playmates—in this activity. Accordingly, it could be inferred that the girls perhaps unintentionally attempted to challenge traditional male and female roles. Nevertheless, since the girls did not dance Barong, perform any of the other characters in the theatrical performance, or play in the gamelan ensemble, their participation in the procession confirms that boys and girls are quite aware of the "nature of socio-political relations in the *banjar* (sub-village unit)" and the respective roles of men and women in Balinese society.[64]

Thoughts on Children's Roles in a Barong Performance

This chapter has focused on Barong performance to illustrate how children's ngelawang are integral to the Balinese New Year celebrations (Galungan and Kuningan) and how its dramatic narrative, mime, speech, music, and dance elements are drawn from several adult dance-drama genres, including Barong, Arja, and Topeng. In so doing, it has examined how the emotional responses of both performer and spectator generated by Barong performance preserve distinct social and moral boundaries, thereby articulating particular gender roles and activities that occur within Balinese society. When examined in this manner, children's Barong provides a way in which fun and enjoyment are linked to the greater and more serious cosmological and geographic concerns that govern the island. Likewise, this chapter highlights a valuable point concerning the music- and dance-learning process in Bali. Through staging Barong, children are enculturated into a Balinese way of understanding and "being-in-the-world" in spatial, sonic, visual, spiritual, human, and nonhuman terms.[65] As a result of this process, boys and girls gradually comprehend how to become mature men and women in Balinese society.

Ultimately children's ngelawang is a socially acceptable ceremonial event that reinforces the significance of Barong in Balinese culture—as both the benevolent deity maintaining the precarious balance with the malevolent Rangda across place and time, and as embodied performance reinscribing gender-normative behaviors intergenerationally. The playful and unpredictable dancing of the children's Barong serves to revitalize the local community by reestablishing a perceived sense of balance between positive and negative cosmological forces. Like adult performances, the dancing of Barong by children is thought to banish the dangerous spirits associated with Rangda at a time of renewal associated with the new year in Balinese society. Such performances also enable humans to reflect on and revitalize an emotional attachment to the landscape and the fundamental kaja-kelod axis of spatial orientation. Consequently, children's Barong performances highlight a sustaining intergenerational activity integral to the spiritual, emotional, and gendered processes of cultural transmission in Bali.

Notes

1. The term "Barong" can also be used to denote masks that represent more or less human figures. These masks are known as Barong Landung and are performed by a single male dancer. The body of Barong Landung takes the form of a large puppet, which is placed over the dancer's head and tied around his waist; this allows the dancer to see out through the puppet's belly button. The puppet's arms are attached to large sticks, which the dancer holds to operate the puppet's arms. There are two common forms of Barong Landung: a male puppet (Jero Gede) and a female puppet (Jero Luh).

2. Galungan is the most important festival of the Balinese-Hindu calendar. On the first day of Galungan the sanctified ancestors of the family descend to their former homes, where they must be entertained with prayers and offerings. Kuningan, ten days after Galungan, marks the end of the New Year celebrations. It is a time for family groups, prayers, and more offerings, as the ancestors ascend once more to heaven.

3. See, for example, Gregory Bateson and Margaret Mead, *Balinese Character: A Photographic Analysis*, Special Publications of the New York Academy of Sciences, vol. 2 (New York: New York Academy of Sciences, 1942); Jane Belo, *Trance in Bali* (New York: Columbia University Press, 1960); Jane Belo, *Bali: Rangda and Barong* (Seattle: University of Washington Press, 1966); I Madé Bandem, "*Barong* Dance," *World of Music* 18, no. 3 (1976): 45–52; Clifford Geertz, "Religion as a Cultural System," in *Anthropological Approaches to the Study of Religion*, ed. Michael Banton (London: Tavistock, 1978); I Madé Bandem and Fredrik de Boer, *Kaja and Kelod: Balinese Dance in Transition* (Kuala Lumpur: Oxford University Press, 1981); John Emigh, *Masked Performance: The Play of Self and Other in Ritual and Theatre* (Philadelphia: University of Pennsylvania Press, 1996); Michele Stephen, "Barong and Rangda in the Context of Balinese Religion," *Review of Indonesian and Malaysian Affairs* 35, no. 1 (2001): 137–93; Walter Spies and Beryl de Zoete, *Dance and Drama in Bali* (Singapore: Periplus, 2002); Angela Hobart, *Healing Performances of Bali: Between Darkness and Light* (New York: Berghahn, 2003); Judith Becker, *Deep Listeners: Music, Emotion, and Trancing* (Bloomington: Indiana University Press, 2004); and Fred B. Eiseman, Jr., *Bali: Sekala and Niskala*, vol. 1, *Essays on Religion, Ritual, and Art* (Indonesia: Periplus, 2004).

4. See Michel Picard, *Bali: Cultural Tourism and Touristic Culture*, trans. Diana Darling (Singapore: Archipelago, 1996); and Annette Sanger, "Blessing or Blight? The Effect of Touristic Dance-Drama on Village Life in Singapadu, Bali," in *The Impact of Tourism on Traditional Music*, ed. Adrienne Kaeppler and Olive Lewin (Kingston: Jamaica Memory Bank, 1988), 89–104.

5. Colin McPhee, "Children and Music in Bali," in *Traditional Balinese Culture*, ed. Jane Belo (New York: Columbia University Press, 1970), 219–20; Margaret Mead, "Strolling Players in the Mountains of Bali," in Belo, *Traditional Balinese Culture*, 137–45; I Wayan Dibia and Rucina Ballinger, *Balinese Dance, Drama and Music: A Guide to the Performing Arts of Bali* (Singapore: Periplus, 2004).

6. See also John Blacking, *Venda Children's Songs: An Ethnomusicological Analysis* (Johannesburg: Witwatersrand University Press, 1967), 31; and Fiona Magowan, *Melodies of Mourning: Music and Emotion in Northern Australia* (Oxford: Currey, 2007), 44–69.

7. See Bandem, "*Barong* Dance"; and Dibia and Ballinger, *Balinese Dance*.

8. The nouns "Barong" and "Rangda" are capitalized because they are the personal names of Bali-Hindu deities.

9. Calonarang is a different theatrical performance to the role of Barong in the festival activities of the New Year celebrations called ngelawang. However, it is referred to here to highlight children's emotional reactions to the appearance of the characters Barong and Rangda.

10. See Bateson and Mead, *Balinese Character*; and Margaret Mead, "Children and Ritual in Bali," in Belo, *Traditional Balinese Culture*, 198–211.

11. Bateson and Mead, *Balinese Character*; Belo, *Bali*; and Mead, "Strolling Players."

12. Bandem, "*Barong* Dance," 48.

13. Ibid., 45.

14. Dibia and Ballinger, *Balinese Dance*, 70.

15. Barong Ketet, or Ket, is also known as Lord of the Woods (Banaspati Raja). Dibia and Ballinger differ from Bandem regarding the translation of the Sanskrit origins of the word "Barong." They translate the Sanskrit word *bharwang* as meaning "two spaces," possibly referring to the two places in the costume-body attached to the animal mask (Dibia and Ballinger, *Balinese Dance*, 70; Bandem, "*Barong* Dance," 45).

16. Mead, "Strolling Players," 138.

17. For teaching purposes the following online resource may be useful: "Cudamani Children Get a Baby Barong," posted to YouTube by "cudamanibali," January 21, 2008, http://www.youtube.com/watch?v=aM-AJAc0-IE. The Cudamani gamelan group comes from the village of Pengosekan, just south of Ubud. This is a children's Barong Ketet—performed by a young boy and his older sister.

18. R. Anderson Sutton, "Asia/Music of Indonesia," in *Worlds of Music: An Introduction to the Music of the World's Peoples*, 4th ed., ed. Jeff Todd Titon (Belmont, CA: Schirmer/Thompson Learning, 2002), 282.

19. See Ward Keeler, "Musical Encounter in Java and Bali," *Indonesia* 19 (1975): 85–126.

20. Due to her associated ambivalent and auspicious powers, Rangda never appears during a children's ngelawang or in children's play activities. Rangda masks, carried in closed woven baskets (*katung*), may sometimes accompany adult Barong performances, although I never witnessed this during fieldwork in Keramas (see Hobart, *Healing Performances of Bali*, 181).

21. Ibid., 182.

22. Ibid., 131.

23. Miguel Covarrubias, *Island of Bali* (New York: Knopf, 1973), 325.

24. In the remainder of this chapter, I refer to the dance studio (*sanggar tari*) simply as the *sanggar*.

25. On this occasion a *gamelan gong kebyar* ensemble (a twentieth-century form of gamelan orchestra) provided the musical accompaniment for the performance. This ensemble, which includes many metallophone instruments, is markedly different to the *gamelan gaguntangan* ensemble that was used to accompany the children's ngelawang in Keramas and Medahan.

26. To reaffirm cosmological balance in this context, it was sufficient on this occasion for villagers in Keramas to witness the theatrical confrontation between Barong and Rangda.

27. Bateson and Mead, *Balinese Character*, 32–38; and Mead, "Children and Ritual," 201.

28. David J. Stuart-Fox, *Pura Besakih: Temple, Religion and Society in Bali*, Verhandelingen 193 (Leiden: Koninklijk Insituut voor Taal-, Land- en Volkenkunde (KITLV) Press, 2002), 4–5.

29. The implications of the kaja-kelod spatial orientation system means that when in the north of the island *kaja* signifies "south," but when in the south of the island *kaja* denotes "north." During lessons at the sanggar, the dance teachers often instruct boys and girls to move toward kaja and kelod, although they rarely employ the terms *kangin* and *kauh*, preferring instead to use the Indonesian words for right (*kanan*) and left (*kiri*). This example of substituting Balinese-specific spatial terms with Indonesian words reflects the dance teachers' tertiary training at the Indonesian Institute of the Arts (Insitut Seni Indonesia), Denpasar, where teaching methods combine aspects of Western pedagogic practices with traditional Balinese approaches.

30. Adults sometimes touch the heads of babies and young children, for example, when singing them to sleep, and young children sometimes touch the heads of their parents and older siblings.

31. Bateson and Mead, *Balinese Character*, 34.

32. Mead, "Children and Ritual," 201.

33. Ibid.

34. Bateson and Mead go on to argue that Rangda represents the mother figure in Balinese society (*Balinese Character*, 36). This finding, however, has been criticized by several scholars: Belo, *Bali*, 38; Gordon D. Jensen and Luh K. Suryani, *The Balinese People: A Reinvestigation of Character* (Oxford: Oxford University Press, 1992), 80–85; and Stephen, "Barong and Rangda," 139. In contrast to the view of Bateson and Mead, these authors acknowledge that Rangda serves only as a representation of the fear aspect of the mother figure; she is not a mother figure herself.

35. Bateson and Mead, *Balinese Character*, 33, 47. The Balinese word *dengen* literally translates as "to inspire fear" in someone. When discussing the appearance of Rangda at the Calonarang performance, children also used the word *takut*, meaning "to be afraid."

36. Belo, *Bali*, 37.

37. Bateson and Mead, *Balinese Character*, 38.

38. Ibid.

39. Mead, "Strolling Players," 140.

40. McPhee, "Children and Music," 218–20.

41. See Colin McPhee, *A Club of Small Men: A Story of Bali* (New York: Day, 1948).

42. McPhee, "Children and Music," 218–20.

43. Colin McPhee, *Music in Bali: A Study in Form and Instrumental Organization in Balinese Orchestral Music* (New Haven: Yale University Press, 1966), 150; Lisa Gold, *Music in Bali: Expressing Music, Expressing Culture* (New York: Oxford University Press, 2005), 82.

44. Michael B. Bakan, *Music of Death and New Creation: Experiences in the World of Balinese Gamelan Beleganjur* (Chicago: University of Chicago Press, 1999), 337.

45. In contrast to children's ngelawang, some adult Barong performances take place on a stage, and many of these are often accompanied by a gamelan ensemble, for example, a gamelan gong kebyar orchestra that includes metallophones and several suling.

46. Gold, *Music in Bali*, 109.

47. In Bali two broad categories of theatrical characters exist: *keras* denotes unrefined or strong characters, whereas *alus* refers to refined or sweet (also known as *manis*) characters. Various differences according to body type, makeup, costume, vocal timbre, and movement serve to reinforce these categories.

48. An *angsel* can also be defined as a rhythmic accent.

49. The foundation of all Balinese dances is an asymmetrical stance (*agem*); *kanan* in Indonesian denotes "right." In this instance, *agem kanan* refers to the basic right male position. For a further discussion of Balinese dance positions and how they relate to male and female styles of performance, see Jonathan McIntosh, "Preparation, Presentation and Power: Children's Performances in a Balinese Dance Studio," in *Dancing Cultures: Globalization, Tourism and Identity in the Anthropology of Dance*, ed. Helene Neveu-Kringelbach and Jonathan Skinner (New York: Berghahn, 2012), 194–210.

50. This is similar to the music that accompanies the entrance of the half-masked servant (*pendasar*) or comic characters (*bondres*) in mask dance-drama (Topeng).

51. Although not necessarily associated with kaja or kelod, the character of a monkey (*bojog*) appears in several traditional Balinese children's stories. In such stories, monkey characters are often portrayed as having mischievous and comedic personalities.

52. After Bateson and Mead, *Balinese Character*, 38.

53. The children's male dance teacher, I Wayan Suarta (also known as Rawit), is a celebrated Topeng and Arja performer. He is renowned not only for the high level of his dance technique but also for his comedic portrayal of bondres characters.

54. Hobart, *Healing Performances of Bali*, 191.

55. Covarrubias, *Island of Bali*, 83; Lyn Parker, *From Subjects to Citizens: Balinese Villagers in the Indonesian Nation-State* (Copenhagen: Nordic Institute of Asian Studies, 2003), 164.

56. Laura Noszlopy, "*Bazar*, Big Kites and Other Boys' Things: Distinctions of Gender and Tradition in Balinese Youth Culture," *Australian Journal of Anthropology* 16, no. 2 (2005): 181.

57. Belo, *Bali*, 53.

58. Hobart, *Healing Performances of Bali*, 171.

59. Bakan, *Music of Death*; Emiko Saraswati S. Susilo, *Gamelan Wanita: A Study of Women's Gamelan in Bali*, Southeast Asia 43 (Manoa: Center for Southeast Asian Studies, University of Hawai'i, 2003); and Sarah Willner, "Kebyar Wanita: A Look at Women's Gamelan Groups in Bali" (paper presented to the Society for Balinese Studies, Denpasar, August 1992) have researched women's gamelan groups in Bali. Such groups have increased since the early 1990s. Nevertheless, it is widely acknowledged among men and women that, although the standard of female gamelan ensembles is gradually increasing, all-female groups sometimes lack the technical and expressive competency demonstrated by male musicians. Moreover, women have also taken to performing mask-dance (Topeng), which was until recently considered a male performance genre. In Keramas, for example, an all-female Topeng group performs regularly, and there is also a female gamelan group. These developments in the Balinese performing arts indicate that one day it might be possible for girls to dance Barong, as well as play in the gamelan ensemble that accompanies a ngelawang. For contemporary research pertaining to girls learning gamelan music in Bali, see Sonja L. Downing, "Arjuna's Angels: Girls Learning Gamelan Music in Bali" (PhD diss., University of California, Santa Barbara, 2008).

60. The children's tiger Barong mask cost approximately five hundred thousand rupiah (approximately fifty dollars). I Wayan Suarta, the sanggar dance teacher, with neighbors and members of his extended family, constructed the frame of the children's Barong over two weeks. The frame was then covered with orange, red, and black material (to represent the fur of a tiger) before being decorated with a mane and tail. All of these materials cost approximately three hundred thousand rupiah (approximately 30 dollars).

61. Belo, *Bali*, 15.

62. Elsewhere, I have noted how the differentiation of gender at this stage in the Balinese enculturation process also leads to a gradual decline of boys and girls participating together in play sessions and song games. See Jonathan McIntosh, "Moving Through Tradition: Children's Practice and Performance of Dance, Music and Song in South-central Bali, Indonesia" (PhD diss., Queen's University, Belfast, 2006).

63. Bateson and Mead, *Balinese Character*, 43.

64. Noszlopy, "Other Boys' Things," 181.

65. See Martin Heidegger, *Being and Time*, trans. John Macquarrie and Edward Robinson (New York: Harper and Row, 1962).

Chapter Three

Performing Emotion, Embodying Country in Australian Aboriginal Ritual

Fiona Magowan

> The saltwater . . . here it rests in the saltwater country, but it all has names. . . . Also the rocks. Rocks that the country holds. Where the water moves . . . where it rests. There are places there, names there, names that are special that Yolngu receive in their heads. And sing and give names to children.
>
> —Djambawa Marawili

Performing the Law

After a rough drive along the dirt road leading away from the township of Galiwin'ku, in northeast Arnhem Land, we came into an outstation on the coast (see map 3.1). Some family members were sitting on their raised verandas in the shade. One of the three Yolngu women traveling in the car gestured that they should go to a thick mangrove cluster close to the sea to gather shellfish and mud crabs.[1] As they departed, I, along with another non-Aboriginal friend who also knew the family and had a long history in the region, took the opportunity to meet with one of the clan leaders. We walked toward the shoreline, where an inlet led around to a rocky headland along the white beach. After some general conversation, and in response to some questions about the genealogy of the area, he offered fragments of information about the ancestor who had traversed the promontory in the distant past, establishing his clan rights and those of his kin there. I had already analyzed a range of song series in the region and knew something of the history of the ancestors in the area. As I listened to him speaking, I recalled the resonant timbre of different singers intoning sacred names of Country, representing its ancestral actions.[2]

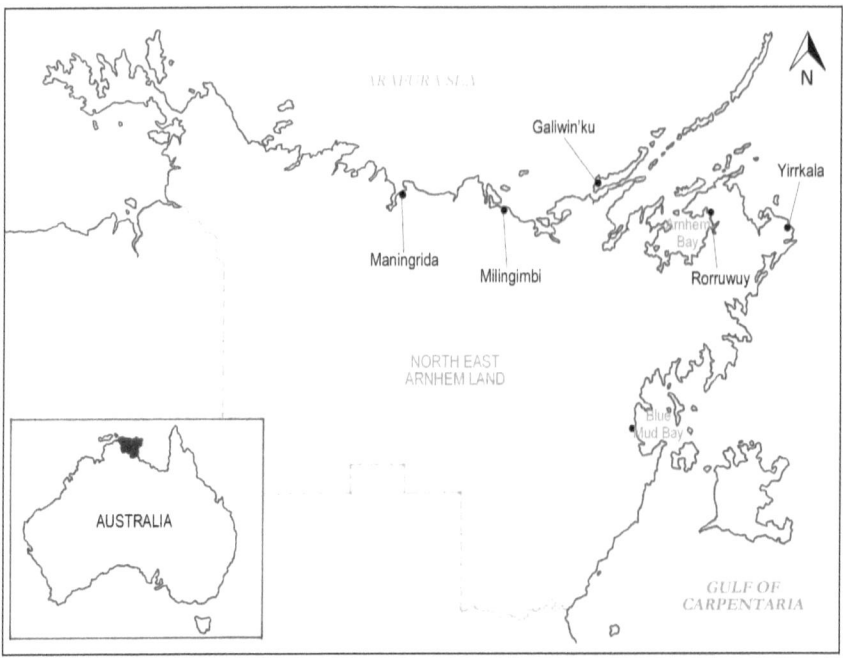

Map 3.1. Australia inset (*bottom left*). Northeast Arnhem Land, with five homeland centers. Map by Angela Snieder.

Ancestors are the foundational source of power for Aboriginal people in many parts of Australia, and their renewing potency within the landscape and seascape continues today. While this generic cosmological belief connects Aboriginals from diverse cultural backgrounds in discourses around identity politics, in this chapter I argue that the cultural specificities of Yolngu ancestral relations with the environment generate particularities of law and performance practice. Their kin-based cosmological relations offer a counterpoint to popular Western views of Aboriginal identity as being based on a generalized spiritual relationship with the land. While Yolngu may, at times, draw on these discourses for political ends, their performance genres are always derived from a consistent core of ancestral ritual practices.[3]

This chapter seeks to explore Yolngu performativity to question how men and women understand the effects of ancestral performance as emotionally embodied in the environment and how they see people's relationships with the landscape as gendered rights in the process. As the interplay between jural processes and spiritual beliefs intractably binds kin to landscape in life and death, I ask in what ways are performative engagements with ecology emotionally affecting and how do sounds and images of ecology shape performative rights in belonging?

Yolngu have been successful in defending some land rights for the courts by translating place-names and terms into legal identifiers of individual and group rights. Thus, while the courts recognize certain forms of evidence, there is a complex, indirect framework of determination between Australian law and Yolngu *rom* (law), especially with regard to legal understandings of how song names encode claimants' rights. Some of these difficulties stem from the restricted and select knowledge of song words by particular clan members over others, combined with the multiplicity and ambiguity of meanings that a single referent can afford.[4] As a result, songs *alone* are not sufficient legal testimony in court, although they are inseparable from other Yolngu judicial processes. In her analysis of the Blue Mud Bay sea claim hearing, Frances Morphy notes that there is no recognition that "the performance of *rom*" translates into "the enactment of *rom*" without other kinds of written or verbal evidence being presented.[5] Furthermore, correlations between metaphysical and physical rights in areas such as seas can be difficult to map onto Western cultural frameworks, yet there is an ongoing need to prove that these rights exist in Australian court settings, particularly since "the settler Australian political geographic imaginary continues to produce and enact boundaries that fracture Yolngu control over Yolngu country."[6]

Not only is the gap between Western legal and indigenous cosmological recognition of rights in singing the land a problem for the courts, it is also paralleled to some extent between scientific and indigenous questions around the term "traditional ecological knowledge." Employed by Western science to capture the complexity of indigenous modes of environmental understanding and knowledge of ecological systems, its use often highlights tensions between scholars who place a biological emphasis on conservation or the governance of different ecological zones and those who attend to anthropological concerns about the performance of indigenous cultural heritage. As Yolngu rangers and scientists from government departments seek to prioritize practical programs to improve resource access, the musical and performance-oriented dimensions of ecological knowledge may be downplayed or, more frequently, compartmentalized and set apart from resource use. However, over the past decade, Yolngu have had opportunities to teach a range of non-Aboriginal people about their own system of legal jurisdiction. They host intercultural arenas and forums of debate and discussion about rom through annual events, such as the Garma Festival of Traditional Culture and the Mawul Rom Mediation Project, which address ancestral rights in song, dance, and art.[7] Various authors writing on different regions of the Australian continent have also foregrounded the politics of Aboriginal cosmology to explain how men and women come to hold ancestral knowledge and acquire rights in songs, dances, and land.[8]

As the Yolngu environment is circumscribed by a gender-specific complex around singing, dancing, and painting, here I argue that the effects generated in one mode of representation have emotional and spiritual affinities with the others. For example, the strong and powerful feelings that Howard Morphy identified in "shimmering" white cross-hatching in Yolngu painting could be said to have their emotive ancestral parallels in vibrant and dynamic dancing and in the deep timbres of the voice in song and the didjeridoo (*yiḏaki*).[9] As we shall see, parallelisms such as these mediate Yolngu performance, circumscribed by the interplay between rights and gendered sentiments toward the landscape and seascape, creating a tightly knit complement of ecologically informed artistic practices.

Kin in Country

In the Northern Territory, as in many other parts of the Australian continent, ecology is integral to the moral dimensions of being human for Yolngu, as it forms the spiritual and cultural basis of their law.[10] The creative actions, dances, and songs of the ancestors who fashioned the sea and land determine the jural relations of Yolngu kinship. The tropical monsoonal region of the northeast Arnhem Land region is home to around seven thousand Yolngu, divided into "sixty patri-groups" and seven language groups split into two moieties, known as Dhuwa and Yirritja.[11] Group orientation is based on the asymmetrical distribution of a set of matrikin (male and female) alliances that occur between wife-bestowing and wife-receiving clans. Rights to land and rights in performance are defined by a range of sociocentric relationships linking all clans to one another in three key dyadic relations: mother-child clans (*ngändipulu-wakupulu*), also known by the term y*othu-yindi* (child-mother); sisters' clans (*yapapulu*), who do not exchange women but are tied to one another spiritually and ritually; and mother's mother's [brother] (*märipulu*) and [sister's] daughters' child clans (*gutharra*), who bestow women as mothers-in-law for their grandchildren.[12]

Each dyadic relation encapsulates different types of custodianship, belonging, and ideals of nurturance with its associated kin group. For example, mother-child relationships are reflected in the proximity of their residence patterns to one another; in the responsibilities of children to work (*djämamirr*) for their mothers' clans in organizing ritual areas, such as buying and collecting materials and constructing a funeral shade or shelter for the coffin; and in their assistance in performances. Men and women who are sisters' children (*wakupulu*) will dance for their mother's clan (*ngäṉdipulu*) as the sister's children "look after" (*djägamirr*) their mother's knowledge. Male didjeridoo players will also accompany the singing of their mother's clan relatives. Mother's clans in turn must look after their child clans, giving them food and compliments in dancing, and in doing so, "one enters the intimate sphere of intersubjective relationships, in which one is emotionally involved and socially accountable for."[13]

Songs of Ancestral Places

Just as residence patterns are circumscribed by kinship rights, so too are rights in performing and learning about songs, dances, and paintings. The majority of ritual contexts for the performance of Yolngu music include three modes of song: unaccompanied men's singing (*biḻma manikay*), unaccompanied women's singing or women's crying songs (*ngäthi manikay*), and ritual singing and dancing led by men (*bunggulmirri manikay*, literally "dance-having songs"), with clapsticks (*biḻma*) providing a steady beat and didjeridoo providing a rhythmic drone, accompanied by men's and women's dancing. Aaron Corn and Joe Gumbula describe how:

> Movement from one note to the next, and the ordering and repetition of each word sung is entirely individuated. Together, the singers' voices delicately intertwine and gracefully permutate around the ideal of a unified melody over the more rigid *biḻma* and *yidaki* patterns that anchors them rhythmically. They give the illusion of hearing a single voice comprised of many: one that is loosely unified, yet full of ever-shifting ever-resolving dissonances.[14]

While many melody lines descend to a low tonic, and others oscillate around particular tones, songs styles vary greatly depending on "the singer's timbre, manipulation of pitch and song text."[15]

Bunggulmirri manikay is the most common performance genre at rituals. All dances are related to the journeys of ancestral beings through the landscape, which follow regular patterns around the shade that constitutes the core focal point of ritual performance. Men lead the dancing, with women either following behind or dancing to one side. Their song templates comprise multiple names and actions of ancestral beings, and sequences of songs are conjoined to create image clusters of particular areas of land and ancestral action. These clusters further coalesce to generate song series of larger tracts of land crossed by several ancestors shared among clans ancestrally connected through kinship relations to these areas. Nancy Williams has analyzed how names are embedded in the land as part of a lexical system of kin and clan recognition. For example, the name *liya-buḻkungu* conjoins the two clans, Djapu and Djarrwark, through the term *liya* (head or thinking about, or with a mind to), together with the word for a beach area replete with stingrays (*bulku*), thereby identifying a set of men and their kin and affines who belong to that area.[16] The mediatory power of ancestors impacting humans and transforming the landscape is a common principle across Australia, as Nancy Munn also describes how among the Walbiri, the acts of ancestral beings are embodied in the landscape through processes of imprinting themselves on it, metamorphosing into and externalizing parts of their anatomy.[17] In doing so, they become "centered mobile fields" of transformative power through the movements they make at particular places.[18] Similarly, the ancestral beings of their neighbors, the Pintupi of the Western Desert, traveled across the land, "performed ceremonies, fought, and finally turned to stone or 'went into the ground' where they remain."[19]

As songs are charters of territory, their lyrics are not interchangeable with other clans' songs, and the texts must conform to specific expectations in performance but also allow for certain kinds of flexibility around naming practices. Singers create songs by drawing from a body of names relating to the features in a particular area and may choose which names are highlighted, as long as references to the environment appear in the right order. Different names may be inserted depending on the singer's preference, and lines may be extended or shortened according to the leader's musicianship, rendering ideas about ancestral subjects as certain kinds of poetic evocation rather than exact textual copies.[20] Thus, songs are improvisatory insofar as the order of the names chosen for a particular ancestor's actions can vary from one version to another.

The power and depth of ancestral song names result in differing degrees of verbal masking in performance. Men, who regularly sing together, know the textual and naming options and pick up their own lines to accompany the clan leader. Women similarly obscure the sounds of the words through the stylistic effect of prolonging song syllables. In working on transcriptions of recordings with both male and female singers, there was no expectation that the transcription should reflect the singer's precise linguistic rendition, as they would often create a new improvisation as part of the transcription process and song interpretation. From a scholarly perspective of accuracy in transcription, this was both instructive and disconcerting since there was no stable version, and capturing the detail of names meant repeating and rechecking the recorded version. At times, this would include recording the newly improvised versions as part of the transcription process, which singers permitted to assist the discussion of how interpretations were made.

Songs are performed separately by men and, at the appointed time, by women in ritual who each sing polyphonically in their respective groups. While male ritual specialists recite deep names of ancestral beings in their sacred areas, older women also sing of these beings in a crying-song style (*ngäthi*), always without accompaniment, using public and unrestricted ritual names. This gender-performative difference has implications for how men and women conceive of the emotional effects of songs. Younger women sit nearby listening and weeping intermittently, calling out terms of endearment to their lost relative. Ritual singing and dancing then have multiple ends: to elicit spiritual power, ensure the continuity of political relations among clans, affirm family responsibilities, and care for the spirit of the deceased on the final journey to the clan homeland.

Sharing Sounds and Images across Gendered Performances

Yolngu sing and name ecological areas and their flora and fauna through distinctions between the seaways (*gapu monuk*) side and the inland or bush (*diltji*) side. To illustrate how the power of ancestors is communicated between the two areas, I consider the extent to which the imagery of one ancestor is shared between men and women across these ecologies in different verses of one song subject. I compare two examples of the song of the dove as performed by a man and woman of two different clans of the Dhuwa moiety. The first song is by Manydjarri Ganambarr, senior leader of the Daṯiwuy clan from the seaways side, and the second song is performed by a woman of the Djambarrpuyngu clan, Murukunn, through the bush side.[21] This analysis highlights the interconnectedness of place-names and journeys associated with the song of the dove set to a separate clan tune (*buku* or *dambu*), as appropriate to the identity of the singer.

Manydjarri gathered his sons together and sat in a semicircle on a tarpaulin in the sand outside the house at his homeland one evening for an impromptu evening's singing, which included the song of the dove.[22] The melody covers a pentatonic scale, starting from a relatively high-pitched fifth and descending stepwise.

Seaways dove song as sung by Manydjarri Ganambarr

What do you see at Ngilamuru?	*Nhaltjan nhängal Ngilamuruli*
What do you see at Gurrmanda?	*Nhaltjan nhängal Gurrmandawuy*
What's that bird called?	*Nhaltjan dhika*
[Names of the dove:] *Larrwalarrwa*, *Yiniyulma*, and *Mamudhuma*	*Larrwalarrwa, Yiniyulma, Mamudhuma*
[The dove sings out]	*Gukuk gukuk gululul gululul*
The bird is over there at Gulurrmun	*Ya—Binaka Gulurrmunli guwarguwar*
The bar-shouldered dove calls out	*Galangam galangam ngapalawal*
Gukuk—he cries	*Gukuk gukuk gululul gululul*
It's raining over at Djulngaymurru *djulngaymurrulil*	*Yä—Waltjan nhängala*
The bird called *Djulwan*, *Larrwalarrwa*, *Mattira*	*Djulwanbuy Larrwalarrwa Mattira*
Also called *Burungga* and *Mamudhuma*	*Burungga Mamudhuma*

Manydjarri's song begins with a questioning tone, naming the areas at his Daṯiwuy clan homeland, Rorruwuy, where the dove is sighted at a long beach leading up to the rocky point. Manydjarri then sings three ancestral names of the bird, which distinguishes it as belonging to his Daṯiwuy clan, in this way imaging relatives who have held these names. The dove calls out, its distinctive, piercing cry clearly audible, naming itself in the process. The singer then begins to lead into the next song with the image of rain clouds brewing, which will whip up the sea, and ends this version by naming the bird with alternative ritual names.

Murukun sang both the seaways and the bush side Djambarrpuyngu version of the dove to me during one of our daily transcription meetings on Galiwin'ku. Despite their musical differences and distinct clan affiliations, these songs are considered to be connected within one ritual complex because of their subject matter. Her song begins at a much lower pitch than that of the Daṯiwuy clan tune and has a narrower range overall, descending stepwise around three notes, beginning on the third note and moving to alternate between the second and tonic. Through her text, Murukun creates an image of the dove at her Djambarrpuyngu clan homeland, Gundangur, which is on the Arnhem Land mainland and connects the grandmother-granddaughter relationship of the Djambarrpuyngu and Daṯiwuy clans through the conjoined ancestral identity of the two sacred sites.

Seaways dove song as sung by Murukun

The bar-shouldered dove calls, "gukuk"	*Ngapaḻawal gukuy*
I saw my child in the muddy water	*Waku nghanal djarrarranmirrinydja*
In the water called Ritjilili Buwanana	*Ritjililimirr buwananmirrnydja*
Crying, the dove calls out, "gukuk"	*Ngäthiny gukuk dhatharram yimingidan gukuk*
He cries at Gulnyirri	*Gulnyirringur ngathi*
I heard him crying	*Ngarra nhangurnydja ngäthi*
Crying at the shark nest Gadulkirri	*Gadulkirringurnydja ngäthi*
I heard him crying the water called Yalwayuna	*Gapu ngama yalwayuna ngäthi dhuwanana*
Also called Murupu and Manybarr	*Murupumirr manybarrmirr*

As the dove is now in a different locale, it is known by the place-specific names, Yimingida and Dhatharra, which distinguish the ancestral origins of the Djambarrpuyngu clan from those of the Daṯiwuy clan. The dove calls out to warn of the ancestor, a shark, this time at Gulnyirri and Gadulkirri—not at Gurrmunli as in the Daṯiwuy song version. He sings the names of the waters at this ancestral area. Murukun directly alludes to her own kin attachment to these waters as she sings, "I saw my child in the muddy water." The dove then calls out other ancestral names for waters; one of these water names is that of a close Datiwuy female relative, reminding me of times I had spent with her as her name is sung.

In performing the *diltji*, or bush-side, version of the song of the dove, the ecology changes and the songs refer to other ancestors associated with inland sacred areas and flora. Instead of crying about the waters at its Djambarrpuyngu ancestral site, the dove tells Yolngu not to stay at the creek but to go and look in the bush, where they will find an abundance of yams, although one of these is sacred and restricted.

Inland dove song as sung by Murukun

He is going to look for food	*Ngatha marrtji nhäma*
He is going to look for food	*Ngatha marrtji nhäma*
The dove cries	*Gukuk ngapalawal ngäthi*
He cries at Wandawuy	*Wandawuyndja ngäthi*
The dove cries	*Gukuk ngäthi*
He is going to look for food	*Ngatha marrtji nhäma*
He is going to these areas	*Marrtji dhuwal yalukulu*
	Wandangurrnydja Milmilngurndja

As we can see in these short song verses, both men and women can assert a range of rights in belonging to place, which determines who can perform songs from that area. Their performance also raises questions about how the environment enters into shared experiences and hence rights in both seaways and inland areas.

Spiritual Affordances of Country

Tim Ingold explains how shared communication is generated among individuals because "sociality is given from the start, *prior* to the objectification of experience in cultural categories, in the direct, perceptual involvement of fellow participants in a shared environment."[23] In ecological psychology, interactions with, and perceptions of, the environment have been analyzed in terms of "affordances," which refer to how the ecological world enters into the physical experience and psychological understanding of the perceiver.[24] Ingold extends James Gibson's perceptual mode of action to include sensory awareness "through looking, listening, touching and sniffing" which allows the individual to be attuned to the environment and "perceive what it affords."[25] By moving in the same environment, people receive the same information and come to understand appropriate language and behavior. Applying his analysis to Australian Aboriginal cosmology, Ingold outlines how variations in affordances coalesce across communicative genres to generate a sentient ecology based in feelings arising from immersion in a particular place.[26]

It is certainly the case that the emotional dynamics of Yolngu relationships are to a large extent intertwined with perceptions of ancestral affordances of the landscape and the rights that these entail. Yolngu have several ancestral names given to them from birth that refer to the sacredness of their bodies, in particular identifying the elbow, head, backbone, and hair. These same names are also topographical markers and, by extension, metaphorical transformations of bodily parts in clan lands. Aaron Corn has explained how, for example, the term *buku*, meaning the head (of a person, ancestor, or headland), further refers to the vocal melody; while the "thigh" of a song refers to "the lyrics of each discrete song item" with full accompaniment.[27] Thus, singing about the features of a homeland, images the presence of humans in the landscape.

The environment then embodies anatomical, kinship, sex, and gender relations within it, bringing humans and the environment together in metaphorical relations that Ian Keen refers to as "figures of network, focus and extension, and strings of indeterminate length."[28] Every aspect of the environment has multiple names and is held or cared for by custodians of different homelands known as *wänga-waṯangu* (place-belongs to [people]).[29] Each clan has its own identity in its ancestral roots, feet, or foundation (*ḻuku*) and in the blood (*mangu*) and backbone (*ngaraka*) of the environment, which in turn are transformations of ancestral beings (*wangarr*). The sinews and tissues of these beings, as well as their umbilical cords, are represented by strings, vines of plants, or tendons of animals tying them to an emotional Country. Inanimate objects such as rocks, moon, sun, and stars also carry ontological power, as transformations of all have anatomical bodies viewed as moving, breathing, life-possessing, and life-imparting beings.

Furthermore, the power and feeling of Country is elicited in references to this anatomy of the environment. Its sounds, movements, and colors evoke love, affection, desire, longing, fear, danger, or concern for those who know how to read its natural dimensions as emotionally and spiritually affecting. For example, among the Dhalwangu clan of the Yirritja moiety, Peter Toner has shown how remembering, longing, and the nostalgia of belonging constitute some of the key emotional resonances conveyed in Dhalwangu men's songs. He details the actions of Birrinydji, a very aggressive fighting ancestor whose brandishing of swords can be heard at nighttime in Gurrumurrru and whose anger, expressed in the sword movements of ritual dancers, transforms into the stingray dance.[30] These laws are performed intergenerationally to teach appropriate moral values and to ensure proper spiritual relations in caring for the land. Children understand, in a general sense, the sentient presence of the environment and why their parents are concerned to sing for those who have died, not just as a mark of respect but as a way of invoking the essence and regenerating power of ancestral life.[31]

Among Yolngu, power is said to exist in the head of the ancestor, whose knowledge is passed on to singers through the patrilineal transmission of songs and sometimes through dreams. In the Dhuwa moiety, the heads and minds of those belonging to the shark clan share the same ancestral name for the head and thoughts of the shark. Mind names for each ancestral being distinguish emotional characteristics that differentiate clans and form the basis of their identities. Michael Christie has argued that language is "co-extensive" and "co-constitutive" as people sing and recount their identities through the activities of ancestors in the land. He contrasts the coconstitutional relations of people and ecology as emergent in movements between places with Western senses of space and place, where concepts are predetermined in an externalized reality. He has explored these philosophical dimensions with Yolngu researchers in terms of clan relations to the ancestral nest, *yalu'* and as part of a program for healthy mothers and healthy babies, run by the Yalu' Marrngithinyaraw Group project in 2000.[32] He notes how one Yolngu researcher, and leader of the Yalu' story, Joanne Garnggulkpuy, has analyzed the use of different attributes and emotional characteristics pertaining to *mulkurr*, or minds, in an effort to solve problems, such as developing responsible patterns of behavior in the mother-child relationship.[33]

The group examined how clan rights are embodied in family histories of naming in the land, along with the transmission of inter- and intraclan knowledge through these names. The clan name Gularri, for example, which pertains to some Yirritja people, was used to convey a "visual sensibility derived from ritual revelation" inherent in the production of a television documentary of the same name.[34] Today, the application of this philosophy runs throughout community concerns over the need to ensure the maintenance of authority over homelands, appropriate engagements with government bodies in determining infrastructure outcomes, and the recognition that ancestral interests underpin all sociopolitical affairs. The idea that "clan minds" have different emotional effects refers to how interactions ought to be carried out with respect to one's situatedness within the clan context. In this way, Yolngu employ the ancestral mind as a conceptual tool that families can draw on to transform sentiments and resolve their differences in conflict situations. As Christie notes, "it is not *what* the other knows, rather it is *how* they know it" that has implications for the ways in which identities and rights to belong are expressed, whether in education or performance.[35]

Conflicts that occurred during ancestral times have also been described by thinking into and through landscapes of connectedness in contemporary popular music. Corn describes how Yothu Yindi songwriter Mandawuy Yunupingu sought to capture a range of emotions by blending clan song concepts with rock styles in the 1983 song "Djapana: Sunset Dreaming." The song refers to the transgressive acts of ancestral "foreign marauders" to the region, and Mandawuy composed it to express "'sorrow,' "homesickness," and "worry'" for his family on the northeast Arnhem Land mainland while he was working on the island of Galiwin'ku as a teacher in the school. Corn notes that drawing on these ancestral sentiments in popular music have been critical to "conveying and contemporizing durable ideas grounded in Yolngu tradition."[36] Recombining song elements in this way has created a new mode of engaging two styles of music making while retaining the emotional impact of the clan song sentiments drawn from the foundation of the ancestral law.

Emotional Journeys in Ancestral Country

As we have already seen in some instances, ancestral metaphors of the Yolngu landscape pertain to nests, as each clan's track of Country has a locus of ancestral power in which different ancestral beings may be found and whose powers must also be managed in ritual. Singers and dancers aim to send a person's spirit after death through the network of waters and homelands to its resting place. This journey inside the spiritual realm is intended to bring the deceased to their mother's mother's land and to the ancestral origins of the clan's sacred site. This is partly why the hidden meanings of the songs are restricted, since they allude to the power, substance, and action of the ancestral being through conception, birth, and death at its sacred site and invite a range of emotional responses channeled through ritual.

An eminent, senior man of the Datiwuy clan (now deceased) sang and told the story of his ancestral foundations to Jennifer Isaacs, describing the waters that flow out to the middle of the ocean as rushing waters within which the shark ancestral being lies sleeping in its depths. Waters are described in the narrative as discussing their chosen journey, deciding where they should stop and which places they will continue on toward. Just as one water calls out the names of the ancestral being on its travels around the coastline, so it meets with another current, and together the waters consider their next ancestral stopping point and foundation of the shark ancestral being. The concept of a clan's ancestral home alludes metaphorically to a cozy shelter where people, nurtured and cared for, can grow and connect with other kin relations. Thus, while the Dhuwa water stayed in the depths of the sea, the Yirritja waters flowed over the Dhuwa ones, imaging the relationship of mother and child: "And there they are together, two mothers and the child. Mother and child. And it is the same with the others; clan by clan by clan. Mingling together in other places."[37]

Metaphors shape ancestral meanings between stomachs and nests, as well as between feet and roots. While each clan is tied to its nest, its waters branch out to other places. The identity of these sacred nests differs for every clan. For one clan it may be the home of the turtle, for another where the crocodile lies, and for another a tree with mangrove worms. Thus, when men and women sing of turtles, crocodiles, and mangrove worms, they are bringing new life to the continuity of their own network of genealogical relations in the land and paying respect to the Country in the process.

The importance of the land as the source of spiritual power and ritual knowledge is a code for how clan members should curb emotional outbursts and behave appropriately toward one another. When fighting breaks out between different families, one way of addressing this is for the mediators to refer to ancestral links of the individuals involved, which provides a set of rules about what can be said between family members.[38] Recognition of the right to belong, then, is a matter of identifying with and being identified by those who are attached to one's own ancestral foundations as well as by their clan aggregate.

As all Yolngu are tied to the land and sea through their ancestral nest and waters, emotions are said to reside variously in the stomach or liver, which holds a deep sense of attachment. The shape of a liver is painted on mother's stomachs in ritual to represent their children and on animals in paintings—which is also said to be their "fat."[39] The location of emotions in the stomach and liver is common to other societies. Among the Uduk of Sudan, for example, Wendy James notes how the idea of the Word of God entering the liver for Christians is "emotionally striking and powerful," as believers will have their sins forgiven, which will cleanse the liver, an action set in opposition to following the stomach or giving in to individual desire, which leads to harm.[40] In this context, James identifies the emotional force of the liver as being stronger than that of the English sense of the heart, as it encompasses *arum* (blood) or life and cannot be separated from the organ itself as a moral force of self-control.[41] Some Yolngu Christians perceive a synergy between ancestral and Christian contexts in the types of moods or feelings (*märr*) expressed. For example, ancestral rocks may speak of an unshakeable faith that is continuously being nurtured and cared for. Thus, just as new life, ancestral strength, and emotional well-being are understood as mediated through cool waters, so they may also be brought into analogical relationship with baptism, purification, and spiritual renewal.

Complementary Rights in Performance: Singing, Painting, and Dancing

Landscapes further mediate the ways in which Yolngu artists sing of images as they paint on bark, canvas, or skin. Songs are sung over individuals as their torsos are painted with ancestral images, thus meshing the evocation of ancestral power through an interpenetration of sound and image. In funerals and other rituals, the majority of dancers smear white ochre over their upper bodies, arms, legs, and hair to protect themselves from pollution from the dead body, and their preparations are accompanied by clan songs during the act of painting. As Morphy's informant Dundiwuy told him, white paint "pushes away the mokuy spirit—and it keeps the bad smell [of the decaying body] so it doesn't get into the skin." For other aspects of rituals, however, yellow and red ochre may also be used. Morphy explains how in the Yellow Ochre Ceremony dancers who are not in danger of being polluted should be painted in yellow ochre, symbolic of the blood of the Yirritja moiety, or red for members of the Dhuwa moiety. Far from being polluting, covering the body symbolically with blood is a renewing act, but it is also ritually ambiguous, since it usually indicates a passage from a polluted state to being free from the dangers of pollution.[42] In addition, kin who stand in close relationships to the deceased have ancestral clan designs painted in yellow and red ochre on their stomachs or full ancestral designs painted on their torsos (such as for a circumcision ceremony that marks a young man's transition to adulthood). The designs painted onto ritual participants directly relate to the ancestral identity of the person and their relationship to that place, and all these modes of body design are enacted through song.

The process of singing and painting entails the ability to recall sounds, movements, colors, and smells of ancestral places, informed by clan rights to vocalize the esoteric names of flora and fauna found there. In the west of the Northern Territory, among Yanyuwa, naming creates a biographical account of places, imbuing the landscape with a quality of endurance that means it will hold those names for ever.[43] Naming continually reanimates landscapes, carrying images and memories from one generation to the next. Songs may also be sung when creating art, as the images conjure memories and expressions of place relatedness through particular sensorial experiences of the area. One Yolngu artist, Dula Ngurruwutthun, has clearly articulated how art evokes other sensory modalities among Dhäpuyngu people when he notes, "Their sacred *design has the tantalizing taste* of the Green Turtle. . . . Sacred art that has [been] *etched by the sea* where the ocean named Wulamba roars."[44]

The turtle is found in a floodplain where three waters meet through songlines, and together these waters create a particular "flavor" of clan design. This encoding of design in water aesthetics references how clans share aesthetic experiences of ancestral domains through the "tastes," "colors," and "temperaments" of waters that meet in specific areas.[45] Turtle designs and patterns evoke a particular flavor and smell of waters, and their colors relate to ancestral knowledge of these designs. Naming ancestral seas is but one poetic mode through which kin may be represented; the relationship between image, naming, and aesthetic form is repeated in many other ancestral contexts, as illustrated, for example, by one of the major Dhuwa ancestral beings, the rainbow serpent. His ancestral power is externalized in "spurting sea water" and by creating serpent-shaped clouds, and his shape and form are identified by voicing names associated with them.[46]

While competent singers must be able to evoke "a powerful image of a specific ancestrally significant place in the mind's eye of the listener," dancers can more readily convey some sense of the ancestor by following the movements of others and embodying their rhythms.[47] Learning to dance is a process of imitation and repetition, which means that girls and boys of any age may participate in unrestricted performances. In singing and dancing the rhythms of songs shape the steps of dancers, in turn imbuing dancers' bodies with power as they respond. Both male and female dancers can be recognized for their ability to preempt movements with precision and clarity. Expert male dancers lead ritual dancing and cue other men to follow changes in their actions. As Mandawuy Yunupingu explained to Aaron Corn, "If you've ever been exposed to those big ceremonies, you see people dancing whether they're Shark [*Mäna*] people or Stingray [*Gapirri*] people, or whether they're *Bäru* [Saltwater Crocodile], the Maralitja man. Maralitja discovered fire in the beginning. So when you're dancing *Bäru*, you become transformed into Maralitja, and that's when you say, 'I'm the Maralitja.'"[48] Women may also be recognized for their affective skill in dancing brightly. As Franca Tamisari has noted, however, compliments for exuberant, clean, and sharp actions are dangerous if they do not result in appropriate payment.[49] Powerful action is conveyed through the act of *guykthun*, which Tamisari refers to as "vomiting" or the "spilling of words," and this invocation creates a special status around the person or object, which needs to be repaid.[50] She recounts one occasion when she was unable to reciprocate the appreciation shown for her dancing with the demand of her loaned vehicle and became ill.[51] By pouring words of praise over her dancing, her body had become infused with the power of voiced rhythms requiring appropriate recompense. Equally, not knowing how to sing words in the right order creates a dissonance potentially disruptive to ancestral country, since it identifies the individual as someone who has not yet learned or does not understand the correct affordances that should be intuited about the sounds and movements of Country.

I have argued that Yolngu men and women understand ecology as the basis of a shared aesthetics for singing, dancing, and painting. Their aesthetic properties are *imaged* in ecological forms, *reflected* in patterns of dancing and painting, and *resonant* in song names. Processes of imaging, reflecting, and resonating inscribe singing, dancing, and painting in one another. This interplay of ecological affordances creates certain kinds of continuity in emotional expression. For example, elsewhere, Steven Feld and Keith Basso have explained how as people "act on the integrity of their dwelling," so they weave experiential and expressive modes of knowing, imagining, yearning for, remembering, living, and fighting for place.[52] Indeed, Yolngu perceptions of place comprise a holistic practice involving colors, sounds, and movements that literally, imaginatively, and affectively touch mind and body. Thus, places are not merely sensuous; they are emotionful, gathering to themselves "experiences," "histories," "memories," and "expectations."[53] Musical emotion is not simply an effect of music on the body; it is an active engagement of the self, attuned to the ongoing creative forces of ecology as they impact its inhabitants.

Ancestral Politics of Performance

Aboriginal people do not simply map their activities onto the landscape. Rather, ancestors were and are, in their spiritual essence, simultaneously perceived as human, animals, birds, and natural elements. They also hold the spirits of deceased people in those forms, and men and women pick up on ancestral sensory cues in the landscape that are legally and spiritually significant to them. Ingold has also argued that there is no division between Aboriginal material and cognitive experiences or "between ecological interactions *in* nature and cultural constructions *of* nature."[54] Instead, he posits that both sets of activities are "ways of dwelling" determined by different kinds of temporalities. Building on Fred Myers's analysis of Pintupi life, Ingold suggests that historical time dwells inside transhistorical time and vice versa, for as Pintupi replicate the transhistorical actions and movements of ancestors, they are "part and parcel of the becoming of the world and are bound to follow the course set by the Dreaming."[55]

The idea that one is emotionally coconstituted by one's own ancestral area through rights to belong there does not preclude holding other kinds of rights and emotional connections to related clan lands. "Co-extensive" dynamics and poetics of selfhood thus arise from perceptual sensibilities and "practical engagements with . . . (ancestrally) lived-in environments."[56]

As Yolngu men and women reclaim clan-specific images in singing, dancing, and painting, they are able to transfer emotional resonances of selves and ancestors as spiritually interconnected. These cosmological principles also have ramifications for identity politics and for the ways in which Yolngu use songs and dances of the landscape to assert their legal authority over the ecological potential of the region. A symbiotic relationship exists between people's identities and their being in the world, circumscribed by combinations of environmental features that define clan ownership and custodianship. Each sound and movement already holds the rights and essences of ancestral personality and gendered sentiments, and their performance recreates political investments in places.

The challenge of integrating complex dimensions of cosmological meaning with legal jurisdictions, resource practices, and ecological discourses remains. In urban centers the potential meanings of places are shaped by planners as they develop cultural strategies around the production of experience, while lawyers require written boundary evidence of ownership. In contrast, Yolngu senses of place are cumulative through knowing how to interact with ancestral environments, and the meanings of places are realized through the jural and emotional effects of performance practices. These differences need to be understood more readily in legal and other contexts if there is to be greater acceptance of how Yolngu conceive of ancestral sentiments of Country and emotional connections to place and one another in performance contexts.

Such an approach could reshape intercultural understandings and outcomes around the multiple agendas inherent in acts of singing, dancing, and painting in the future.

Notes

1. "Yolngu" is the term that identifies Aboriginal people of the northeast Arnhem Land region. It is contrasted with the term "Balanda," which means non-Aboriginal person.

2. The term "Country" is frequently used without the article by scholars in Aboriginal Australian contexts to indicate the agency of land and spiritual sentience arising between one's Country and feelings perceived within and because of it, as well as one's attachments to it (see also Muriel Swijghuisen Reigersberg, this volume).

3. An extensive body of scholarship exists on Australian Aboriginal ritual performance, with a large proportion of it relating to northeast Arnhem Land, through song styles, structures and metaphors. See for example, Steven Knopoff, "Value in Yolngu Ceremonial Song Performance: Continuity and Change," in *Beyond Price: Value in Culture, Economics, and the Arts*, ed. Michael Hutter (Cambridge: Cambridge University Press, 2008); Peter Toner, "Tropes of Longing and Belonging: Nostalgia and Musical Instruments in Northeast Arnhem Land," *Yearbook for Traditional Music* 38 (2005): 1–24; and Aaron Corn, "Ancestral, Corporeal, Corporate: Traditional Yolngu Understandings of the Body Explored," *Borderlands* 7, no. 2 (2008): 1–17. For relationships of art to land, see Howard Morphy, *Ancestral Connections* (Chicago: Chicago University Press, 1991). For the politics of ritual performance, see Nancy Williams, *The Yolngu and Their Land: A System of Land Tenure and the Fight for Its Recognition* (Canberra: Australian Institute of Aboriginal Studies, 1986); and Ian Keen, *Knowledge and Secrecy in an Aboriginal Religion* (New York: Oxford University Press, 1994). For dance and emotion in ritual, see Franca Tamisari, "Body, Vision and Movement: In the Footprints of the Ancestors," *Oceania* 68, no. 4 (1998): 249–70; and Tamisari "Writing Close to Dance: Expression in Yolngu Performance," in *Aesthetics and Experience in Music Performance*, ed. Elizabeth Mackinlay, Dennis Collins, and Samantha Owens (Cambridge: Cambridge Scholars, 2005). The rich ethnographic and theoretical insights of these Arnhem Land works complement ritual studies in other parts of Australia that deal with the "commemorative, revelatory and instrumental" purposes of ritual. Stephen Wild, "Men as Women: Female Dance Symbolism in Walbiri Men's Rituals," *Dance Research Journal* 10, no. 1 (1977): 15. For performative relationships to land, ritual, and politics, see Deborah Rose, *Dingo Makes Us Human* (Cambridge: Cambridge University Press, 1992); and Helen Payne, "Rites for Sites or Sites for Rites? The Dynamics of Women's Cultural Life in the Musgraves," in *Women Rites and Sites: Aboriginal Women's Cultural Knowledge*, ed. Peggy Brock (Sydney: Allen and Unwin, 1989).

4. As songs take listeners to ancestral sites, their arrival is signaled by the intonation of deep power names (*bundurr*) which can be sung only by male ritual specialists (*djirrikaymirr* or *dalkarramirr*) who have the authority to invoke the ancestors. Ritual entails the expectation of controlling the correct iteration and address of these restricted clan names (*guykthun bundurr*). See Richard Moyle, *Alyawarra Music: Songs and Society in a Central Australian Community* (Canberra: AIAS, 1986); and Jill Stubington, *Singing the Land: The Power of Performance in Aboriginal Life* (Strawberry Hills, New South Wales: Currency House Press, 2007), 80.

5. Frances Morphy, "Performing the Law: The Yolngu of Blue Mud Bay Meet the Native Title Process," in *The Social Effects of Native Title: Recognition, Translation, Coexistence*, ed. Benjamin R. Smith and Frances Morphy (Canberra: ANU ePress, 2007).

6. Frances Morphy and Howard Morphy, "The Blue Mud Bay Case: Refractions through Saltwater Country," *Dialogue, the Journal of the Academy of the Social Sciences in Australia* 28, no. 1 (2009): 15–25.

7. Aaron Corn, "When the Waters Will Be One: Hereditary Performance Traditions and the Yolngu Re-invention of Post-Barunga Intercultural Discourses," *Journal of Australian Studies* 84 (2005): 15–30.

8. See, for example, Diane Bell, *Daughters of the Dreaming* (Sydney: Allen and Unwin, 1983); Françoise Dussart, *The Politics of Ritual in an Aboriginal Settlement: Kinship, Gender and the Currency of Knowledge* (Washington, DC: Smithsonian Institution Press, 2000); Keen, *Knowledge and Secrecy*.

9. See Howard Morphy, "From Dull to Brilliant: The Aesthetics of Spiritual Power among the Yolngu," *Man*, n.s., 24, no. 1 (1989): 21–40. For ancestral parallels in dancing, see Franca Tamisari, "The Meaning of the Steps Is in Between: Dancing and the Curse of Compliments," *Australian Journal of Anthropology* 11, no. 3 (2000): 274–86. For parallels in song, see Toner, "Longing and Belonging."

10. Yolngu men and women perform ancestral songs and dances at funerals and commemoration, initiation, and fertility rituals, as well as at contemporary events such as graduations, visits of dignitaries, openings of key buildings, conferences, art exhibitions, and tourist activities.

11. Corn, "Ancestral, Corporeal, Corporate."

12. Morphy, *Ancestral Connections*, 52, 54.

13. Tamisari, "Meaning of the Steps," 277.

14. Aaron Corn and Joe N. Gumbula, "Budutthun Rajta Winyimirri," *Australian Aboriginal Studies* 2 (2007): 116–20.

15. Stubington, *Singing the Land*, 157.

16. Williams, *Yolngu and Their Land*, 71.

17. Nancy Munn, *Walbiri Iconography: Graphic Representation and Cultural Symbolism in a Central Australian Society* (Ithaca: Cornell University Press, 1973), 132.

18. Nancy Munn, "Excluded Spaces: The Figure in the Australian Landscape," *Critical Inquiry* 22, no. 3 (1996): 446–65.

19. Fred Myers, *Pintupi Country, Pintupi Self: Sentiment, Place and Politics among Western Desert Aborigines* (Washington, DC: Smithsonian Institution Press, 1986).

20. Ibid., 9.

21. An example of Datiwuy song and dance can be found online at "Datiwuy manikay & bunggul, Milingimbi, with Terrence Gaypalani, Wilson Manydjarri, Brendan Ganambarr," posted on YouTube by "ididjaustralia" on February 3, 2010, http://www.youtube.com/watch?v=0G03d_qfvWk. Murukun Buyu-Djarrakmirr died in 2000.

22. Both recordings are transcribed from field recordings made with each of the singers in 1990.

23. Tim Ingold, "Culture and the Perception of the Environment," in *Bush Base: Forest Farm; Culture, Environment and Development*, ed. Elisabeth Croll and David. Parkin (London: Routledge, 1992), 47.

24. James J. Gibson, *The Ecological Approach to Visual Perception* (Hillsdale, NJ: Erlbaum, 1986).

25. Adopting Paul Friedrich's notion of polytropy as a language of poetic effect, imagination, and interpretation, Peter Toner uses five tropes to analyze the sounds

of the drum (*dhamburru*) and the didjeridoo of two ancestors: Birrinydji and Ganbulapula. These comprise (1) image tropes that evoke visual depictions of musical imagery, (2) modal tropes that shape affective responses, (3) formal tropes that influence poetic construction, (4) contiguity tropes that create aesthetic links with other contexts and times, and (5) analogical tropes involving resemblances between one element and another. He describes how echoes of the drum are felt around the community of Gurrumurru, generating a sense of elation for performers and listeners who imagine themselves in the ancestral time and place of performance ("Longing and Belonging," 7, 13). Although the sound invokes joviality in performance, it hides an undercurrent of war and bloodshed related to earlier times of conflict. Thus, emotional ambivalence and multiple emotional resonances are engendered in the use of the drum.

26. Tim Ingold, *The Perception of the Environment: Essays in Livelihood, Dwelling, and Skill* (London: Routledge, 2000), 25.

27. Corn, "Ancestral, Corporeal, Corporate," 8.

28. Ian Keen, "Metaphor and the Metalanguage: 'Groups' in Northeast Arnhem Land," *American Ethnologist* 22 (1995): 502–27; here 520.

29. Frances Morphy, "Whose Governance, for Whose Good? The Laynhapuy Homelands Association and the Neo-assimilationist Turn in Indigenous Policy," in *Contested Governance: Culture, Power and Institutions in Indigenous Australia*, Centre for Aboriginal Economic Policy Research (CAEPR) Research Monograph 29, ed. Janet Hunt and Diane Smith, Stephanie Garling, and Will Sanders (Canberra: Australian National University ePress, 2008).

30. Peter Toner, "Ideology, Influence and Innovation: The Impact of Macassan Contact on Yolngu Music," *Perfect Beat: The Pacific Journal of Research into Contemporary Music and Popular Culture* 5, no. 1 (2000): 22–41.

31. For an extended analysis of how children understand their relationships to the environment musically, see Fiona Magowan, *Melodies of Mourning: Music and Emotion in Northern Australia* (Oxford: Currey, 2007).

32. Michael Christie, "Yolngu Language Habitat: Ecology, Identity and Law in an Aboriginal Society," in *Trends in Linguistics, the Habitat of Australia's Aboriginal Languages: Past, Present and Future*, ed. Gerhard Leitner and Ian G. Malcolm (Berlin: Mouton de Grutyer, 2007), 57, 62–63.

33. Michael Christie and John Greatorex, *Yolngu Life in the Northern Territory of Australia: The Significance of Community and Social Capital* (Darwin, Australia: Charles Darwin University, 2006), 8, accessed December 16, 2012, http://www.cdu.edu.au/centres/inc/pdf/Yolngulife.pdf. See also Michael Christie, "Teaching from Country, Learning from Country," with the assistance of Yiŋiya Guyula, Dhäŋgal Gurruwiwi, John Greatorex, Joanne Garnggulkpuy, Kathy Guthadjaka, *International Journal of Learning in Social Contexts Australia* 2 (2010): 6–18.

34. See Jennifer Deger, *Shimmering Screens: Making Media in an Aboriginal Community* (Minneapolis: University of Minnesota Press, 2006).

35. Christie, "Yolngu Language Habitat," 76.

36. Charles Mountford, *Art, Myth and Symbolism* (Melbourne: Melbourne University Press, 1956), 333–38, cited in ibid., 89; Aaron Corn, "Land, Song, Constitution: Exploring Expressions of Ancestral Agency, Intercultural Diplomacy and Family Legacy in the Music of Yothu Yindi with Mandawuy Yunupiŋu," *Popular Music* 29 (2010): 81–102, 89.

37. See Manydjarri Ganambarr, quoted in Isaacs, *Saltwater*, 17.

38. For more information, see Dorothy Bepuka Garawirrtja, *Yalupuy Dhawu*, as transcribed by Joanne Wirrinywirriny and Emma Kowal, Galiwin'ku, October 21, 2002, http://yalu.cdu.edu.au/philosophy/text/bepukay/html.

39. See also Tamisari "Meaning of the Steps," 281.

40. For emotions in the stomach and liver, see Barley Norton, this volume. See also Wendy James, "Uduk Faith in Five-Note Scale: Mission Music and the Spread of the Gospel," in *Vernacular Christianity: Essays in the Social Anthropology of Religion, Presented to Godfrey Liendhardt*, ed. Wendy James and Douglas H. Johnson. JASO Occasional Papers, no. 7 (Oxford: JASO, 1988), 40.

41. Wendy James, *The Listening Ebony: Moral Knowledge, Religion and Power among the Uduk of Sudan* (Oxford: Oxford University Press, 1988), 230.

42. Howard Morphy, *Journey to the Crocodile's Nest* (Canberra: Australian Institute of Aboriginal Studies 1984), 85.

43. Amanda Kearny and John Bradley, "Too Strong to Ever Not Be There: Place Names and Emotional Geographies," *Social and Cultural Geography* 10, no. 1 (2009): 77–94.

44. Dula Ngurruwutthun, quoted in Isaacs, *Saltwater*, 9.

45. Ibid.

46. Franca Tamisari, "Names and Naming: Speaking Forms into Place," in *The Land Is a Map: Placenames of Indigenous Origin in Australia*, ed. Luise Hercus, Flavia Hodges, and Jane Simpson (Canberra: Australian National University, 2002): 94–96.

47. Toner, "Longing and Belonging," 6.

48. Mandawuy Yunupingu, quoted in Corn and Gumbula, "Bu<u>d</u>utthun Rajta Winyimirri," 5.

49. Tamisari, "Meaning of the Steps."

50. Tamisari, "Names and Naming," 95.

51. Tamisari, "Meaning of the Steps," 280.

52. Steven Feld and Keith H. Basso, introduction to *Senses of Place*, ed. Steven Feld and Keith H. Basso (Santa Fe, NM: School of American Research Press, 1996), 8.

53. See Edward Casey, "How to Get from Space to Place in a Fairly Short Stretch of Time: Phenomenological Prolegomena," in Feld and Basso, *Senses of Place*, 24.

54. Ibid., 57.

55. Myers, *Pintupi Country, Pintupi Self*; Ingold, *Perception of the Environment*, 57.

56. Christie, "Yolngu Language Habitat," 57; Ingold, *Perception of the Environment*, 168.

Part Two

Memory and Attachment

Chapter Four

Christian Choral Singing in Aboriginal Australia

Gendered Absence, Emotion, and Place

Muriel Swijghuisen Reigersberg

This chapter examines the relationships between choral singing, gender, and emotion in the Lutheran Australian Aboriginal community of Hopevale, northern Queensland (map 4.1). It is based on applied ethnomusicological research undertaken in collaboration with the Hopevale community between 2004 and 2005. During this period I worked as a choral music facilitator, conducting the Hopevale Community Choir (see fig. 4.1) and occasionally teaching music at the Hopevale state primary school. I developed an ethnographically informed approach to choral facilitation that incorporated Hopevalian understandings of musical preferences and performance aesthetics and what it means to "sing in a choir."[1] Through conducting, singing, and socializing with the Hopevale Community Choir, I began to question how emotional responses to choral singing in Hopevale are influenced by gender and place. In this chapter I explore whether contemporary Lutheran choral singing can strengthen the formation of a specifically Lutheran, Hopevalian identity or whether changes in musical preferences and the decline of active church-based Christian worship mean that hymnody is no longer as important in sustaining local identities as it once was.

In particular, I examine how the relative absence of young men from the community choir, and from the community more generally, can affect emotional responses to choral hymn singing of Hopevalian choral singers and choir audiences.[2] I do so through an analysis of a performance given by the almost entirely female Hopevale Community Choir in the Lotus Glen men's correctional facility in Mareeba, northern Queensland. First, I elaborate on Aboriginal concepts of place and Hopevalian history to demonstrate that the frequent, often enforced, relocations of the Hopevale community have impacted negatively on the maintenance of precolonial cultural, religious, and

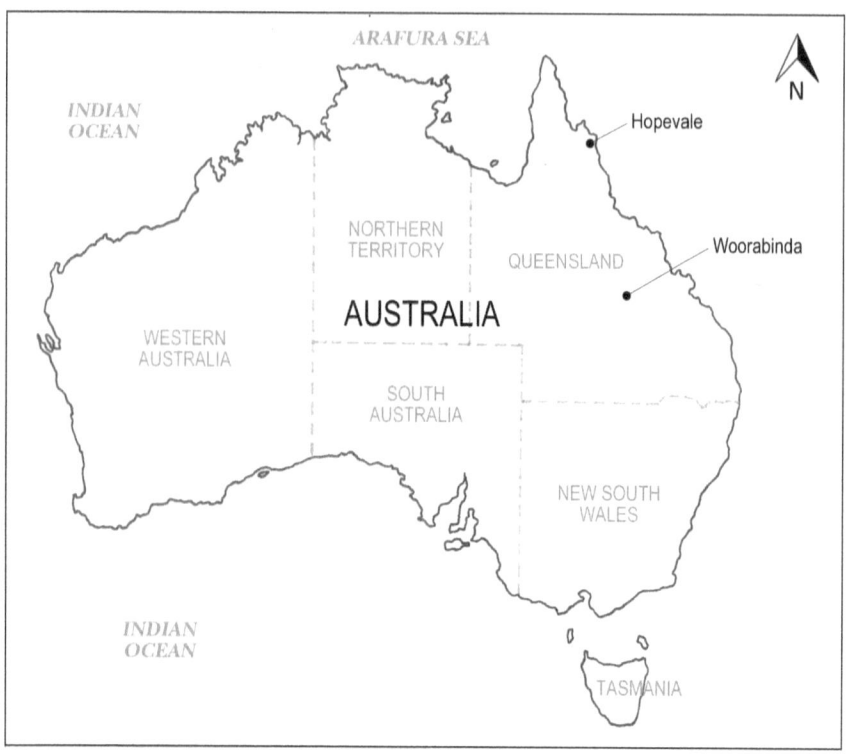

Map 4.1. Australia and the former Queensland missions, Hopevale and Woorabinda. Map by Angela Snieder.

musical practices. This elaboration explains why Lutheran and Anglican hymnody and congregational singing have flourished in the region. The historical background informs discussion about why generational differences exist in emotional relationships to place.

The Cultural and Historical Significance of Place and Relocation in Hopevale

The concept of place, or "Country," as it is often referred to by Indigenous Australians, is particularly important in Aboriginal Australia. The word "Country" does not just refer to a geographic area or a commodity with definite boundaries tied to notions of material ownership, sale, and purchase, as is the case under European Australian law. Instead the concept contains topographical subtleties often unrecognizable to non-Indigenous people. Similarly, the spiritual connotations that the word "Country" carries are fluid

Figure 4.1. Hopevale Community Choir, Anglican Church, Ravenshoe, April 2005. Photograph by the author.

and contested. In many areas of the continent, the term "Country" can refer not only to a geographic area but also to the ancestral spirits and people who inhabit a locality, as well as the flora, fauna, and natural elements and phenomena that form part of a region. For example, among the Yolngu of northeast Arnhem Land, local geographic areas intimately relate to gender, kinship affiliations, local fauna, and spirituality in such a way that Country is synonymous with a person's social identity, and Aboriginal ritual music and dance are intimately related to aspects of Country.[3]

Historically, missionization altered the relationship between Country and people in Indigenous groups, introducing a nonland-based spirituality, monotheism, and a heavily enforced dichotomy between good and evil, light and dark, heaven and earth. Missionaries attempted, and often failed, to introduce agricultural practices to Indigenous groups together with the demand that they abandon their nomadic practices. Western understandings of sexuality, family, and gendered role divisions were also propagated, since they were part and parcel of what the missionaries believed to be a Christian way of living. Global processes of missionization, together with responses to it, have been discussed extensively, as has the transplantation of a religion to another geographic area.[4] Several works provide compelling accounts that problematize transplanted religions to vastly different cultures in ways that resonate with the situation elaborated here.[5] When comparing the outcomes and processes of missionization globally, the Indigenous Australians have most in common with North American Indigenous peoples and the Maoris of New Zealand. In all three cases the colonizer never left, and these groups remain as minorities in their own country. All have also been coerced into adopting and adapting the settlers' language and social customs, have suffered from social disadvantages (as compared to their non-Indigenous peers), and have had to struggle to maintain their local traditions.

Missionization, however, was not a heterogeneous process globally, Australia being no exception. Various authors have addressed the subject of missionization in Australia generally and more specifically, documenting the local history of individual missions and aspects of the missionization process and its aftermath.[6] The ways in which Aboriginal people responded to missionization very much depended on the character of their local missionaries; the proselytizing denomination and its attitudes toward Indigenous customs; the time at which missionization occurred (the Northern Territory being affected later than, for example, New South Wales, South Australia, and Victoria); the conduct of other non-Indigenous settlers in the region; and the reasons for settlement.

Many of these texts mention the importance of hymnody and the eventual use of Aboriginal traditional ceremonial music in Christian contexts as a route to conversion. In Hopevale, however, such ceremonial music is no longer performed; instead Christian music and Westernized worship practices have taken its place. Missionary intervention combined with cultural decimation resulted in a declining familiarity with precolonial Indigenous spirituality. The concept of Country in Hopevale, therefore, means that flora, fauna, ancestors, natural elements, and kinship affiliations are not accorded the same spiritual significance as elsewhere in Australia. Neither have Hopevalians formally adopted the concepts of an Indigenous theology into local church music, due to a lack of familiarity with and opposition to its ideas.[7] This has resulted in the absence of any direct or oblique references to Country in church hymnody, choral singing, and sermons. To understand how such changes have come about, it is necessary to elaborate on how Hopevale's history as a Lutheran mission has impacted the relationship between men, women, and Country.

The Lutheran Aboriginal community of Hopevale lies about a five hours' drive north of Cairns, northern Queensland, on the Cape York peninsula of Australia. The nearest town is Cooktown, approximately forty-five minutes away by car. It is the main township on the lands now belonging to the Aboriginal Guugu Yimithirr people. The township moved its location several times during the course of history and was renamed Elim, Cape Bedford, Hope Valley, and Spring Hill. Now named Hopevale (sometimes spelled Hope Vale), it has a fluctuating population of about sixteen hundred inhabitants split into thirteen Aboriginal kinship groups. A small percentage of non-Indigenous church, teaching, health, and administrative staff also live there. The three languages used regularly by Hopevalians are Aboriginal English and two Indigenous languages: Guugu Yimithirr and sometimes Guugu Yalanji.

The former mission settlement was created by missionary Johann Flierl in 1886 for the purposes of protecting, proselytizing, and settling or resettling the historically nomadic Indigenous groups living in the area. The first mission, initially named Elim and then Cape Bedford, was a response to the brutal slaughter of the local Aboriginal population by settlers arriving during the 1873 Palmer River Gold Rush. This devastation of Indigenous people caused a loss of oral culture and musical as well as spiritual knowledge. The resettling of the nomadic Indigenous family groups, in turn, led to changes in the ways in which local Aborigines related to Country socially and musically. Historical literature suggests that there had been relationships between Indigenous spirituality and local Country.[8] With restrictions imposed on the nomadic movements of Indigenous groups, some kinship groups could no longer perform particular ceremonies. Disassociated from the local landscape to which their ceremonies were bound, these (new) inhabitants were inappropriately related to their new home and its original Indigenous inhabitants, which also resulted in the loss of ceremonial and musical knowledge.

Several other events compounded the loss of ceremonial knowledge. First, the implementation of the Aboriginals Protection and Restriction of the Sale of Opium Act in 1897 in Queensland made it legally possible for government officials to detain people of Indigenous descent on missions and reserves. The act also sanctioned the removal of Indigenous children from their Aboriginal parents to missions, a practice that continued into the 1960s and 1970s. Many children at Cape Bedford (the historical name for the mission on Guugu Yimithirr territory located thirty kilometers away from Hopevale) were members of what is now known as the "Stolen Generation"—children with an Indigenous ancestry removed by officials to live on the Cape Bedford mission.[9] Children were forced to abandon what missionaries considered to be the heathen ceremonial practices of the bush-dwelling Indigenous people. The effect of the removal of children was not just a loss of cultural knowledge but also an intense personal trauma for them and for their families.

Second, ceremonial knowledge was further damaged between 1942 and 1949 when Hopevalians, or the Cape Bedford people as they were then known, were forcibly evacuated to Woorabinda in southwestern Queensland as a result of the German nationality of their missionary, George Heinrich Schwarz.[10] This forced evacuation came unannounced, and the people were unable to adequately prepare themselves for the journey and change in local temperatures. It is due to the dramatic change in climate experienced during the evacuation that over a quarter of the Cape Bedford Aborigines died of influenza, including many elders who possessed vast amounts of oral history and musical knowledge.

Finally, the Australian federal government's introduction of integration and assimilation policies in the 1960s and 1970s advocated abandoning Indigenous spiritual beliefs, languages, and other cultural practices in favor of the wholesale adoption of Westernized modes of living. During this period many Hopevalians moved to larger, predominantly white, cities in southern Queensland to work or attend school, here influenced by policies that further emphasized the undesirability of engaging in precolonial modes of worship and spirituality. These numerous turbulent episodes of relocation, death, and removal in the community's history have altered the musical practices transmitted through generations. More specifically, these relocations, combined with missionary intervention and spiritual conversion, led the community to adopt Christianity and its music, which in turn affected how people relate both to music and to place. Before exploring two specific contemporary examples of this, the following section provides a brief history of the introduction of choral singing to Hopevale.

Hopevalian Hymnody, Spirituality, and Place

Writing about earlier missionary activity in Hope Valley (or what is today Hopevalian land), the reverend Howard J. Pohlner records, "Singing was traditionally an important means of communication. When Pastor Bartholomaeus came to Hope Valley in 1939 there was an elderly aborigine Toby, camped in the stable. He had come to the Mission as an old man. When the young pastor asked how he had come to know Jesus he replied, 'Through listening to the boys singing hymns every night.'"[11] Missionaries found hymnody to be an effective way of transmitting spiritual knowledge, and Christian services in Hopevale started to incorporate regular hymn singing to draw in the local Indigenous population. A strong choral tradition based on more formalized congregational hymn singing developed when the Cape Bedford people were evacuated to Woorabinda, with the result that hymn singing provided more than a Christian resource.[12] Church organist June Pearson refers to this, while also alluding to the emotional longing experienced by the Cape Bedford people for their home in northern Queensland through this singing, when she recollected that "quite a lot of the old fellas . . . learnt to sing in the churches in Woorabinda, because they sang a lot to stay happy to come back home."[13] Interviews and literature suggest that the congregational singing of Lutheran hymns, particularly in the Guugu Yimithirr language, strengthened the community's resolve to return home during the evacuation and provided an emotional outlet for the grief experienced by the community as a result of the high mortality rate.[14] These themes of loss and longing as articulated through singing recur throughout the episodes considered in this chapter.

The absence of a permanent white Lutheran pastor in Woorabinda in the 1940s led the Cape Bedford people to start ministering among themselves; this included leading one another in congregational song. These activities stimulated the formation of a core Aboriginal spiritual leadership among the Cape Bedford men, including responsibilities these Cape men had not been entrusted with by their previous Lutheran missionary, George Heinrich Schwarz.[15] Perhaps not coincidentally, it was during this period, in 1946, that Schwarz sent them their first translated hymnal in Guugu Yimithirr.

The hymnal incorporated a translated Order of Service and twenty-seven hymns, including "King of Creation," the Christmas hymn "Praise God the Lord," and "Wake, Arise"—with most translated by Pastor Wilhelm Poland (in Cape Bedford between 1888 and 1905). It was a text-only edition, with no English translations, and stimulated singing and worshipping in Guugu Yimithirr at a time when local Woorabinda churches offered no services in this language due to the linguistic differences between the local Woorabinda Aborigines and the evacuated Cape Bedford people.[16] The Lutheran hymns also helped the Cape Bedford people maintain their denominational practices as distinct.[17] Most notably, congregational hymn singing and, later, choral singing became a unique way in which the congregation's Lutheran Guugu Yimithirr identity was performed during the turbulent years of the evacuation.

In 1949, when the first group of men was finally allowed to return to Hopevale, pastors Frank Behrendorf and Vic Wenke started teaching the choir in earnest. Pastor Wenke first taught the newly returned men to sing their hymns in harmony by playing the various voice parts on his violin to the singers, who would then repeat the vocal lines and learn them by ear. Pastor Wenke had also used this method during his occasional periods of ministry in Woorabinda. Women and children who had returned from Woorabinda also joined the congregational hymn singing.[18] They learned to sing in three- or four-part diatonic harmony from choir members who led the singing during the compulsory church services. The practice of congregational singing in harmony was still practiced between 2004 and 2005 during important Christian festivals such as Easter and Christmas, when a relatively large number of elders attended church services.[19] Piano, electronic organ, or keyboard now provide standard accompaniment in church (with the guitar sometimes used outside of church).

Some hymns have since become associated with specific Hopevalian individuals and localities. This is made obvious in obituaries or in the order of service, where family members often list the favorite hymns of the deceased and request that they be sung in commemoration. Some obituaries even mention the locations where hymns were last sung by the deceased and the language used in connection with place. For example, the unpublished obituary of the elder Walter Bowen contained the following details:

> Walter and Ella [Walter's wife] then went up to Elim [area on the coast] and pulled weeds out of [Walter's mother's] grave.... On Sunday the 23rd of January Walter was up early, moving around, doing his own thing. Ella, his wife, started singing "I am coming Lord" and surprisingly, he joined in and the two sang the hymn, followed by a few more. They then sat and watched the beach, with Walter describing each bird, and naming them in language [in Guugu Yimithirr].... In his last days, on earth, Walter, continually spoke in language, and pointed out areas in language.[20]

Walter was speaking "in language"—an expression often used by Hopevalians to refer to an Aboriginal language or another foreign language. Many church elders were particularly supportive of the use of Guugu Yimithirr in speech and hymnody (as opposed to Aboriginal English in daily conversation), particularly if they had kin links with traditional owners of Guugu Yimithirr Country, and would frequently name flora and fauna in the vernacular.[21] Walter Bowen was a Birri-Guba clan member through his father, George Bowen. Although the Birri-Guba people are not traditional owners of Guugu Yimithirr Country, Walter could claim some ownership rights through his mother, Dora Dharrpa, who was a member of the Dharrpa traditional owners and taught her son Guugu Yimithirr. The explicit references made to Walter's use of Guugu Yimithirr, as opposed to English, emphasize the fact that he had rights to Country and that he knew how to name Country in his mother tongue. These obituary details, therefore, carefully asserted Walter's relationship to place and the memory of loss through singing and language.

The ways in which the hymns mentioned in Walter's obituary relate to Country differ from some expressions of Christian song and place in northeast Arnhem Land.[22] In Hopevale all Christian hymn melodies and texts sung are taken from published sources such as the *Australian Lutheran Hymn-Book* (1950),[23] the *Lutheran Hymnal with Supplement* (1989),[24] and *Together in Song* (1999)[25]—or from popular chorus bundles such as *All Together OK* (1996).[26] In contrast, in northeast Arnhem Land some Yolngu Christian songs are set to melodies and rhythms of the ancestral law. Fiona Magowan analyzes how two Yolngu ministers composed the Christmas story to their own clan song styles, while another Easter song incorporates references to the transformation of water into honey and blood through ancestral imagery as a vehicle for Christian interpretation.[27] Hopevalians, therefore, have lost the ancestral rhythmic and melodic references as well as song texts linking spirituality, local geographic areas, flora, fauna, and kinship groups through song performance. Although they might sing in the vernacular, the Christian texts are direct translations from English or sometimes German (introduced by missionaries and pastors). As a result, the hymns do not refer to Country as they might in some Yolngu areas where Aboriginal Christians have composed their own songs.

In both church worship and daily life, hymns are meaningful to Hopevalians because their performance facilitates the sharing of a social history and a Lutheran spirituality. Hymn singing also stimulates listening and performative pleasure that may be place bound even when the singing is used to commemorate deceased elders. However, Lutheran spirituality and commemoration do not formally acknowledge the importance of Country in church worship through sermon and song. While individuals such as Walter Bowen might assert links to Country in private, such views are not seen as collective expressions of an Indigenous approach to the interpretation of Christian doctrine. Links to Country in Hopevale are not accorded theological importance, even if acknowledged and mentioned, partly due to the difficulty in developing an Aboriginal theology within the Lutheran Church in Queensland.[28] The absence of an Aboriginal theology and corresponding music in Hopevale contrasts with such developments in Arnhem Land, where ancestral traditions have been debated in the church and where ancestral Christian songs have been composed and performed on special occasions.[29]

In Hopevale, church services are no longer compulsory, and many people attend only at Easter, Christmas, weddings, and funerals. The diminished levels of church attendance have reduced the pool of people who might wish to sing in the choir, as well as the opportunities for transmitting hymns orally. As a result, fewer people are singing and learning hymns, and there is less opportunity for people to discuss the hymns' significance in the past in building and maintaining a Hopevalian identity.

The linguistic evolution of Guugu Yimithirr has also affected the practice of choral hymn singing. Some singers and youths are unable to pronounce or understand some of the more archaic words used in the Guugu Yimithirr hymnal, *Gunbu Guugu Yimithirrbi*.[30] Due to falling levels of school attendance and literacy in Hopevale, reading hymn texts in any language is problematic, making it particularly discouraging for younger people to learn the older hymns. Furthermore, unlike community elders who have greater experience of other Australian communities as a result of traveling to different regions, younger Hopevalians have not moved around as much and therefore do not need to use hymnody to create a specific identity for themselves in relation to other Australians—resulting in the decline of choral singing. A further deterrent for younger people, especially men, is that choral singing has evolved into an almost single-gender activity.

Gendered Absence: "Choir Is for *Gamba Gamba*"

From 2004 to 2005 the Hopevale Community Choir consisted of primarily older women aged between fifty-two and seventy-five. As with Fiona Magowan, Louise Wrazen, Christine R. Yano, and Tina K. Ramnarine in this volume, the age of my research partners and singers informed my research methodology and subsequent discussions of the outcomes. I initially wondered if the absence of men from the choir was due to socially constructed, gendered musical domains where choral singing belonged to the female domain. Scholars such as Magowan, Françoise Dussart, Diane Bell, and Linda Barwick have shown that other Aboriginal communities still operate along gender segregated lines that influence social conduct and performativity.[31] Christian choral singing in some parts of the Northern Territory can also be an activity undertaken only by women, as illustrated by the renowned Ntaria Ladies Choir of Hermannsburg.[32]

Although all forms of music making, including congregational hymn singing, are open to both genders in Hopevale, Christian choral singing was associated predominantly with *gamba gamba* (older, married, or respected women) in 2004–5. There was no historical or social precedence for this. Rather, I argue that this relative absence of men from Hopevalian social and musical life is a consequence of the influence of Western gender models and the unwillingness of church and state officials to give leadership roles to Indigenous men. The overall lack of confidence in Indigenous ability has indirectly led to the incarceration, demoralization, unemployment, ill health, and early deaths of Hopevalian men. As the following section shows, choir membership and responses to choral performances reflect this historically constructed absence of men.

The enlightenment and salvation of women were perceived as being particularly urgent in Cape Bedford, with numerous instances of sexual exploitation and abuse of Aboriginal women and children recorded in the Cooktown area after 1873.[33] Thus, when the Cape Bedford mission was first established, George Heinrich Schwarz felt it was his Christian duty to protect the most vulnerable Aborigines, namely women and children, from local Aboriginal men and settler society. These missionary interventions also were believed to restore the Edenic state of relations between the sexes by introducing the social relations characteristic of Christian nations. Missionaries simultaneously aimed to convince Indigenous women that their enlightenment could come only through the adoption of the Christian faith and morality and to demonstrate to non-Indigenous congregations that missionization was urgently needed and morally justifiable.[34] Through Schwarz's efforts a group of young Christian women and children made the mission their permanent home. They, in turn, attracted the attention of young Indigenous men who were unable to find suitable brides within their own kin groups. Schwarz agreed to allow the young men to marry the Christian girls, provided the men themselves became faithful converts and refrained from seeking contact with their non-Christian relatives in the area. By manipulating marital opportunities, the Cape Bedford missionaries thus established an isolated Lutheran community with a core of permanent, settled residents.

While focusing their efforts on women and children, the missionaries at Cape Bedford were simultaneously determined to destroy what they perceived to be all non-Christian ceremonial practices.[35] Aboriginal pastor George Rosendale commented on missionaries Schwarz's and Poland's unwillingness to consider the possibility of any benefits in precolonial spirituality: "And they have, that burn time ceremony. All the people get together and they have that ceremony. The old missionary here, *jurra*, never looked into these ceremonies, what it's all about. All he did was rubbish everything, you know, 'No, you can't do that, that's heathenism' and all that."[36] This condemnation of ceremonial practices eroded the spiritual and social roles of non-Christian men at Cape Bedford. By discrediting ceremonial knowledge, missionaries ensured that gradually the older Aboriginal men who held positions of ceremonial responsibility were accorded less respect by younger men, which in turn resulted in fewer initiates coming forward. Eventually missionaries managed to halt initiation ceremonies altogether. However, these ceremonies were crucial to the maintenance of a system that accorded men respect and social rights based on the volume of spiritual, musical, and other ceremonial knowledge they carried. Now in a position where they were unable to fulfill their ceremonial responsibilities due to their lack of spiritual knowledge about Country, the uninitiated Christian men at Cape Bedford had very few political, marital, or social rights and were rejected in non-Christian circles. Since these men were unable to assert themselves as leaders of worth in their traditional communities, they turned to Christianity and aspired to be religious leaders in their new faith. Yet upon their return to Hopevale (and in contrast to Woorabinda), Aboriginal men were denied positions of formal spiritual responsibility until the 1960s, causing disillusionment with the Lutheran church among Hopevalians—a situation only slightly ameliorated in 1969 when pastors George Rosendale and Alick Cameron were ordained.[37] As has been well documented, Aborigines were similarly denied rights of ownership of their lands. Even when the Deed of Grant in Trust resolution of 1986 awarded the Hopevale Aboriginal Council 110,000 hectares of land, the transition was problematic and is yet to be resolved.

Despite the assimilationist policies of the 1960s and 1970s encouraging Hopevalians to move south and acquire jobs and a Western education, many non-Indigenous Australians did not believe Aborigines to be capable of more than domestic or agricultural labor. As a result, very few Hopevalians were trained and prepared with the skills and experience to manage Hopevale when it acquired its own Indigenous council in the 1980s. Additionally, when Hopevalians returned home after their studies or work they found it difficult to find meaningful employment and housing; local jobs were scarce and few employers offered positions of responsibility and land ownership or management, since these were occupied by white men.

Men increasingly found that their political, social, and religious aspirations were being thwarted by the government, church, and, later, from within the

Hopevale community itself. In contrast, Hopevalian women were able to fulfill their roles as domestics, mothers, religious helpers, and singers. With very little to fill the gap created by the loss of significant employment, community support, and spirituality, many young men sought refuge in alcohol and drugs. This has resulted in community violence, high levels of incarceration, suicide, diabetes, and renal failure among Hopevalian men today.[38] Due to the relatively early deaths of male community elders who had an extensive knowledge of hymns, very few men were able to function as role models or to contribute to hymn and choral singing in Hopevale between 2004 and 2005.

As a result, men were largely absent from Hopevalian social life during this period, and very few participated in church-related activities such as choral singing or worship services. The Hopevale Community Choir had only one regular male participant, for example. There were, of course, positive male role models in Hopevale, but they were often based elsewhere and did not sing in the choir (e.g., Hopevalian football player Matthew Bowen and Indigenous politician Noel Pearson). Other men were unable to participate in rehearsals due to work commitments in and around Hopevale itself; during my attempts to recruit male choir members, I encountered only two men who openly declared they wished to join, but both were unable due to work obligations. In this absence of men, therefore, choral singing has become a specifically female musical activity. Furthermore, with choir members ranging in age from fifty-two to seventy-five and only older, devoutly Lutheran Hopevalian women singing regularly, younger women are reluctant to join. By 2004, therefore, youths perceived choral singing as something that only the deeply religious *gamba gamba* did.

The general decline of choral hymn singing suggested earlier, combined with its development as an almost single-gender activity, has not, however, diminished its significance to the community. Choral singing is still deeply appreciated by both singers and audience members, many of whom find that musical enjoyment can elicit joy as well as heightened feelings of nostalgia, loss, and longing for Country. The following section focuses, in particular, on specific circumstances when the feelings of loss and longing for Country can be more pronounced: during a concert at Lotus Glen men's correctional facility, the absence of Hopevalian men was especially emphasized.

Choral Singing, Emotions, and Absence Today

During my time as choral facilitator, the Hopevale Community Choir of eleven women and one man undertook a four-day tour through northern Queensland in April 2005.[39] According to choir members, this was the first time they had been on an official choir tour that received publicity in the local media (where it was featured on local Australian Broadcasting Corporation radio

Figure 4.2. Lotus Glen Correctional Centre, Mareeba, April 2005. Photograph by the author.

and received some coverage in the local press). The tour involved performing for tourists, fellow Christians, inmates, and clients at Lotus Glen Correctional Facility in Mareeba (see fig. 4.2) and Douglas House Rehabilitation Centre in Cairns, singing once at each venue over the course of four days.

In this analysis of the concert in the Lotus Glen Correctional Facility, I use the concert as a platform to discuss emotions experienced during the choral performance of hymns and consider how the hymns heightened feelings of longing for Country in the prison among inmates and choir members. I compare the prison context with choral music making in Hopevale and describe how these occasions differ emotionally and performatively. The discussion is based on my own performative experience as a conductor and singer with the choir, combined with written feedback and discussions with singers and audience members outside of Lotus Glen. For reasons of security and time, we were not able to interview inmates within our twenty-minute slot. My description, therefore, necessarily relies on my own experiences and my interpretation of those of others, together with the questionnaire outputs; in so doing, I acknowledge the methodological challenge of knowing and writing about performative emotions and the difficulties of ascertaining what other people feel.[40] I have included here materials of a brief questionnaire that I used, but I do not have extensive recorded interview materials. Most of what I write here is based on casual conversations I had after the event, which were recorded in my field diary. I argue that during the Lotus Glen concert, choral hymn singing elicited greater emotional responses than when the choir sang the same hymns in Hopevale and that these expressions were freed from conventional expectations of gendered displays of emotion. Additionally, I posit that the emotions experienced by singers and the audience during the Lotus Glen concert in relation to Country were heightened feelings of loss and longing for Country, combined with mixed emotions of joy, pride, and apprehension.

Lotus Glen is the nearest all-male correctional facility to Hopevale where local and other Aboriginal men from northern Queensland are interned, some for life. The choir's concert had been eagerly awaited and discussed through the teleconferencing link between Lotus Glen and Hopevale. Although the prison surroundings were intimidating, the choir was warmly received on the day by both the prison staff and the young men attending the concert. Greetings, jokes, and hugs were shared after the performance, and inmates were happy to see their family members. The performance lasted less than half an hour and was hosted in the prison gym. While the single-sex prison held both Aboriginal and non-Aboriginal men, the audience consisted of predominantly Aboriginal men, several from Hopevale. Not all Hopevalian men were able to attend, as some had to remain in their cells or work on the farm lands surrounding Lotus Glen. During the concert the choir sang unaccompanied hymns and gospel songs such as "King of Creation" and "In the Sweet By and By" in Guugu Yimithirr and "Swing Low Sweet Chariot" in English. I conducted the English items and joined the choir as an alto for the Guugu Yimithirr hymns.

When singing in the choir and facing the audience, I noted that most young men sat very quietly. Singer Pamela Kemp remarked, "All eyes were on the singers at all times and there was no fidgeting." Choir member Ella Woibo commented on the silence: "You could hear a pin drop." Many men had sad expressions on their faces; others were smiling wistfully; some even cried or had tears in their eyes. When I asked the choir what they had observed, they gave mixed responses. Choir members interpreted these reactions positively, saying they indicated that the audience enjoyed the singing. In a questionnaire, I asked how choir members could tell that they (the audience at Lotus Glen) did or did not enjoy the singing.

Three women commented on the fact that the facial expressions of the audience suggested they were enjoying the concert or were moved in some way. Mavis Yoren said, "I think it made most of the people homesick." Daisy Hamlot-Bowen believed she knew they were enjoying it because "their faces . . . were listening and smiling." Violet Cobus also remarked on the "quality" of the smiles, observing, "I think they enjoyed it very much. I could see it in their faces how they smiled." Physical displays of emotion were also noted after the concert. Gertie Deeral wrote on her questionnaire, "Our

Aboriginal *Bama* were excited and many friends were happy to see us when we sang. They were excited and happy to see us there, they put their arms around us and cried with joy." After Henry Deeral had spoken to audience members, he remarked, "Well, all the *bama* [Aboriginal people or in this case the inmates specifically] was in there was excited and happy to hear us sing," while Myrtle Bambie simply said, "If they didn't like it they wouldn't be there." Concert attendance was optional, a fact she felt explained the lack of non-Indigenous men in the audience.

I asked choir members to complete three questionnaires to understand how their emotions changed (1) prior to entering the prison, (2) during singing, and (3) following the concert. The results show that the emotions they experienced while performing at Lotus Glen ranged from joy to sadness, apprehension to pride. Table 4.1 shows the range of responses when I asked choir members how they felt when coming into the prison. As mapped on table 4.1, positive feelings outnumber those of nervousness, fear, or sadness. Pamela Kemp and Henry Deeral noted that the unusual prison environment made them ill at ease to begin with. Pamela Kemp said she was "a little bit apprehensive, not being sure at the reception and not familiar with the setting," and when coming into the prison Henry Deeral felt "scared a bit and nervous and shy. A bit of everything." Gertie Deeral also experienced mixed feelings, saying she felt "nervous. . . . I was proud to be there and excited. I was scared and worried they might not like our singing." Mavis Yoren also articulated how her emotions changed during the concert, saying, "At first a bit shy, then later I felt happy." The fluctuations in emotional experience reflect the unknown context and the opportunity to share their music.

I then asked choir members how they felt when they were singing (see table 4.2). As shown in both tables 4.1 and 4.2, feelings of sadness figured prominently, along with mixed emotions of excitement and happiness. Some of their unsolicited comments were more expansive. Phylomena Naylor and Gertie Deeral mentioned a sense of joy at seeing the audience members and pride at singing for the young men. Phylomena Naylor wrote, "I was so excited when we all walk[ed] into the (gym building) to sing our song with all the boys we know and the surrounding area up north, east, south and west it gave me love in myself because I was there singing." Gertie Deeral said that she felt "scared, nervous because I was there for the first time. I was proud to be there singing to them in prison a bit of everything above." Pamela Kemp reflected on her audience's lack of liberty and how it affected her. She noted, "it was an emotional experience realizing that we were in that gym voluntarily and were free to leave at any time, but our audience did not enjoy that freedom. I also reacted to the knowledge that the clean, fresh-faced men had all made some mistakes in life and that choir members cared for their well-being."

Table 4.1. Hopevale Community Choir responses before the concert at Lotus Glen

Response	Frequency
Excited	10
Happy	9
Proud (to be there)	8
Sad	8
Nervous	6
Scared	5
Worried (that inmates might not like the concert)	4

Table 4.2. Hopevale Community Choir responses during the concert at Lotus Glen

Response	Frequency
Happy	8
Excited	7
Sad	7
Proud (to be there)	6
Worried (that inmates might not like the concert)	5
Nervous	5
Scared	3
Shy	2

In the last questionnaire (see table 4.3), I asked how they felt after they had finished singing, and, interestingly, members' responses to a mixture of sorrow and happiness had not changed radically. Unsolicited comments mainly focused on the absence of some of the men who had still been in their cells during the concert or those who had been out working on the facility's grounds during the session. Henry and Gertie Deeral and Violet Cobus all commented on this. Gertie wrote, "I felt relieved and I was happy to see our boys from HV [Hopevale] and I was sad and worried because I did not see the other boys from Hopevale." Violet Cobus wrote that the choir members "were sad because we [the choir] didn't see our boys at the gym room." Pamela Kemp also noticed that not just the inmates and choir were moved but that members of the prison staff also were affected. She wrote, "Many people in the audience, including the guards, were moved by the songs and the emotion spilled over to the after-concert mixing."

These emotions were among those I also personally experienced in empathy with the singers and in response to the performance location. At Lotus Glen I found it physically difficult to sing, given the lump in my throat. I could

Table 4.3. Hopevale Community Choir responses after the concert at Lotus Glen

Response	Frequency
Happy	9
Relieved	8
Sad	7
Content	5
Worried (that inmates did not like the concert)	2
Energized	2

hear and see that other singers were experiencing these same difficulties singing, which I interpreted as performative evidence that our emotive and physical responses to the performance context and songs were similar.

This strong response contrasts with the emotions experienced during the performance of the same repertoire in Hopevale. Singers acknowledged that when performing the same hymns in the church in Hopevale, their experiences were less extreme and less diverse emotionally. Choir members also explained, more specifically, that when singing Guugu Yimithirr translations of "King of Creation" and "In the Sweet By and By" at Lotus Glen, the songs and the use of their native language became more meaningful to them and their audience, since both stimulated memories related to Hopevale Country, ancestors, and living family. Choir members commented that singing in English and Guugu Yimithirr was, by contrast, equally meaningful in everyday circumstances.

Music and hymnody were believed to possess the power to bring about an emotional response more generally. Hopevalian church organist June Pearson said, "I feel that whatever type of music comes out, you know, whether they're singing or playing, it always touches the heart in some way, you know? It makes you feel good or makes you feel sad. I mean, you can sing a song that'll make you very sad and make you cry! But then again, it can touch the heart in a different way."[41] The phrase "touches the heart" was one often used in Hopevale when referring to the emotional arousal experienced when listening to or performing hymnody. The quote from June Pearson demonstrates that the phrase might refer to feelings of both joy and sadness. Another Aboriginal English word used in Hopevale to describe an emotive response was that of "crying." In Hopevale "crying" may refer to the act of deeply missing a person or place (usually Country) as well as the physical act of weeping. During my fieldwork both men and women said they had cried for a person or place, would physically weep in public, or sometimes wept when alone out of sadness. Crying, therefore, can be both a public and a private emotion, resulting either in physical tears being shed or feelings remaining internalized. The extent to which a person cries in public is dependent on personality and the ability to contain grief. During the funerals I witnessed at Hopevale, crying was never accompanied by wailing, self-harm, or other forms of physical emotivity as reported elsewhere in Australia.[42] I found the funereal ceremonies and the concomitant emotive responses to death similar to those I have witnessed in Europe, although relatively more men cried or admitted to experiencing feelings of grief in Hopevale.

In Hopevale all music is deemed capable of stimulating crying or "touching the heart," and crying is not related to a particular song genre. There are also no social expectations based on gender, age, or authority to perform regulated crying practices (unlike mortuary singing in Arnhem Land). Hopevalian crying, however, does share one aspect with the complex of emotions that Magowan analyzes in Yolngu funeral crying, which is "personal nostalgia or inner emotivity resulting from experiences that are not regulated by ritual participation."[43] At Lotus Glen nostalgia was a key emotion among the singers and audience: many choir members said that the choral singing or listening to hymns caused them to cry, as they missed the young men in prison. Hymn favorites sung in Guugu Yimithirr were seen as particularly effective in stimulating an emotional response, leading both singers and the audience to remember Country and ancestors more vividly. These emotions were experienced together with the joy and pride at seeing one another again. It was this mixed set of emotions that made the performance so poignant.

The same hymns, therefore, which would have been quite ordinary to the Hopevale Community Choir and its audience when sung in Hopevale, carried a greater significance in the Lotus Glen prison context, where they became associated with crying for Country and people.[44] These emotions became even more pronounced when the hymns were rendered in Guugu Yimithirr, since the associations were more vivid and included memories of a shared social and linguistic history. The fact that both men and women said they experienced similar emotional responses to hymnody suggests that these responses were not gender specific nor socially restricted. In this way, this situation is consistent with Judith Becker's view that "groups of people who are focused on a common event and who share a common history of that event act, react, and to some extent think in concert, without sacrificing their bounded personal identities."[45]

Musical and Social Change: Toward an Indigenous Future

The emotional responses to hymnody in Lotus Glen and the emotional experiences of those elders who were evacuated to Woorabinda during the war years notably share sentiments of loss and longing as well as common wishes to return to Hopevale. In the contemporary prison context, these feelings were intensified by the use of Guugu Yimithirr and by the choral performance of hymns. As suggested in this chapter, both this language and the song performance genre form an intimate part of Hopevalian history, and when combined they become particularly capable of stimulating the memories of older people, friends, and family. Conversations and observations suggest that this loss, remembrance, and longing for Hopevale, combined with the joy of singing and sharing time together, were experienced by both the almost all-female choir and its all-male audience. In seeing prisoners cry, emotions of loss and longing for Country were clearly heightened by the current reality of the inmates' continued absence from the community. This absence of predominantly young men from Hopevale added additional intensity to the emotions of loss, longing, and Country already raised through hymnody.

It is the power of association and memory combined with the performance context that determines to what extent Hopevalian choral singing is able to offer an emotional outlet and catharsis for singers and audiences, as opposed to simply providing an opportunity to sing hymns. This is partly due to the fact that the older Christian hymns once favored by the choir are being performed less in Hopevale and that younger Hopevalians are not joining the choir because it is viewed as being an activity suitable only for older, devout Christian women. Equally significant, younger people now prefer different musical genres; in fact, they told me that they would like to see bands using guitar, bass, keyboard, and drums perform in church, playing faster, more upbeat songs. Younger schoolboys, in particular, were keen on band performances since many of them play the guitar.

While many Hopevale community members welcome the idea of new musical genres being introduced as a prominent feature in church, bands are reluctant to commit themselves to regular Sunday services. Many performers are also wary of being too closely associated with the church due to its patronizing approach to evangelization in the past. This colonizing legacy discourages both church attendance and the introduction of new musical genres into regular church worship.

Today, ongoing Indigenous interpretations of the Christian gospel are influencing the future of choral singing; this might in turn result in more songs being composed for church services incorporating references to Country. Notably, in 2004 and 2005 new songs integrating themes of community history, Lutheranism, and references to Country were being performed outside the church context, often using a country-and-western-style band. Choir members enjoyed these songs, and some expressed the wish to have songs like these composed for the choir. Upon returning to Hopevale in the summer of 2009, I noted that a non-Indigenous visiting leading figure of the Lutheran Church actively supported the introduction of an Indigenous Christianity.[46] He referenced Pastor Rosendale's contribution to *Rainbow Spirit Theology* in his sermon, stating that a Christian God had been present in Hopevale prior to the arrival of missionaries and that it was time for Australian Lutheranism to embrace this concept and for Hopevalians as Indigenous Christians to reinvigorate their relationship with Country.[47] The sermon was positively received by Hopevalians who attended the service. Elder Shirley Costello said, "I never thought about it that way, but it makes sense, doesn't it?" I also discovered that local male elders were leading their own church services in the absence of the pastor (who has recently retired) and that male elders participated as occasional members of the choir to sing at the biannual Queensland Music Festival, where they had been asked to represent the local traditional owners of Country for the third year running.[48] When I left after my visit in 2009, Hopevale was awaiting its new non-Indigenous pastor. This is a critical juncture, for it is the extent of his willingness to accept an Indigenous theology and leadership, and the level of his encouragement of new musical practices, that will largely determine the development of musical worship and choral singing in Hopevale in the future.

Notes

1. I use the terms "Hopevalian" and "Hopevalians" to refer to Indigenous people living in Hopevale. Local Indigenous people call themselves Guugu Yimithirr or Guugu Yalanji. These two groups divide into subgroups called *warra*. Occasionally, they might also call themselves "Murri," the word used to describe Aboriginal people from Queensland. All people living in Hopevale, both Indigenous and non-Indigenous, were said to "belong to Hopevale."

2. It was this absence of young men that provided the initial impetus for this chapter, as I was emotionally affected by the suicide of Max Bowen, son of my Indigenous friend (a choral singer) and my fieldwork partner Daisy Hamlot-Bowen.

3. See, for example, Max Charlesworth, Françoise Dussart, and Howard Morphy, eds., *Aboriginal Religions in Australia* (Aldershot: Ashgate, 2005); Andrée Grau, "Sing a Dance—Dance a Song: The Relationship between Two Types of Formalised Movements and Music among the Tiwi of Melville and Bathurst Island, North Australia," *Dance Research* 1, no. 2 (1983): 32–44; Grau, "Dance as Part of the Infrastructure of Social Life," *World of Music* 37, no. 2 (1995): 43–59; Grau, "On the Acquisition of Knowledge: Teaching Kinship through the Body among Tiwi of Northern Australia," in *Common Worlds and Single Lives*, ed. Verena Keck (Oxford: Berg, 1998), 71–93; Fiona Magowan, "'The Land Is Our *Märr* (Essence), It Stays Forever': The Yothu-Yindi Relationship in Australian Aboriginal Traditional and Popular Musics," in *Ethnicity, Identity and Music: The Musical Construction of Place*, ed. Martin Stokes (Oxford: Berg, 1997), 135–55; Magowan, "Globalisation and Indigenous Christianity: Translocal Sentiments in Australian Aboriginal Christian Songs," *Identities: Global Studies in Culture and Power* 14, no. 4 (2007): 459–83; and Peter Toner, "Melody and Musical Articulations of Yolngu Identities," *Yearbook for Traditional Music* 35 (2003): 69–95.

4. See, for example, James Axtell, "Were Indian Conversions Bona Fide?" in *After Columbus: Essays in the Ethnohistory of Colonial North America*, ed. James Axtell (Oxford: Oxford University Press, 1988); Fiona Bowie, Deborah Kirkwood, and Shirley Ardener, eds., *Women and Missions: Past and Present; Anthropological and Historical Perspectives* (Oxford: Berg, 1993); Jean Comaroff and John Comaroff, "Through the Looking-Glass: Colonial Encounters of the First Kind," *Journal of Historical Sociology* 1, no. 1 (1989): 6–32; Comaroff and Comaroff, *Of Revelation and Revolution*, vol. 1, *Christianity, Colonialism and*

Consciousness in South Africa (Chicago: University of Chicago Press, 1991); Steve Kaplan, ed., *Indigenous Responses to Western Christianity* (New York: New York University Press, 1995); and Selva J. Raj and Corinne G. Dempsey, eds., *Popular Christianity in India: Riting between the Lines* (Albany: State University of New York Press, 2002).

5. See, for example, Jeffrey A. Summit, *Abayudaya: The Jews of Uganda* (New York: Abbeville, 2002); and Raj and Dempsey, *Popular Christianity in India*.

6. For general studies, see, for example, John Harris, *One Blood: 200 Years of Aboriginal Encounter with Christianity: A Story of Hope*, 2nd ed. (Sutherland, Australia: Albatross Books, 1994); Anna Johnston, *Missionary Writing and Empire, 1800–1860* (Cambridge: Cambridge University Press, 2003); Noel A. Loos, "A Conflict of Faiths: Aboriginal Reaction to the First Missionaries in North Queensland," in *Lectures on North Queensland History: Second Series* (Townsville: James Cook University of North Queensland, 1975), 47–55; and Tony Swain and Deborah Bird-Rose, *Aboriginal Australians and Christian Missions: Ethnographic and Historical Studies* (Bedford Park, South Australia: Australian Association for the Study of Religions, 1988). For specific studies, see, for example, Annette Hamilton, "Bond Slaves of Satan: Aboriginal Women and the Missionary Dilemma," in *Family and Gender in the Pacific*, ed. Margaret Jolly and Martha Macintyre (Cambridge: Cambridge University Press, 1989); Max Hart, *A Story of Fire, Continued: Aboriginal Christianity* (Blackwood, Australia: New Creation, 1997); Tony Scalon, "'Pure and Clean and True to Christ': Black Women and White Missionaries in the North," *Hecate* 12, no. 1–2 (1986): 83–105; and Robert Tonkinson, *The Jigalong Mob: Aboriginal Victors of the Desert Crusade* (Sydney: Cummings, 1974).

7. See Norman Habel and the Rainbow Spirit Elders, *Rainbow Spirit Theology: Towards an Australian Aboriginal Theology* (Blackburn, Australia: HarperCollins, 1997).

8. Walter E. Roth, documenting initiation ceremonies, for example, records that the dances and song cycles he observed at Cape Bedford (near the Hopevale town center) referred to animals such as the native companion or Brolga (a type of bird), owl, pheasant, and the body louse, as well as plants such as the black palm. "On Certain Initiation Ceremonies," *North Queensland Ethnography* 12 (1909): 172.

9. Some members of the Stolen Generation were still alive while I was working in Hopevale between 2004 and 2005. They very kindly shared with me their experiences of this traumatic time in their lives. While many were removed by force, some were left on the mission by their parents, who may have felt that it was safer for their children to live on the mission due to the violent clashes that occurred between settlers and Indigenous people in the area.

10. George Heinrich Schwarz arrived in 1887 from Germany and lived and worked in Hopevale as a missionary until his incarceration during the war in 1942. The Australian government feared Schwarz might collaborate with the Japanese due to his German nationality and imprisoned him as a result. After the war he was released, but did not return to Hopevale to minister.

11. Rev. Howard J. Pohlner, *Gangurru* (Milton, Queensland: Hope Vale Mission Board, 1986), 110–11.

12. I refer to Hopevalians as the "Cape Bedford people" when discussing the period of the evacuation to Woorabinda between 1942 and 1949, because this is how Hopevalians refer to themselves when speaking about this period in their history. At the time of the evacuation, their main mission town was at Cape Bedford, thirty kilometers from what is now Hopevale. Hopevalians use "Cape Bedford people" due to the Indigenous importance placed on Country in their worldview. Although the same people moved from Cape Bedford to Woorabinda and then to Hopevale, because Cape

Bedford is not in the same geographic location as Hopevale, according to local custom, one cannot use "Hopevalians" and "Cape Bedford people" as synonyms.

13. June Pearson, interview with the author, Hopevale, November 29, 2004.

14. Pohlner, *Gangurru*, 123.

15. Ibid., 114.

16. Ibid., 121–23. Schwarz and Poland created an orthography for the Cape Bedford people to translate the Bible and hymns. This orthography was taught in the local school, and the Cape Bedford people were able to speak, write, and read in Guugu Yimithirr. Today Guugu Yimithirr is no longer taught, but elders are trying to revive this practice.

17. Between 1942 and 1949 Woorabinda had a Roman Catholic Church, a Church of England, and an Aboriginal Inland Mission. Personal communication with choir members Daisy Hamlot and Myrtle Bambie indicated that younger people were keen to worship with other churches because they enjoyed the hymns being sung. The Cape Bedford elders, however, chose to maintain their Lutheran practices rather than amalgamate with other churches and led their own church services in the absence of a regular Lutheran pastor.

18. Pohlner, *Gangurru*, 132, 135.

19. With choral singers in the congregation, the meanings of choral singing and "singing as a choir" merged in the local Hopevalian English vocabulary. Harmonized congregational singing would sometimes be referred to as "choir singing," as would singing by a specific group of vocalists who might choose choral singing as a personal hobby. In this way, choral singers are not accorded a special status as everyone in Hopevale can be a choir member. This flexibility is demonstrated on public occasions, when Hopevalian audience members might feel inspired to go to the front and join the choral singing for a particular song. They become choir members for the duration of the song, as they might in congregational singing. Everyone is considered a potentially good singer if they are willing to be a good listener first. There is no Guugu Yimithirr translation for the words and concepts of "choir," "choir singing," or "congregational singing," but there are words for the verb "to sing," namely, *gunbu-gundal*, or song and hymn *gunbu*. *Gunbu* can refer to both secular and sacred songs. Interestingly, the term "to dance" is *gunbu-wuuril*, suggesting that previously there may have been strong links between song and dance as in other communities. However, in Hopevale, Christian worship never includes dancing.

20. Obituary of the elder Walter Bowen (unpublished, January 2005), Hopevale.

21. The rights to land ownership through kinship affiliations are heavily disputed in Hopevale, however, due to the various relocations experienced by the community, the deaths of many elders, and the difficulty of ascertaining the descent of some Stolen Generation elders. In 1997 thirteen clans of Guugu Yimithirr people were acknowledged as the original inhabitants of these lands. During my 2009 visit to Hopevale, I was informed that the negotiations as to when, how, and to whom these lands would be handed over were still ongoing.

22. See Fiona Magowan, "The Joy of Mourning: Resacralising 'The Sacred' in the Music of Yolngu Christianity and an Aboriginal Theology," *Anthropological Forum* 9, no. 1 (1999): 11–36; and Magowan, "Globalisation and Indigenous Christianity."

23. Lutheran Church of Australia, Adelaide: Lutheran Publishing House.

24. Ibid.

25. Ecumenical Songbook Committee Australia. Sydney: HarperCollins.

26. Mann, Robert (ed.) Adelaide: Openbook Publishers.

27. Magowan, "Joy of Mourning," 18.

28. See Rev. David Thompson, ed., *Milbi Dabaar: A Resource Book* (Cairns: Wontulp-Bi Buya College, 2004); and Habel and Elders, *Rainbow Spirit Theology*.

29. Magowan, "Globalisation and Indigenous Christianity," 459–83.

30. George Rosendale, trans. *Gunbu Guugu Yimithirrbi* (Hopevale: Hopevale Lutheran Congregation, 1986).

31. See Magowan, "Land Is Our *Märr*"; Magowan, "Joy of Mourning"; Magowan, "Globalisation and Indigenous Christianity"; Fiona Magowan, *Melodies of Mourning: Music and Emotion in Northern Australia* (Oxford: Currey, 2007); Françoise Dussart, *The Politics of Ritual in an Aboriginal Settlement: Kinship, Gender, and the Currency of Knowledge* (Washington, DC: Smithsonian Institution Press, 2000); Diane Bell, *Daughters of the Dreaming*, 2nd ed. (Minneapolis: University of Minnesota Press, 1993); and *Yawulya Mungamunga*, ed. Linda Barwick, Festival Records 0139686, 2000, compact disc.

32. See *Journey to Horseshoe Bend: A Cantata Based on the Novel by TGH Strehlow*, composed by Andrew Schultz and Gordon Kalton William, performed by Sydney Symphony, John Stanton, Aaron Pedersen, Rodney Macann, Ntaria Ladies Choir, Sydney Philharmonia Motet Choir, David Bruce, and David Porcelijn, Sydney, 476 2266, 2004, compact disc; and *Ekarlta Nai!*, performed by Ntaria Ladies Choir, Label CD 29684, 1993–99, compact disc.

33. See John Haviland and Leslie Haviland, "'How Much Food Will There Be in Heaven?' Lutherans and Aborigines around Cooktown to 1900," *Aboriginal History* 4, no. 2 (1980): 137.

34. Johnston, *Missionary Writing and Empire*, 45, 56.

35. See Muriel E. Swijghuisen Reigersberg, "Choral Singing and the Construction of Aboriginal Identities: An Applied Ethnomusicological Study in Hopevale, Northern Queensland Australia" (PhD diss., Roehampton University, University of Surrey, 2009).

36. Pastor George Rosendale, interview with the author, Hopevale, March 23, 2005.

37. Noel Pearson, *Ngamu-ngaadyarr, Muuri-bunggaga and Midha Mini in Guugu Yimidhirr History (Dingoes, Sheep and Mr Muni in Guugu Yimidhirr History): Hope Vale Lutheran Mission, 1900–1950* (Sydney: University of Sydney, 1986).

38. Nationally, the average life expectancy of an Aboriginal male living today is between fifty-three and fifty-eight years, but often less; Aboriginal males are twenty-nine times more likely to be detained in custody than non-Aborigines. Colin Tatz, *Aboriginal Suicide Is Different: A Portrait of Life and Self Destruction*, 2nd ed. (Canberra: Aboriginal Studies Press, 2005), 5–6.

39. The tour was made possible by a Queensland Arts Council grant, which I had successfully applied for on behalf of the choir.

40. Magowan records that on Galiwin'ku men's clan-song style and women's funeral crying-song style may be used in specific compositions to transmit understandings of Christian doctrine. These song styles are based on traditional song melodies, rhythms, and pitches that reflect the Yolngu identity of the composer and his or her clan. "Joy of Mourning," 24–25.

41. Pearson, interview.

42. Magowan, *Melodies of Mourning*, 85–86.

43. See Magowan, *Melodies of Mourning*, 72. Using performative writing, I have questioned my own "emotional knowing" (see Swijghuisen Reigersberg, "Choral Singing," 22–32, 254–91).

44. See, for example Swijghuisen Reigersberg, "Choral Singing," 245–53, 290.

45. Judith Becker, "Anthropological Perspectives on Music and Emotion," in *Music and Emotion: Theory and Research*, ed. Patrik N. Juslin and John A. Sloboda (Oxford: Oxford University Press, 2001), 152.

46. While there may have been many changes since 2009, I am unable to comment on these as I have not been able to make my way back to Hopevale for any length of time since 2009. As a self-funded, independent scholar without institutional support, completing further research has not been possible. Similarly, due to the technical divide, the time difference between the United Kingdom and Australia, and the age of my friends in Hopevale (fifty plus) Internet and telephone communications have become (increasingly) problematic.

47. Habel and Elders, *Rainbow Spirit Theology*.

48. I had organized the choir's first appearance at the Queensland Music Festival in 2005 as part of a series of engagements prior to my departure to ensure that the choir did not stop singing and had something to work toward. On the basis of their successful engagement and a lot of local support in Hopevale and Cooktown, the choir was asked to sing again in 2007 and 2009.

Chapter Five

Transforming the Singing Body

Exploring Musical Narratives of Gender and Place in East Bavaria

Sara R. Walmsley-Pledl

This chapter examines how issues of place and gender, specific to German East Bavaria, are mediated through song imagery. Taking the arena of choral music as a locus of social and musical production, I also analyze how singers' musical narratives and memories of music making embody and reflect their emotional relationships with this region. The physical and emotional effects of singing raise questions about differences between male and female German choral singers as they narrate their bodily experiences of music making. I ask, how do gender roles determine male and female experiences of singing in a choir and to what extent does singing offer an experience capable of transcending the constraints of gendered expectations?

This analysis is based on ethnographic research conducted with an amateur choir in East Bavaria between 2004 and 2005.[1] Bavaria has a distinct regional identity within Germany, characterized by its own dialect, a conservative government, the predominance of the Catholic Church, and the strength of local customs and tradition. The market town of Deggendorf in East Bavaria is known as the gateway to the Bavarian Forest. Its inhabitants express a strong sense of belonging and pride about the area, which they refer to as *Heimat* (home). The concept of Heimat and the associations it evokes are central to understanding how a sense of belonging emerges in this region. Peter Blickle asserts that Heimat is the outcome of living in small communities where "everything in the locality is known."[2] Music making is one activity central to feelings associated with Heimat, as Chor Kreis Deggendorf singers' narratives demonstrate. By comparing choir members' musical stories, or narratives, I show how contrasting perceptions of "the local" and other localities are shaped by musical participation to create distinctive attachments to and emotional affinities with place. These "formalized narratives" of musical engagement are "the negotiated end product of the narrative process" and are one of the ways in which language and experience may be mediated by the singing, musical body.³

Chor Kreis Deggendorf Choral Repertoire

A secular choir of about twenty-five active members, the Chor Kreis Deggendorf is directed by Stefan Trenner, a conductor, organist, and composer. The choir sings from a wide repertoire that includes German comic songs of the 1920s, songs from English-language musicals such as *My Fair Lady*, French folk songs, and sacred material used within the setting of a mass. Each genre evokes performance contexts that have different kinds of associations for individual members of the choir. For example, older members of the choir have clear memories of popular songs from the 1960s, whereas younger members do not. Equally, younger members found singing in English much less of a tribulation than older members. While all the singers expressed preferences for one genre over another, it was accepted that not all the choral repertoire might be to their taste.

Chor Kreis Deggendorf meets once a week (and occasionally on weekends) to rehearse in a local school. Some of the singers are highly proficient musicians and others are music novices. The choir is under the direction of a professional choirmaster, who receives a small retainer for his work, including arranging and composing. The choir performs in public three to four times a year, which can include singing in staged concerts and taking part in masses in local Catholic churches.

A unique feature of this choir is its constitution as a Verein. Loosely translated, this means a club or society, but within the German, and specifically East Bavarian, context, membership brings with it very distinct expectations around involvement, with an emphasis on sociability as much as musicality. Indeed, the strong regional identity of East Bavaria is reaffirmed by inhabitants' associations with and feeling for place, further influencing their experiences of singing in a choir. Such familiarity brings with it a sense of belonging best encapsulated by the concept of Heimat. The essence of Bavarian identity extends from this sense of belonging, or Heimat, and is a highly gendered experience.

The Concept of Heimat and Its Relationship to Musical Narratives

Heimat is considered a key concept for German-speaking peoples: "Deeply embedded in language, deeply involved in German self-identity and regional self-understanding beyond the political domain—[Heimat] is one of the main elements in contemporary German renegotiations of what it means to be German and to live in a German-speaking environment."⁴ While Heimat can be understood as an abstraction promoting positive communal values, it can also be an expression of belonging that emerges out of individual experience of local environments. The sense of Heimat is evoked by familiarity. Although there is general consensus as to what constitutes the familiar, which includes dialect, landscape, folk music, the Catholic Church, and the *Wirtshaus* (inn), how individuals experience a sense of belonging depends on the particular way in which their engagement with the familiar ties them to home.

Heimat can be tied to an understanding of implicit knowledge that relates to how Pierre Bourdieu has discussed knowledge and institutionalized practices. While Bourdieu's outline of a theory of everyday experience highlights the concept of habitus as pertaining largely to nonreflective and embodied knowledge, he also underlines the importance of recognizing the role of institutionalized practices within the life of the individual.[5] This embodied knowledge, or "implicit knowledge," is acquired through experience—often without being consciously learned through verbal transmission.[6] This point is relevant to the choral experience discussed in this chapter. By analyzing choir members' musical narratives, I illustrate how the interconnectedness of their experiences arises from a shared sense of Heimat, or familiarity and attachment with the local that involves both explicit and implicit knowledge of East Bavarian people and place. Consequently, regional distinctiveness in East Bavaria is the result not of an abstract construction but rather of strong emotional attachments to the areas in which people live out their lives. These connotations of Heimat have changed over time, in line with changing perspectives on identity and belonging; as suggested by Blickle, "*Heimat* has become increasingly associated with an inner emotional capacity to attach oneself through personalized memories of experience to a place, a family, a specific landscape."[7] In other words, it has become something intrinsic to the individual, influenced by a variety of factors, including the environment.

The members of Chor Kreis Deggendorf have a shared local knowledge that they use to negotiate musical participation, practice, and interpretation, which in turn influences the relationship with music they are able to develop. The concept of Heimat therefore can be seen as a type of local knowledge—one that makes daily life feel more secure insofar as it includes a sense of warmth, a feeling of "being at home."[8] As I became aware of the importance of the regional quality of life in East Bavaria and how this was having an impact on the organization and experience of music making, the notion of Heimat emerged as prominent in the narratives of choir members as they reflected on the practice of singing.

Narrative Processes

The study and interpretation of narrative is rich. Michel de Certeau sees the creation of narrative as a process where "the narrativizing of practices is a textual 'way of operating' having its own procedures and tactics."[9] For Nigel

Rapport narrative is "the form in which individuals habitually recount the created order of their meaningful lives, self, and world to themselves." He associates narrative closely with consciousness, asserting that it is through narrative that the individual becomes conscious, and therefore "cognition turns life into text, whether implicit or explicit."[10] In other words, narrative refers to an active process whereby individual experiences are given an expressive dimension through deliberately chosen language, reflecting the experiences of the speaker. Meaning then emerges from the experiences of the individual through the practice of narration.[11]

Narrative is also a "storytelling event" where "members of a culture share some ways of . . . knowing the world" but still retain individual comprehension.[12] It becomes a way of making private sentiment into public meaning, since stories offer the speaker a means of organizing experiences into some sort of order—whether chronological or prioritized by personal choice. Such strategies of telling in turn enable the analyst "to regain some purchase over the events that confound." Thus, narrative never contains just the personal, because "storytelling mediates our relations with worlds that extend beyond us."[13] Individuals can place themselves within their perception of the story, and the narrative can provide an indication of the framework within which people conceptualize their experiences—and reveal how they connect to specific places, people, and events.[14] In this way, the content of narrative can provide some indication of how social expectations accompanying a particular gender can influence music making and an individual's subsequent participation in a musical life.

In this chapter extended narratives are drawn from interviews with one male and two female members of Chor Kreis Deggendorf. The singers articulate the physical nature of their musical experience as one that grows out of a gendered singing body engaged with other singing bodies. Rather than being a litany of where they had played and with whom, their narratives endeavor to express how music has affected them throughout their lives. As well as being personal biographies, they reveal the extent to which music has a physical presence and an impact on their sensory and emotional well-being. Although most of these singers can play an instrument to some degree, suggesting a certain level of general musicianship, the majority of them have chosen to put their musical energy into ensemble singing.

Sonic Memories of Place

The existential condition of human experience means that the issue of place, whether as a physical entity or as a backdrop for social interaction, is an underlying theme of all personal discourse. All the singers' narratives highlighted locality; however, the meanings that they held for an individual varied depending on their personal biography. The links between music making and places were highlighted as choir members recalled memories of childhood, and the role that gender could play in dictating musical opportunities within a conservative, rural society also became apparent.

I begin by illustrating this through the narrative of one soprano, Agnes, who joined the choir about three years ago and recounted her story with some passion.[15] Agnes was brought up in a village in the German-speaking part of the South Tyrol. She was keen to sing or play an instrument, but her parents were busy and did not prioritize her desire. She recalled her childhood home in terms of musical restriction: while her brothers were allowed to join a brass band, girls were not; the church choir was not open to her because it would entail walking alone. This was acceptable in her parent's eyes for a boy but not for a girl. Her mother had sung in a choir, and this had seemed very unfair to Agnes and still rankled with her forty years later. Music, therefore, was an important part of Agnes's life, yet one that she felt had been thwarted in her childhood. When I asked her what music had offered her as a child, she said, "Freedom, a way of letting emotion out without having to consider what is allowable and what is not." Now that she has her own family, she has used her own children to assuage some of her own thirst for access to music making by ensuring they have all the musical advantages that she had been denied.

Agnes began attending Chor Kreis Deggendorf once her children were old enough. This allowed her time away from her family obligations and gave her a space to pursue her abiding interest in participating in active music making. Her one remaining musical wish was to play the piano; she tried to pick it up as the children were learning but did not get very far. However, she has promised herself one last go with a good piano teacher at some stage in the future. Active participation in performing music clearly has a profound personal significance for Agnes: when I asked her what music offers her now as an adult she affirmed, "Something where I can be me."

Agnes's narrative draws attention to a musical nature being silenced by artificially imposed boundaries. Yet she was not surrounded by silence in her childhood: there was the sound of the church choir and of her brothers playing in the brass band. For Agnes these familiar sounds reinforced the sense of musical exclusion that she was already feeling as a child. The sounds of music were not absent, but only out of her reach, and they mingled with other sounds around her.

All the Chor Kreis Deggendorf's members' narratives contained memories of nonmusical as well as musical sounds. This emphasizes the role of hearing as a broader experience and extension of a particular place, with the result that all kinds of sounds become imprinted in accounts of remembered experience within a specific time and place. The place of the environment is key to understanding individual experience helping to foreground the role of the familiar. Sounds such as those described by Agnes and other choir members shaped a sense of familiarity, suggesting that "soundscapes" act as a critical link between place and the body.[16] Therefore, the sense of familiarity that a person feels in connection with a certain place (and through which Heimat is experienced) is also shaped by the presence or absence of sounds. Memories of soundscapes emerged as a significant means of evoking connections to place and life stages among the choir members. Singers' personal and social accounts of bodily and sonic experiences revealed how their relationships with music developed.

When choir members talked of their music making located in the village, in the church, in school, and at home, they all evoked personal associations with Bavarian life—thus connecting with an underlying concept of Heimat. An alto choir member, Gertrud, spoke of her childhood and the role of music in the home, where relatives played the guitar and would entertain everyone.[17] Folk songs were often sung, although she also had a strong memory of her grandfather singing endless verses of May songs (*Marienlieder*).[18] Before coming to Chor Kreis Deggendorf, Gertrud had sung in the school choir and in the youth choir. "I sing with great enthusiasm," she maintained and went on to detail how she had met her husband in the choir. She explained how they took turns to come to choir when their children were small and concluded by remarking, "Singing is our shared hobby, the one thing that is left!"—thus revealing the special role that the choir holds in their relationship. Luise, another alto who sits beside Gertrud in choir, also connects singing with home, remembering that her mother enjoyed singing.[19] She commented rather wryly that since this was Catholic Lower Bavaria, the choice of what was sung was the "usual May songs." She also recalled, however, that there was also music at parties, especially birthday parties. The only opportunity to take part in music for her as a child had been to join the church choir she described as "dusty with old women." Gertrud had been shy, and it was difficult to feel involved in this group because of the cliques within it, which clearly influenced her experience.

In both of these narratives about musical experiences in childhood, musical sounds play an important role in recounting a sense of belonging when brought up in East Bavaria—whether given access to musical training or not. Both Agnes and Gertrud framed their experiences in relation to music. Tim Ingold refers to this manner of directing attention to something as "educating attention," and Kay Milton suggests that emotions, along with interest, are active in directing attention.[20] According to work in cognitive science, the brain forms neural circuitry to cope with specific stimuli if it receives sufficient exposure to them, thus contributing to this directed attention and helping to explain why Agnes's and Gertrud's narratives of childhood foregrounded music, but as adults changed to narratives about their love of singing.[21]

Sensuous Experiences of Music Making

Singing begins unequivocally with the body, and within a choral setting it is extended outward to include interaction with others and the sonic environment. In what follows I show how the interaction of the body and musical sound, fundamental to music making, is crucial in determining the nature of an individual's relationship with music. The nature of musical experience challenges musicians to find a language for sensations generated within the body that have both physical and emotional aspects. For singers, there is the added complication insofar as the body is an instrument producing sound while at the same time being immersed in sound. The body feels sound from both within and without and, therefore, "sound is the more encompassing because of physical reverberation."[22] The performance of music is above all an acoustic event, as the whole body is enveloped in sound, thus creating a sensuous, somatic experience. Yet music in the sense of sound, although spoken of as if it had a permanent existence somewhere, comes into existence only by virtue of a social performance.[23] Music making is also a creative process that may be preceded by some degree of anticipation, through which the sonic manifestation of music surrounds the players and audience. Some choir members were very explicit about this process of sound as interacting within and between bodies. In three detailed interviews with three female choir members of Chor Kreis Deggendorf, I explore this process. Through references to their surroundings, the narratives also reveal how men and women write gendered senses of being into the landscape through their musical experiences.[24]

The following account comes from Gabriela, who has made the rather unusual choice to sing tenor in Chor Kreis Deggendorf, a musical choice that she is able to make despite the seemingly gendered overtones. She also sings in another choir that gathers every year to perform large-scale choral works and provides her with an opportunity to sing first bass. Although she cannot reach every note, Gabriela feels that it is closer to her range. A key aspect of choral singing in contrast to that of solo singing is the requirement to blend voices in the interest of the overall sound. In a mixed choir, women conventionally take the two highest voices (soprano and alto) and men the two lower voices (tenor and bass). The practical consideration of dividing and harmonizing voices, therefore, leads to people being grouped with others singing in the same vocal range. This raises questions about how space influences the perception of sounds created while singing, as well as the personal experience of singing itself. Gabriela's awareness of her natural pitch and range has led her to ally with male voices in the choir rather than with women's voices. Elizabeth Ekholm, in a study of the acoustic quality of singing for soloists and choirs in Canada, reported that seating people beside those with whom they could most easily blend was a commonly used technique to achieve a desirable choral sound.[25] Gender in this instance becomes a secondary feature. This suggests that in considering Gabriela's position within the choir, it is not her gendered body but the voice that it contains that is of primary importance.

James Daugherty considers how spacing in the choir and the formation used (mixed voices or blocks of voices) influences the perceptions of an audience and the singers in evaluating the overall choral sound.[26] All singers, regardless of gender, stated a preference for standing in the middle of the choir (a position giving access to a blended version of sound rather than exposure to the sound of a single concentrated voice). Interestingly, bass voices preferred to sing in blocks (surrounded by fellow basses), whereas the female voices preferred a mixed formation (not confined to being surrounded by women's voices). Gabriela's behavior conforms to what might be expected of a low-pitched voice that has been shaped throughout her childhood, as revealed in her story of her musical heritage. Gabriela spent a lot of time with boys while growing up and found no problem being one of the "boys" in the choir. This earned her the honorary title of "Fred" among the men in Chor Kreis Deggendorf, who accept her presence unquestioningly. She further elaborated on music in her life:

> I grew up with music. My grandfather played a number of instruments and was in the church choir. My granny would sing songs for me, and then we would sing them in three parts with my cousin. I remember those songs still. I recently heard an elderly lady sing, and it was a flashback. My parents played instruments and sang. I couldn't live without music; it accompanies me daily. When I was small I was in a children's choir. Then I went to a music grammar school where the music master was worshipped. The only problem was that one unlearned spontaneity. I can't improvise on instruments. Later I took up percussion and relearned what I had lost. I want to be spontaneous. I want to get away from notated rhythm. Singing can be spontaneous. I was invited to sing with the gospel choir of an Episcopalian church and experienced what it was like to sing with no sheet music at all. I learned to trust myself, and this was very freeing.
>
> Singing and playing instruments are two different things. With an instrument I produce music. I am completing only what was already on the page. There are sounds but not just melody that is produced. The piano has a wave of sound. With singing, it can be dictated and written, but more feeling can be expressed. In the choir there is more a sense of being bathed in sound; the body feels this. With friends, I can also express my feelings. A song that one knows produces a mood, and there is a sound that goes along with that. I have a deep voice, and so the women sing too high and the men too low. I feel comfortable in the middle range, where I am producing a resonating sound. There is improvisation in the gospel choir especially with expressing feelings because there is no notation. There are various aspects of being in the choir. There is that of togetherness and feeling. And of course there is the sound being produced. When we were at school we made a record, which included a Distler motet.[27] Some of us in the rehearsal intentionally made mistakes so that we could repeat certain bits. It was so wonderful that sound! The body really registered it.[28]

For Gabriela, the surround of sound is one of her main reasons for singing in a choir. The physical affect of sound as a sensual quality of music washing over and around her has been an aspect of her music making for a long time. Notably, Gabriela's narrative suggests a focus on the quality of sound. Although her relatively deep voice resonates at a pitch that does not follow the traditional divisions of choral singing, she is comfortable with her unusual decision to sing tenor or bass. By interweaving concrete experiences with abstract concepts, Gabriela used the metaphor of water to communicate what she found significant in the quality of her singing. She talks of "being bathed in sound," alluding to ideas of luxuriating, being submerged in water. Her other themes of spontaneity, freedom, expression of feeling, and improvisation also relate to water through which a degree of freedom can be experienced. Physical freedom is associated with water and musical freedom with improvisation, an absence of notation, and experimentation with rhythm.

For Gabriela, experimentation allows room for spontaneity and a freer expression of feelings. The gospel choir singing had given her some sense of what she was searching for. Her desire for freedom of expression could be seen as a foil for her daytime job: Gabriela is a psychologist in a psychiatric hospital, where patients are contained mentally in their own distress and physically within the institution. Singing, therefore, offers her a degree of freedom that distinguishes it from a workplace characterized by aspects of confinement.

Singers' narratives variously attempted to convey the physical quality of voice production. This could be seen in the singers' use of gestures and actions to me during interviews, as well as their use of metaphors. Regina sings soprano in the choir, and her story illustrates this attempt. She is a small, light person who radiates energy, and she talks of the renewal of energy through music making. Indeed, her way of thinking about music is closely related to how she experiences her own body. As I found, her very being is implicated in how she understands her world: she uses small fine hand movements to emphasize points while speaking, and she has an unusual speech style with clipped words that, in contrast to the slurring and legato common in Bavarian speech, tends far more toward staccato or pizzicato. In fact, she is very clear in stating that rhythm dominates how she relates to music:

> I need rhythm; it belongs to my life. I lie in bed and tap out rhythms until my husband cries, "Will you give me peace!" Music runs through my head and body. I can't explain it. It's the same when I look at sheets of music. I cannot imagine how it would be without music. At home we always were making music, the whole family. We took it as completely normal to make music. I feel sorry for people who have no connection with music. Often it is that the family had no music. It starts in childhood; one simply grows into it.[29]

Her musicality used to be expressed through playing the guitar and organ, but now, due to an injury, this is not an option. Regina always had a good voice and has turned to her singing to satisfy her desire to make music. She described this desire as a physical experience: the rhythms that exist in her are not consciously there; she just has them. Since singing has become her only means of making music, she took on the role of cantor in her Catholic parish church in Deggendorf in 1993, having learned this skill from a former organist at the church. At this time, their church was the only one in the area that had the position of cantor. With rhythm permanently percolating in her head and body, she is continuously aware of the presence and vitality of music. When she imagines people who are without music she describes them as mutilated, using a very strong term, *verstümmelt*, which suggests that the very essence of an ordinary life has been taken from them.

For some choir members, the physical experiences of music can be traced back to one event involving a significant memory. Beate, who sings soprano, went to the same school as Gabriela and sang in the same school choir under the directorship of Dr. Konrad Ruhland.[30] A number of the musicians I met had been taught at this "musical" grammar school, where music is treated as a core subject.[31] This choir director's influence was significant both in the musical opportunities he provided and through the attitudes that he held about music. The reason that Beate joined Chor Kreis Deggendorf was because she had heard Stefan, its choirmaster, performing with an American gospel choir singing from shape-note notation. Although singing for a number of years with another choir, she was becoming jaded for lack of getting what she was hoping for: Beate was searching for a feeling she had when singing in the school choir many years before. She made no effort to try to describe this but commented that when she heard the choir "singing shape notes" she felt something special. Beate left the choir she had been in and joined the Chor Kreis Deggendorf. Her continuing membership is sustained by the joy she feels in singing, which Stefan, as conductor, brings to his choral direction.

As Chor Kreis Deggendorf singers recounted their stories of what music making meant to them and how their current musical practices had come about, they were also trying to explain the active relationship they had with the physicality of music making. This was not done simply for my benefit; it was confirmation for them that they had an active, meaningful relationship with music as a physically vibrant experience. These examples show that women in the choir form unique understandings of their musical engagement derived from their personal biographies and experiences. This diversity occurs in spite of sharing musical practices and drawing on a common narrative stock of metaphors that reference a life lived in Bavaria.

Men's and Women's Emotional States While Music Making

How musical narratives reveal personal reflections and experiences of music making is not straightforward. I begin by drawing attention to two opposing perspectives on the emotional effects of music on men and women. One view of emotion concentrates on its role in communication and argues that socially produced differences in gender may find expression in communication style or content and that "a full theory of emotion should be directed at the real-life contexts for the use of emotion discourse and the effects that such discourse may have on the conduct and formulation of ongoing relationships between people."[32] This operates at a group level in choral singing. The second view, in contrast and as argued by Maria Sandgren, maintains that the shared experience of choral singing removes any significant gender differences in expressions of emotion.[33] Following a study using well-being as a means of accessing "emotions" to investigate whether men and women differed in "their ratings of emotional states on, before and after . . . a regular choral rehearsal," she found that while women had a tendency to report more positive emotions than men, there was no discernible gender difference as to how these were reported. (A long-term membership in the choir, together with shared experiences and similar expectations, may account for this similarity, even across differences).[34] These two juxtaposed positions provide an interesting base line from which to view the issue of gender and emotion in the group setting of a choir.

I now turn to the example of Andreas, a bass singer in the choir whose heartfelt account of his musical experience supports Sandgren's findings that men have a tendency to reveal more of the negative aspect of music making than women. In addition, his story offers a good example of how experience and meaning are always mediated within an idiosyncratic understanding of what it is to live in East Bavaria. When I met Andreas, who is in his early thirties, he had not been singing long with Chor Kreis Deggendorf. He had come because Stefan, the choirmaster, was a gifted musician able to communicate his love of music to those around him. Andreas, an experienced musician, had a beautiful voice and was an asset to any group he joined. He was exceptionally articulate in explaining how his relationship with music had begun and what it involved. His narrative evocatively illustrates how one male singer conceptualizes his relationship to Bavarian music, land, and culture:

> There is a relationship between music and the land. I am from Franconia, where there are lots of trees; they are part of me. I put my arms around the trees, and I look up high. There is power [*Kraft*]; I sing with joy. Nature has a quietness [*Stille*], but there is always a ground tone; the wind moves the trees. But when I sang with my sister this was a catastrophe! Boys should play football; why do I have to sing? My mother always wanted me to sing. No one else in the class sang! Then I had to join the choir. All girls! How embarrassing! I could fight against them, but that would have been impolite; I had to behave so decided to get to know the people and be the best singer. People then said, "Oh, you can sing beautifully" or "What a lovely voice." I didn't understand the importance of that then. My father wanted me to learn an instrument. I decided on a little drum, and so I joined the village band [*Dorf*

Kapelle]. I then began the trumpet. Evenings after school, I went to practice through winter and summer. It was cold. After a loud practice I would come home in the quietness of nature.

I was asked to help out at a funeral. I was twelve years old. There was music to accompany the carrying [of the coffin] to the grave. The coffin was lowered into the grave. It rained and there were umbrellas and people cried. It was summer and twenty-eight degrees. Nature again. I wanted to be a musician. My week was full with making music in the choir and with the brass band. My parents said, "You have to learn a trade." I was sixteen; they sent me to a weaving factory. I hated the work; it was loud, you couldn't talk. I began to practice yodeling. In Austria it was used [to communicate from] mountain to mountain, and here we are again back at nature. When I was last at home there was a beggar on the street who sang really badly. I didn't give him any money; he was ruining the music. I was sorry for him, but what he was doing was wrong. He should practice. Here, the other day, there was a woman with an accordion. She played from the heart and was really good; the noise of the street disappeared.

I joined a band. We toured through Germany. There was no free time. You had to do as you were told. We played from 8:00 p.m. in the evening to 2:30 in the morning, always the same songs. I tried to understand what the audience found so wonderful in these songs. Music should encourage honesty, but they didn't understand that. After two years they set my trumpet at the door and said, "You don't fit."[35] My mother said, "Now you know." I had shaking legs. I have never touched the trumpet since. It was very intense and hurtful. I left the village. Everyone knew. I never forgot the "you don't fit" and didn't want to hear the "so you're not with the band anymore."

I have spent the winter singing in a gospel choir. The woman who runs it is arrogant. She sings so much solo, you must ask, who is she there for, her or the choir? We sang at weddings, and the money was good. She said that the money had gone to music and photocopying, but I don't understand why. The singers who are there are honest. There is nothing they can do. I came to all the rehearsals even when I was sick. My sore head disappeared, and my mood changed. I need to do this to find the source to build up my soul. Music builds me up; it gives me strength.[36]

In this rich response to being asked about his musical biography, Andreas revealed far more than just details of the people and events in his life. His narrative contains concrete examples of experiences that relate to place, sound, and the body. It also contains metaphysical allusions to nature, power, and purpose. He makes it clear through his interweaving of the real and abstract that his connection to music takes a tangible form. Because music is a substantial force within his life, his narrative recounts concrete embodied experiences and uses these as a springboard for expressing a relationship with music. As Bradd Shore has suggested, "through narrative, the flow of events is given an articulate form, made into a kind of model.[37] Experience is literally talked into meaningfulness."

Andreas begins by talking of the forest and the sounds within it. At first sight, this appears poetic, but by the end of his narrative it can be understood as key to his experience of music. After establishing this link between nature and music, he gives an account of growing up in a tightly knit village community, where the church and local community organizations offer structure and routines. Through his music making he became actively involved with the rituals of life. The purity of nature is emphasized and associated with music, though nature is a fundamental that humans cannot control. Music has rhythm, which he links to the reality of learning the drum and also to life's rhythms as marked by the seasons and by his own rites of passage—from the protection of musical learning in the home to becoming a teenager in a band. Music is a source of strength for him because of its link to nature and hence to the power it commands. This close relationship between the body and the power of music is bidirectional: Andreas was able to resort to using music to escape the horrible reality of the weaving factory by yodeling under the clatter of the looms and thus soaring to the mountains. Music was not frivolous nor used for tawdry aims, and it upset him greatly that the band he joined was abusing the power of music by primarily seeking personal gain—an agenda that he found sordid.

Andreas's understanding of music is unique to him. It emerges from his interpretation of concrete examples that he deliberately organizes to conceptualize music as something powerful and virtuous, in other words, as something to be treasured and treated with respect. As an example, he cites the accordion player who is to be praised for playing from the heart, in contrast to the beggar whom he condemns for killing the music, which is a depraved act. His own dream of being a professional musician led to his illusions being shattered by the tedium and lack of freedom when playing in a band. But he was also scandalized by the behavior of band members who used music to get girls and money. Deeply hurt by the band's treatment of him, he left his area and moved south. Andreas's relationship with music has been central to his life, guiding his actions and decision making in a significant fashion. His relationship with music, therefore, has been intense and resides in his very core of being; as a result, the episode with the band has taken on catastrophic properties for him personally.

Insofar as his narrative at times entered a confessional mode, it provides an example of how "narrative ... mediates a reinvention of identity."[38] As I listened to Andreas revealing the intense role that music making had played in his life, I became uncomfortable with his "confession" at times. Yet I also recognized that in trusting me with the narrative reinvention of himself through choral music, he allowed me to see the power that music exercised for him. The strictures of choir membership allowed Andreas to experience personal transformation and transcendence through singing. It also created a moment of liberation from situations he found upsetting. The effect of singing in Andreas's life resonates with how Liz Garnett has theorized musical participation in terms of "technologies of the self," after Michel Foucault:[39] "Musical practices can be simultaneously independent from and constructed within the power structure of day-to-day social relations: while the mechanisms that regulate choral behavior index political axes of identity such as class, educational level and regionality, they do so with an agenda that is more focused on the transformation than on the exclusion of the individual."[40] By capturing autobiographical stories of musical lives, we can gain an idea of how these singers locate themselves within a larger web of narratives. Although choir members' narratives necessarily are incomplete accounts of their experiences of music making (since there are experiential elements beyond the linguistic remit), they still offer compelling evidence of how their relationship with music has developed.

Narratives of Experience and Expression

In this chapter I have used autobiographical stories to access the experiences of a number of choral singers. As I have shown, for some of the Chor Kreis Deggendorf singers in East Bavaria the structure of the Verein as a social unit brings two processes to bear on choral performance. The first is musical, whereby the conventions of choral singing ensure that "the idealized state that these technologies of the self are designed to attain is that of choral unity."[41] A striking feature of both men's and women's narrative in Chor Kreis Deggendorf was the positive quality attributed to the act of music making, even when the surrounding circumstances were unhappy. This finding accords with Sandgren's observation that choral singing can lead to an increase in reported positive emotions and a decrease in negative emotions.[42] The second process in operation concerns the role of the local, personal, and familiar apparent in the Verein structure within which the choir operates. The knowledge of how to behave in a socially acceptable fashion within the context of East Bavaria is gathered through experiences of everyday life. This lived experience in turn generates a sense of belonging and sense of identity for choir members, which is encapsulated within the notion of Heimat.[43]

As these narratives reveal, individual relationships with music emerge through the development of personalized associations with acoustic and nonacoustic elements of musical experiences, confirming that "the function of music is to reinforce, or relate people more closely to, certain experiences which have come to have meaning in their social life."[44] These narratives suggest that the interaction of place, soundscape, and the body are crucial in developing a relationship with music. Singers' narratives also raised issues about the gendered body within the context of choral singing. While the very nature of choir organization is usually based on gendered subdivisions according to vocal range, Gabriela was able to subvert these gender divisions and still find acceptance. In addition, the very opportunity to make music and sing is influenced by gender; this was demonstrated by Agnes, whose desire to play an instrument or sing was denied to her but not to her brothers.

The challenge for these singers was how to maintain the experiential quality of music making in telling their stories. All respondents expressed their experiences of choral singing in terms of physical sensations and remembered emotions. The strongly embodied sense of the sonic affect of singing led them to foreground its emotional impact, while the physicality of singing also found echoes in the metaphors and images used. Notably, this talk about music revealed how personal understandings of the body become linked through the experience of music making to place, people, and gendered events; music making becomes part of the familiar and local realm of a singer's life. Singers' reflections on their musical experiences were also viewed as special and transformative at a level of physical experience that often transcended gender considerations.[45] The narratives presented in this chapter show similarities, especially regarding efforts made to articulate the physical sensations of singing. This suggests that a key aspect of the experience of choral singing lies in the bodily based nature of such an activity. This is not to deny that these bodies are gendered but rather to suggest that the overwhelming experience of singing and being with others in musical unity is a very powerful one. Gabriela, for example, highlighted how unity occurs through voices merging in song, confounding prescribed gender roles. The analysis presented in this chapter has also emphasized the importance of place in forming individuals' relationship with music. Singers' reflections about their experiences suggest that emotions generated in music making can propel individuals to move beyond normative gender and social restrictions, facilitating a sense of transcendence and personal transformation.

Notes

1. I am grateful for the award of an AHRC grant, which funded fourteen months' fieldwork for my doctoral research on voluntary music making in East Bavaria during 2004–5.

2. Peter Blickle, *Heimat: A Critical Theory of the German Idea of Homeland* (New York: Camden House, 2002), 32.

3. Bradd Shore, *Culture in Mind: Cognition, Culture, and the Problem of Meaning* (New York: Oxford University Press, 1996), 58.

4. Blickle, *Heimat*, 154.

5. Pierre Bourdieu, *Outline of a Theory of Practice* (Cambridge: Cambridge University Press, 1977).

6. Robert Borofsky, *Assessing Cultural Anthropology* (New York: McGraw-Hill, 1994); Maurice Bloch, "Language, Anthropology and Cognitive Science," *Man* 26, no. 2 (1991): 183–98.

7. Blickle, *Heimat*, 78.

8. See Nigel Rapport and Andrew Dawson, eds., *Migrants of Identity: Perceptions of Home in a World of Movement* (Oxford: Berg, 1998).

9. Michel de Certeau, *The Practice of Everyday Life* (Berkeley: University of California Press, 1988), 78.

10. Nigel Rapport, *I Am Dynamite, An Alternative Anthropology of Power* (London: Routledge, 2003), 29–30.

11. Nigel Rapport and Joanna Overing, *Social and Cultural Anthropology: The Key Concepts* (London: Routledge Key Guides, 2000), 284.

12. Ibid., 287.

13. Michael Jackson, *The Politics of Storytelling: Violence, Transgression and Intersubjectivity* (Copenhagen: University of Copenhagen, Museum Tusculanum Press, 2006), 17–18, 23.

14. Nigel Rapport, *Transcendent Individual: Towards a Literary and Liberal* (London: Routledge, 1997), 13.

15. Agnes, interview with the author, Deggendorf, February 15, 2005.

16. R. Murray Schafer, *The Tuning of the World* (New York: Knopf, 1977), 7.

17. Gertrud, interview with the author, Deggendorf, February 15, 2005.

18. Mary, mother of God, is revered within the Catholic Church, and in Bavaria the month of May is "Mary month." A repertoire of sacred songs is sung at this time.

19. Luise, interview with the author, Deggendorf, February 15, 2005.

20. Tim Ingold, *The Perception of the Environment: Essays in Livelihood, Dwelling and Skill* (London: Routledge, 2000); Kay Milton, *Loving Nature: Towards an Ecology of Emotion.* London: Routledge, 2002), 64–65.

21. Merlin Donald, *A Mind So Rare: The Evolution of Human Consciousness* (New York: Norton, 2001).

22. Ruth Finnegan, *Communicating: The Multiple Modes of Human Interconnection* (London: Routledge, 2002), 90. The body provides the means of knowing as well as being known. Paul Stoller exhorts anthropologists to reference the all-encompassing bodily experience when writing ethnography to be truer to the actual experience. *The Taste of Ethnographic Things: The Senses in Anthropology* (Philadelphia: University of Pennsylvania Press, 1989).

23. Andrew Killick offers an interesting discussion on musicians playing alone for their own private satisfaction, in contrast to experiences of public performance or the social experience of playing as part of an ensemble. "Holicipation: Prolegomenon to an Ethnography of Solitary Music Making," *Ethnomusicology Forum* 15, no. 2 (2006): 273–99.

24. Sinead McDermott, "Memory, Nostalgia, and Gender in 'Thousand Acres,'" *Signs* 28, no. 1 (2002): 399.

25. See James F. Daugherty, "Spacing, Formation, and Choral Sound: Preferences and Perceptions of Auditors and Choristers," *Journal of Research in Music Education* 47, no. 3 (1999): 224–39; and Elizabeth Ekholm, "The Effect of Singing Mode and Seating Arrangement on Choral Blend and Overall Choral Sound," *Journal of Research in Music Education* 48, no. 2 (2000): 123–35.

26. Daugherty, "Choral Sound," 235.

27. Hugo Distler (1908–42) was a German composer known for his melismatic style of choral writing.

28. Gabriela, interview with the author, Deggendorf, February 25, 2005. Gabriela uses the German word *wahrnehmen* to indicate the reality and physical presence of sound moving through her body as she sings in a choir. *Wahrnehmen* has to do with perception and awareness. Given the context of what she is trying to convey, I have expressed this as her body "registering" the sound.

29. Regina, interview with the author, Deggendorf, April 11, 2005.

30. Beate, interview with the author, Deggendorf, March 15, 2005.

31. Within the Bavarian school system, some grammar schools are recognized as specializing in particular subjects such as languages or music. A number of the choir members had attended a *musisches Gymnasium* in Niederalteich. Since this type of school does not exist within the British and Irish school system, I have indicated the special nature of such a school by putting the word musical in quotation marks. In this school music is a core subject and is given exactly the same weight as math or German.

32. Brian Parkinson, *Ideas and Realities of Emotion* (London: Routledge, 2001), 21. See also Brian Parkinson, Agneta H. Fischer, and Antony S. R. Manstead, *Emotions in Social Relations: Cultural, Group, and Interpersonal Processes* (New York: Psychology Press, 2005).

33. Maria Sandgren, "Evidence for Strong Immediate Well-Being Effects of Choral Singing: With More Enjoyment for Women than Men," in *Proceedings of the Seventh Triennial Conference of European Society for the Cognitive Sciences of Music*, ed. Jukka Louhivuori, Tuomas Eerola, Suvi Saarikallio, Tommi Himberg, and Päivi-Sisko Eerola (Finland: Department of Music, University of Jyväskylä ESCOM, 2009), 475–79.

34. Sandgren, "Effects of Choral Singing," 478.

35. While Andreas has a wonderful voice, he is also an accomplished trumpet player. However, when his trumpet case was set at the door by the other band members to signify that he should leave the band, this marked the end of his trumpet playing. When I met him several years later he said he had never touched the trumpet again.

36. Andreas, interview with the author, Deggendorf, April 26, 2005.

37. Shore, *Culture in Mind*, 58.

38. Michael Jackson, *Minima Ethnographica: Intersubjectivity and the Anthropological Project* (Chicago: University of Chicago Press, 1998), 24.

39. Luther H. Martin, Huck Guttman, and Patricia Hutton, eds., *Technologies of the Self: A Seminar with Michel Foucault* (Massachusets: University of Massachusets Press, 1988), 16–49.

40. Liz Garnett, "Choral Singing as Bodily Regime," *International Review of the Aesthetics and Sociology of Music* 36, no. 2 (2005): 250. Although this analysis does not examine political or class affiliations within the choir, it is helpful to say a few words on these within the context of Bavaria and the choir. Choir members were keen to stress the irrelevance of job status in connection with choir membership and often stated that they were unaware of the nature of others' jobs. However, it became apparent that this was more an espousal of an ethos of equality that singers felt the choir should engender rather than fact. Choir members worked in a wide range of jobs from dentistry to hairdressing, farm work, and truck driving. Politics in Bavaria are conservative and, at the time of my fieldwork, the ruling party was the Christian Socialist Party. It espouses traditional family values and a sense of belonging to Bavaria. Thus, choral practices that encourage musical togetherness and social bonding are commensurate with wider-held views of how society should operate.

41. Ibid., 265.

42. Sandgren, "Effects of Choral Singing." See also Robert J. Beck, Thomas C. Cesario, Shookooh Yousefi, and Hiro Enamoto, "Choral Singing, Performance Perception, and Immune System Changes in Salivary Immunoglobulin A and Cortisol," *Musical Perception* 18 (2000): 87–106; Stephen M. Clift and Grenville Hancox, "The Perceived Benefits of Singing: Findings from Preliminary Surveys of a University College Choral Society," *Journal of the Royal Society for the Promotion of Health* 121 (2001): 248–56; and Gunter Kreuz, Stephan Bongard, Sonja Rohrmann, Volker Hodapp, and Dorothee Grebe, "Effects of Choir Singing or Listening on Secretory Immunoglobulin A, Cortisal, and Emotional State," *Journal of Behavioral Medicine* 27 (2004): 623–35.

43. Some of the choir members were not born in East Bavaria and had different views as to what choir membership should entail. They attended for the purposes of singing but viewed the social functions beyond the rehearsal room as optional. This attitude was received unfavorably by other East Bavarian choir members who understood sociability to be integral to the performative experience.

44. John Blacking, *How Musical Is Man?* (Seattle: University of Washington Press, 1973), 99. Nonacoustic elements of musical experience refer to the aspects of experience that are felt rather than heard. One example of this is the sensation of core muscles contracting as female singers make an effort to support the voice for high notes or at the end of a phrase when the column of air is threatening to collapse.

45. See Garnett, "Choral Singing."

Chapter Six

A Place of Her Own

Gendered Singing in Poland's Tatras

Louise Wrazen

Hej kie jo se zaśpiywom,
puscem dolinom głos;
Hej ustysys mnie chłopce,
Ale mnie nie poznos.

[Hey, when I sing,
I'll let go of my voice in the valleys;
Hey, you will hear me, fellow,
but you will not recognize me.]

In this song from southern Poland, the women singing engage in a first-person narrative in which they position themselves discursively within a surrounding mountain landscape of the Tatra Mountains by sending their voices into this land (see fig. 6.1).[1] At the same time, depending on where they are singing, they may or may not actually be placing themselves—through their singing voices—physically into the hills and valleys that this text describes. What is the significance of this song and this singing within the experience of place? What is the relationship between singer, landscape, and song? How is this affected by gender, age, and modernity? This chapter addresses such questions in considering gendered musical performance among the Górale of Podhale, Poland (map 6.1).[2] By locating women's singing within its environment, this chapter aims to show how singing, place, and gendered identity coalesce. It also elaborates on the individual experience of singing by examining one exceptional singer's negotiation of gendered performance practice and her ongoing attachment to the landscape.[3]

In exploring the particularities of one woman's musical life, this discussion builds on ongoing research in ethnomusicology on the individual[4] and also contributes to what Margery Wolf has identified as an important task of anthropology to discover "all we can about the diversity of women's lived

Figure 6.1. A view of the Tatra Mountains: Rusinowa Polana, Poland, July 2006. Photograph by the author.

experience."[5] But doing so here leads to the challenge of accessing lived (musical) experience—which may best be undertaken by considering musical behaviors. As Ruth Finnegan has suggested, "we can productively focus not on trying to penetrate and pin down hidden internal states but rather on the *manner*, variably practiced and conceptualized in different contexts, in which people are personally involved in their musical engagements."[6] Such personal experience, as understood through engagement, functions as a form of agency that also can contribute to distinguishing difference.[7] By exploring one specific set of musical experiences, this chapter, therefore, is concerned with the larger theoretical project of understanding and explaining the active subject. By detailing the manner in which people are personally involved in their musical engagements in a certain place, it also situates the experience of the individual within a performative context-specific dynamic.

More particularly, this chapter focuses on gender difference within the normative practices of performance options available to men and women in the region of Podhale. In drawing on the intimacy of one woman's musical life, I am deliberately retrieving some gendered music experiences from among the Górale to include in a discourse drawn largely from men's perspectives.[8] This exposes gendered musical variation as an inherent constituent of a dynamic larger narrative, while also detailing some of the qualities of these differences through one individual's story. In so doing, this chapter contributes to charting "the ways that individuals and communities are incorporating, resisting, or

Map 6.1. Poland and the region of Podhale. Map by Angela Snieder.

reformulating these discourses and practices through musical means, at times interrogating the concept of gender itself."[9] As shown here, the poetics and performance of singing are directly implicated in a gendered experience of place. Women's singing, in particular, is considered as it contributes to the process of emplacement, which is bound to an understanding of ways to encounter places, perceive them, and invest them with significance.[10]

This discussion is organized into three main sections. The first introduces the Górale, the ideals of Górale life and behavior as related to the land, and the gendered performance forms that have emerged. The second introduces women's singing as a possible departure from the constraints of other normative gendered music forms and as it can be understood in relation to a contextualizing landscape. The third section focuses on the music experiences of Aniela and on ways in which these experiences reinforce and articulate her own subjective place in the Tatras.

Men, Women, and Music in Podhale

The legends and stories on which Górale men's and women's songs are based are animated by heroic and virtuous men. Arguably most notable among these is Janosik, who actually was not from Podhale but from the southern side of the Carpathian Mountains. This legendary Robin Hood-like figure was born Juraj Jánošík in 1688 in Terchová, Slovakia, and led a band of brigands from both sides of the Tatras until he was captured, tortured, and killed in 1713. The story of Janosik and his men provides the inspiration for a body of strophic songs popular in Podhale called Janosikowe.[11] Constructed primarily as narratives of male bravery, references to women in these songs are rare and generally brief (although at least one song refers to a woman's role in betraying the hero, reflecting one version of this tale).[12] The story of Janosik's courageous adventures with his men in the Tatras also serves as the basis for the dance known as the *zbójnicki*, a group dance for men that features a virtuosic display of strength and agility through a series of coordinated leaps and steps, many involving the *ciupaga* (weapon-cum-walking stick) that they all carry.

The imposing landscape of the Tatra Mountains is the main setting for all these stories and is central to local conceptualizations of identity and worldview. Most of Podhale actually stretches beyond the foothills of the Carpathians and into a sweep of land between the Tatras (to the south) and Gorce Mountains (to the north). Yet Górale regional identity is very much rooted in the harsh conditions and topography of the rough mountain terrain; it also is indebted to a strong association with traditional forms of transhumant pastoralism and history spanning both sides of the Carpathians.[13] The prominence of these mountains in Górale life and imagination has resulted in a mythology and an expressive culture constructed around themes of heroism, stamina, and ingenuity (as embodied in the hero Janosik). As the central protagonists in these stories, Górale men continue to reenact and promote these ideals through their leading roles in the traditional music and dance forms that derive from these same narratives.[14] Men initiate and lead the prominent regional dance for a single couple (known as the *góralski*), play instruments, and sing; in the zbójnicki dance men are the sole participants.[15]

Not surprisingly, women's roles are more narrowly circumscribed: they do not generally play instruments; they are to follow the man's movements and gestures in dancing the góralski; and, although they sing, they can do so only outside the parameters of the dance.[16] In the góralski dance for a single couple, for example, the woman who is to dance does not enter the dance floor by herself. Instead, women watch from the sides as a man approaches the musicians, sings a tune and text, then turns and waits for his partner to arrive. She is brought to the floor either by another man or by female friends, who complete a brief sequence of turns before leaving her to dance with her partner. The couple dances, without physical contact, for as long as the man chooses. When he has had enough, he stops, leaves the floor, and returns to the musicians to sing another tune. The woman returns to the side and waits until she is again brought to the floor for the next tune (this usually happens from three to five times for one set of the dance). Once he has had enough, the man signals the musicians and takes his partner to dance briefly together before leaving the floor—when another man is then free to approach the musicians for his dance. A woman, therefore, does not enter the dance floor alone and is silent in this dance, where she should enact the muse, ornament, or foil while men around her direct the action through their dancing, singing, and playing.

Women's relative silence on the dance floor, and largely supportive roles in stories and legends, is not inconsistent with their position in local music histories. These histories are well defined, and the story of music among the Górale is charted through the names of prominent male musicians and dancers. Virtually without exception, notable male fiddlers are identified as icons of Górale music—their musical styles emulated, and their names sometimes attached to prominent monuments or regional ensembles (for example: Sabała, Obrochta, Chotarski, and more recently Karpiel-Bułecka and Trebunia-Tutka). The one possible exception here is Bronisława Konieczna-Dziadoń from the town of Bukowina and known as Dziadońka (1894–1977). Anna Czekanowska refers to her as the "first woman to be recognized as an instrumentalist in the Polish Tatra region"—a reputation supported as I heard her vehemently promoted for her passionate playing at a cultural gathering in the main hall of the Związek Podhalan (Podhalan Alliance regional cultural organization) in Zakopane in 2006.[17] Those women who are known for their singing, however, have not received comparable attention. The following discussion turns to consider women's voices in song in an effort to redress at least some of this silence in historiography.

Women and Singing

Unaccompanied singing presents a departure from male-dominated performance practices. Characterized by a vocal quality designed to carry across distances, this singing is associated primarily with the outdoors, although it also frequently occurs indoors—in other words, wherever an opportunity presents itself or whenever women choose to participate through song. Though men also sing in this manner (alone or together with women), this style of singing comes closest to defining a "women's repertoire" among the Górale. Typically, one person begins and others then join in with lower parts. Unlike instrumental music and the góralski dance cycle where men dominate, this singing has allowed women to exercise some musical authority and define a performative space—be it in the open fields and hills or on the outskirts of the dance floor. Although women do not sing as part of the góralski dance, for example, it is nonetheless possible for them to engage in the event by singing from the sides. In so doing, they may even extend some control over the dance: by beginning to sing before a man has had a chance to sing a tune to the musicians in his dance set, women's singing can interrupt the sequence of the dancing and prevent the man from continuing to dance. Or a woman may begin to sing quite independently of any musicians who may simultaneously be playing (either for dancing or for listening), thereby adding to the musical density of the event with an interjection of female vocality.[18]

Such vocal interjections by women do not significantly alter the balance of power within this dance event, however. Furthermore, such explicit gendering of control does not necessarily go unnoticed by the women themselves, as was suggested in a conversation with Aniela (whom I discuss later) and her friend Ludwisia. Reflecting on these dances, perhaps drawing on their own memories, these two Górale women did not hesitate to point out that women have a distinct disadvantage during these events. In the midst of this conversation, they referred to the following saying as though to further prove their point:

Słomiany kawaler się orzeni
A złota dziewcyna się nie wyda.

[A bachelor of straw will marry
But a girl of gold will not.]

In other words, while any young man (that is, as common as straw) can marry, the same is not true for a young woman, even one who is as precious (virtuous and good) as gold. Among desirable female virtues, singing certainly does not go unnoticed; given the vibrancy of Górale social life, a woman's ability (knowledge of tunes and texts) and willingness to sing (thereby contributing to social conviviality) are as important as the strength and quality of her voice.

In singing, a woman may take the lead, choosing both the tune and text with which the others will join in after several notes. Her choices may depend on a variety of factors: the occasion and setting, her comfort with the tune, the other singers present, and the possibility of layering any personal feelings onto the situation through a more distinctive text. In contrast to the narrative songs (Janosikowe) introduced earlier, these songs are typically brief: the music may consist of a single melodic phrase repeated three times or of two phrases with the second one repeated, with texts comprising two lines (twelve to fourteen syllables each, with a caesura in the middle). These texts are generally drawn from a common repertoire, though they may be varied through extemporization, especially in the second half. In contrast to the Janosikowe narratives and those songs that accompany the zbójnicki dance, which are inspired by the bravery of men, these brief texts address a variety of themes and can present a woman's distinctive perspective. Jan Sadownik has edited 1,250 of these texts and organized them into eleven categories that provide some insight into their thematic range: reflective, social, soldier, brigand, hunting, shepherds, men's bravado and swagger, courtship, love, family, and comic.[19] Brief couplets, these song texts express a complete, synoptic thought or idea in a haikulike fashion that may juxtapose a potentially revelatory personal expression with a reference to the surrounding landscape.

The potential emotional resonance of many of these texts is unmistakable given their frequent first-person voice or poignant juxtaposition of personal and natural worlds. Furthermore, they offer a level of emotional disclosure that contrasts with normative social interactions unmediated by music. Attempting to explore this possibility further within a now-changed social discourse no longer built on a vibrant practice of singing, I was nonetheless advised that it was possible to express through song what would have been difficult or impossible to express through speech; in the notable words of one Górale man: "If you don't want to tell me, then sing it to me."[20] Deliberately chosen song texts, therefore, were not inconsequential. The emotional valence of these songs became potentially more pronounced within a broader cultural practice where, as one Górale man suggested, "Górale ... dislike an honest opinion or explicit revelation of true thoughts and feelings. Therefore, it was through the music and songs that true thoughts and feelings were revealed."[21] While carefully chosen song texts can inspire one level of personal revelation and emotional commitment, the performative act of singing initiates another affective level of engagement. Where elsewhere I have also considered the relationship between song and personal expression, here I turn to focus on the experience of singing as part of a gendered attachment to place.[22] In so doing, this chapter aligns itself with Finnegan's concern to explore the manner of musical engagements rather than attempt to penetrate hidden states—while still concerned with individual subjectivities.[23]

Górale singing of these texts is linked unequivocally with the local landscape through local identification, performance practice, and particular details of text. Known as *wierchowe* (derived from *wierchy*, mountain peaks) or *pasterskie* (referring to shepherds; pastoral), the songs bear names that suggest both their outdoor performance and possible provenance. They are characterized by a loud, resonant vocal quality and free-rhythmic performance, with long pauses possible between the three phrases that contribute to making this singing style ideal for outdoor open spaces. Melodic contours are frequently descending or quickly rise to sit in an upper tessitura before descending, as though to capture the natural resonance of this upper register. One woman even suggested to me that one really cannot sing these songs indoors. In this way, the surrounding landscape is implicated in the very act of performance. By choosing to sing outside, beyond the enclosures of the home or hall, women access an open, unhindered, natural space for their voices. By casting their voices through the fields, hills, and valleys around them, women performatively reach into and connect with their natural environment, thereby establishing a type of intimacy with the surrounding land. At the same time, they also ensure that they are heard—just as the mountains are always seen. Indeed, I have often been told stories that include memories of hearing women sing across valleys or fields.

Numerous song texts, such as the one that opened this chapter, also refer to the resonance of the singing voice in this landscape. Many of these texts represent the woman through a first-person narrative while also positioning her (often through a reference to her voice) within this natural environment. Indeed, both poetics and performance present the mountain landscape as a participant in the singing. By providing the very means to communicate with others, the carrying power of the outdoors—with their acoustic vistas provided by hills and valleys— allows the voice to extend far beyond its normal range. Here sounds (acoustics) become the object of recognition rather than any visuals.[24] Such sounds may remain unrecognized (as in the opening text) or recognized, as here:

Hej zaros jo cie zaros
poznała po głosie;
Ej ino se zarąbał
siekiereckom w lesie.

[Hey, immediately I
recognized you by your voice;
As soon as you struck
your axe in the woods.][25]

In this text, the man is immediately identified by the woman by the sound of his voice as he swung his axe. Though recognition is not even possible in the following text, this does not prevent the woman from singing into the hills nonetheless:

Choćby jo śpiywała
góry powolała;
Mój miły nie cuje
Daleko nocuje.

[Even though I may sing
and call the hills;
My love does not hear
he sleeps far away.][26]

This connection between the landscape and women's singing is pronounced. Such texts, which are not unrepresentative of Górale songs and which frequently make their way into performances (live and recorded), attest to the intersection of poetics and performance in engaging the landscape in a sensual and personal experience of place. The importance of place for the Górale (and in particular the imposing landscape of the Tatra Mountains) has already been well established, and the nuances of this association as attenuated through time, distance, and memory have also been variously explored.[27] I qualify this compelling association of music and place as it intersects with experiences of gendered Górale identity. In singing, the female voice becomes part of the hills and valleys through both text and performance. Thus extended, women's voices performatively create a personal space beyond the confines of an immediate, and limited, local reality to access the infinite parameters of a broader, outer world of and through nature. Within Górale gender-performative expressions of identity, where men's dancing may be seen to reference narratives of heroism and control of place, women's singing, in contrast, can establish an intimacy celebrating the transcendence of this landscape.

These performances, therefore, access inner and outer worlds (used here in subjective, social, and spatial terms) differently and suggest a binary that has already been explored by anthropologist Frances Pine in her work on the Górale. In her analysis of Górale society, Pine has suggested that "Górale ideology places enormous moral legitimacy on the house, its production, consumption and ritual."[28] This is where full personhood is derived and social relations emerge and develop to allow access and participation in an "outside space" beyond the containment (and conformity) of the home and village community. She characterizes gender relationships in Podhale as fluid, negotiable, and apparently flexible and recognizes the active role that women have historically played in the outside world of a larger market economy as a result of a long history of migration and participation in a "second economy." Much of Pine's work revolves around a nuanced economic analysis that considers this home and village community in relation to the state (and state-controlled or affiliated ventures). In so doing, she argues for the relevance of analyzing Górale society in terms of binary opposites, where the major contrast is defined not by gender but by marital status and self-definition relative to the rest of the world (an inside-outside binary, rather than male-female). The inside is associated with married life, conformity, mutuality, house and family interest, and house and village community, whereas the outside is associated with being single, autonomy, individuality, self-interest, and that which lies beyond the village community. Yet, as she suggests, these worlds are not necessarily mutually exclusive, as Górale (men and women) have operated in the outside (economic) world for some time. At such times, "the gender and generation rules that operate within the village are suspended or even reversed; what is applauded is individualism, entrepreneurial skill, and innovation."[29]

While such individualism and extroverted behavior may be lauded in dealings with the outside, the inside is more controlled, especially for women and, in particular, for married women, whose primary responsibility of looking after children and home places significant constraints on them. Whereas this control is reinforced in the góralski dance sequence, unaccompanied singing allows women, sonically and symbolically, to access greater possibilities through the experience of placing themselves musically within the framework of a larger conceptual and physical coexistence with the landscape. Where the dance may provide men with an access to the outside from the inside, singing may offer women the possibility of an emplacement that renders their inside existence coterminous with a larger outer world.[30]

Such gender-performative attachments to place become displaced when performances move from the field to the stage or are often recreated through the mediation of recordings (which often attempt to recreate outdoor acoustic space). The voices of such women singing have in fact been heard across valley, recording, and auditorium for many years. For example, as early as 1929, a program for a concert in the northern town of Poznan at 3:30 on Friday, September 27, 1929, announced an "ensemble of Górale women with their own band" (*Zespół Góralek z Poronina z własną orkiestrą*), thus suggesting that singing has for some time not only provided Górale women with a special relationship with the outside natural world but also facilitated entry into a larger outside social world. In the following section, this discussion continues by turning to Aniela, whose musical experiences elaborate on ways in which these worlds intersect and for whom singing has consequently offered the possibilities of broadening her horizons of a local place.

A Woman's Voice

Podhale has been filled with the voices of women singing, just as it has been characterized by the sounds of men playing. Although their names are often noted in association with tunes and texts that have found their way into various collections over the years, these women remain relatively unknown.[31] Now over seventy, Aniela Fiust has lived in Podhale all her life and has long been active singing in a variety of contexts. Even while singing in ensembles for much of her adult life, however, she has maintained a strong musical bond with the natural environment around her. This intersection of experiences is explored here.

Born in 1936 as the second of five daughters on a farm on the periphery of the small village of Gliczarów (west of the town of Poronin), Aniela grew up in the hardship and poverty on which Górale legends are based. She also grew up at a time when music and dance such as described earlier formed an integral part of local village life in Podhale. Although shy and not particularly healthy as a child, with a poor appetite and pronounced stutter, Aniela remembers always being quick to sing. She learned from a young age and remembers singing all the time—when working in haying, when digging potatoes. These early recollections of singing inevitably revolve around the outdoors, and some remain particularly memorable. They include memories of working in the fields with her cousins when she was quite little and of then being told by her uncle to leave the work and instead go to a particular place to sing. This must have been a spot with especially fine acoustics, because when she and her cousins would go there and sing together "people from all around" would stop and listen. Such contexts provided the opportunity to learn how to sing—a process she described haltingly, as though searching to retrieve these images (her many pauses are indicated by the subdivision of her narrative into separate lines):

I learned to sing
I—that is really—I learned by myself [and she laughs].
They sang because a long time ago, they sang
when digging potatoes.
One would sing
when raking
like when there—one beside the other—so we'd run and huddle together and
sing
and to sing.
And so in this way there with them—
and so I with these cousins [male and female]—so we in this way from a young age—so in short from the time of a young child [I sang].

Aniela must have distinguished herself as a singer from a young age, for she explained that although everyone sang in her village, and many sang well, she was usually the one to sing the top—the most important—voice. In 1956 or 1957 she joined the ensemble in the neighboring town of Biały Dunajec, a village well known for its fine singers and dancers. Aniela recalls that everyone brought the repertoire they already knew from home to the rehearsals. This was an ensemble led by Zofia Solarzowa (1902–88), who was not from the region but who was given the mandate to organize a regional ensemble and finally settled on Biały Dunajec for the location. Aniela suggests that the large number of good singers and musicians in the area must have contributed to this decision. She stressed, however, that neither she, nor the others, learned to sing or dance in the ensemble: they all knew this from home already—although the director and ensemble work assisted them in presenting this effectively to others. With as many as forty people attending a rehearsal (held twice a week and sometimes more often) Aniela recalls that the ensemble was like "one big family" and that these rehearsals provided a much-appreciated break from the routines of work and an otherwise difficult life. It was also a pleasure to sing, and she emphasizes that it was this essential pleasure that sometimes led them to go out even after a long rehearsal to sing some more.

During this Soviet-driven era ensemble participants were paid, which provided enormous assistance to Aniela and others, who otherwise had very little income. Ensembles also provided an opportunity for travel at a time when this was virtually impossible.[32] They also wanted to go to be together and to sing:

> Everyone wanted to go, well, because we met
> we socialized, we sang
> so all of this pulled us one to the other.

Aniela remembers traveling to Bulgaria, the former Czechoslovakia, Hungary, the former Yugoslavia, and even Finland during these years. Not married, nor with any responsibilities tied to a farm, Aniela was free to travel with the ensemble.[33] A number of such ensembles existed in the region during this period of communist rule in Poland—many under the patronage of a local industry that would provide the costumes and a focus for the proceedings. Aniela's narrative traces her involvement with several of these ensembles from different towns over the years, for, as her reputation as a singer grew, she was invited to participate in a variety of ensembles, performances, and festivals.

Aniela's remarkable voice first became known to me through an early recording she made with an ensemble from the town of Poronin in the late 1950s (the date is not provided on the recording and Aniela does not remember the precise year). This recording is notable as one of only a few commercial recordings of the music of Podhale available from this period and attests that this repertoire was performed without any musical elaboration and stylization (as opposed to the practices of other ensembles, such as Mazowsze, during this period).[34] Aniela recalled that the recording was made in a hall in Zakopane in a series of continuous takes that lasted most of the night: by the time they had finally finished, everyone was exhausted. Although instrumentalists are listed on the liner notes by name, the singers remain anonymous. On the first side of the record, in a grouping of several songs inserted between bands devoted to the fiddle and string ensemble, Aniela's voice opens the first song, which is one of the most well known of Górale tunes and texts. In it, the singer is able to see (or imagine) the entire world through these most valued—golden—mountains:

> *Góry nase góry*
> *hej pozłociste skały;*
> *Jak sie wos zapatze*
> *hej to widze świat cały.*

> [Mountains our mountains
> Hey, gilded rocks;
> When I look upon you
> Hey, I see the entire world.]

Aniela's exceptional voice subsequently led her to be recognized and sought by a number of ensembles throughout her life, and she has continued to sing (despite a period of serious illness) within the framework of the ensemble or festival for more than fifty years.

Despite her extensive ensemble experience, however, Aniela admitted to me in 1989 that she sings better in natural surroundings among friends than on the stage. Notably, therefore, even with this extended ensemble-performance experience, she continues to associate singing with the outdoors. As she explains, normally when she sings indoors, she has to sing with half a voice (*pół głosem*); only outside can she sing in full voice. The singing should be loud and high; this was the ideal sought. She recalls, for example, times when she and her friends would be making their way to or from a dance and "at such times we would let it rip" (*to sie darło*). Similarly, she remembers going to dances with her cousins, where they would go outside during the breaks explicitly to sing. This was more problematic during a period of the communist era, however, when the government imposed a 10:00 p.m. curfew, forbidding singing (as too loud) after this hour. The will to sing out of doors in conjunction with such dances imposed itself, however, for Aniela reminisces about singing one last time before being silenced by the government curfew: "And so at ten to 10:00 we run outside so we can sing some more." This ruling, she suggested, was more strictly enforced in certain towns than others. They could sing more freely, for example, in the fields beyond the main hall, but not near the road, where they would be given a warning.

Aniela's preference for singing outdoors continues. When I first met Aniela and asked if I could record her singing, she insisted that we go to a particular valley to do so. She subsequently arranged a meeting with her friend Ludwisia, and we headed out to her valley of choice (fig. 6.2). The result was a convivial afternoon of eating, drinking, and singing among the intimacy of the hills, wind, and birds around us. Now living alone in a small apartment in a newer suburb of low-rise apartments in Nowy Targ (a larger town on the northern fringes of Podhale), Aniela seeks every opportunity she can to be outside and also to get together with friends with whom she can still sing. She relates that often on Sundays after Mass, they congregate in a particular valley where there are shepherds' huts (*szałas*) no longer in use. They will light a fire, have something to eat and drink—and sing.

Aniela continues to frame herself, and her voice, within the natural landscape through her recollections. Her voice is never tinged with any sense of regret nor nostalgia when she relates her past experiences of singing to me.[35] As she says, she still has her voice: she can still sing. Singing for her, therefore, has less to do with referencing the past than with maintaining an ongoing sense of a present embedded in a sensory experience of place. Aniela continues to implicate herself in this place that has, in turn, so informed who she is. The nature of this experience can be understood in terms of an acoustemology

Figure 6.2. Aniela (*right*) and Ludwisia (*left*) singing, outside Nowy Targ, Poland, July 1989. Photograph by the author.

where, as Steven Feld has suggested, "the local conditions of acoustic sensation, knowledge, and imagination [are] embodied in the culturally particular sense of place." The sound of Aniela's voice in these places is for her "central to making sense, to knowing, to experiential truth," which is ultimately particularly relevant to her sense of emplacement and making a place for herself.[36]

This story of Aniela also offers a perspective on a musical life that elaborates on the normative. Though born at a time when expectations clearly prescribed marriage or religious ministry as the two main options for a woman, Aniela has avoided both. Music performance (and singing in particular) has allowed her to navigate gendered roles and expectations to create an alternative space for herself within Górale society. Performing at a time when musical opportunities were much more limited for women than for men, Aniela nonetheless established a position for herself through her voice within the ensemble structure of institutionalized traditional music making.[37] This in turn forged her entry and participation in broader social circles as well.

In her modest life today, Aniela conspicuously and creatively maintains her ties with the natural world in which she grew up. With her small apartment overflowing with plants (both inside and on the small balcony in the warm weather), she goes out often and regardless of the weather: even one of the hottest days (of 2006) provided an ideal opportunity for us to go to a mosquito-infested forest to pick tiny wild blueberries. She recounts how often she has been to the river or gathered together with friends on a hillside to visit and to sing. Singing—both in constructed and natural worlds—perpetuates this strong association with the land. As this chapter has argued, by singing into and about the landscape fundamental to her, Aniela's experiences illustrate how women can performatively inscribe, or emplace, themselves within and through their environments to articulate alternative subjectivities and associations. Furthermore, in the midst of modernization, a postsocialist market economy, and globalization—in addition to the personal reality of aging—the landscape created through song remains reliably the same. It is no surprise, therefore, that such a place, now performatively articulated and embodied, continues to provide a compelling frame of reference.

More generally, in focusing on Aniela and engaging with the particularities of the local, this study responds to Ellen Koskoff's call to "put real people and the truth of their musical lives back into the picture."[38] It also supports a theoretical position that draws on the musical subjectivities of individuals as an entry into an inquiry into the active subject to address experience in terms of gendered difference. This chapter has considered the poetic and performative dimensions of localized singing as gendered experiences contextualized within the specifics of place. At a time when the very future of our natural world is in jeopardy, any example of the dynamic relationships of women and men with their landscape—such as provided throughout this volume—can be posited as an argument for the indispensable role of expressive culture in global environmental sustainability.

Notes

1. All translations are my own. I have erred on the side of literal translations, rather than poetic, in an effort to provide a sense of the words and images evoked in these short texts.

2. Sometimes translated as Highlanders (from "góra," hill). I adopt the plural "Górale" as both noun and adjective, singular and plural, masculine and feminine, as a way to apply gender-neutral designations and to avoid the complexities of declensions.

3. I am grateful to the support of the Social Sciences and Humanities Research Council of Canada for support for fieldwork in 2006, which built on earlier research that began in the 1980s.

4. See, for example, Timothy Rice, *May It Fill Your Soul: Experiencing Bulgarian Music* (Chicago: University of Chicago Press, 1994); Virginia Danielson, *The Voice of Egypt: Umm Kulthūm, Arabic Song, and Egyptian Society in the Twentieth Century* (Chicago: University of Chicago Press, 1997); Beverley Diamond, "The Interpretation of Gender Issues in Musical Life Stories of Prince Edward Islanders," in *Music and Gender*, ed. Pirkko Moisala and Beverley Diamond (Urbana: University of Illinois Press, 2000), 99–139; Jonathon P. Stock, "Toward an Ethnomusicology of the Individual, or Biographical Writing in Ethnomusicology," *World of Music* 43, no. 1 (2001): 5–19; and Jeff Todd Titon, ed., *Worlds of Music*, 4th ed. (New York: Schirmer, 2002).

5. Margery Wolf, *A Thrice Told Tale: Feminism, Postmodernism and Ethnographic Responsibility* (Stanford: Stanford University Press, 1992), 118.

6. Finnegan, "Anthropology of Emotion," 188 (italics in the original). See also Ruth Finnegan, "Music, Experience and the Anthropology of Emotion," in *The Cultural Study of Music: A Critical Introduction*, ed. Martin Clayton, Trevor Herbert, and Richard Middleton (New York: Routledge, 2003), 187, 188. For other perspectives see Joan W. Scott, "Experience," in *Feminists Theorize the Political*, ed. Judith Butler and Joan W. Scott (New York: Routledge, 1992), 37, who has been tempted to abandon the word "experience" altogether "given its usage to essentialize identity and reify the subject."

7. See historian Joan W. Scott, who suggests that ultimately "the evidence of experience . . . becomes the fact of difference," though she also maintains that the project of making experience visible is not enough, but must be a way of exploring how difference is established: "It is not individuals who have experience, but subjects who are constituted through experience. Experience in this definition then becomes not the origin of our explanation, not the authoritative (because seen or felt) evidence that grounds what is known, but rather that which we seek to explain." Scott, "Experience," 25, 26.

8. For an exception, see Anna Czekanowska, "Is Music Crucial to a Sense of Identity? Traditional Stereotype vs. the Capacity to Adapt," in *The Individual and Collective in Traditional Culture*, ed. Toimetanud Triinu Ojamaa and Andreas Kalkun (Tartu: Toid Etnomusikoloogia [Alalt 4], 2006), 105–11; also see Timothy J. Cooley, *Making Music in the Polish Tatras: Tourists, Ethnographers, and Mountain Musicians* (Bloomington: Indiana University Press 2005), 49–57.

9. Jane C. Sugarman, *Engendering Song: Singing and Subjectivity at Prespa Albanian Weddings* (Chicago: University of Chicago Press, 1997), 32.

10. Steven Feld and Keith H. Basso, introduction to *Senses of Place*, ed. Steven Feld and Keith H. Basso (Santa Fe, NM: School of American Research Press, 1996), 8.

11. See Cooley, *Making Music*, 30–31.

12. See Władysław Motyka, *Śpiewnik Górali Polskich* (Milówka: Beskidzkie Towarzystwo Oświatow, 2004), 232.

13. Louise Wrazen, "Relocating the Tatras: Place and Music in Górale Identity and Imagination," *Ethnomusicology* 51, no. 2 (2007): 185–204.

14. Although these normative descriptions derive from an ethnographic present that is decidedly in the past, these patterns continue to guide performance practice today— as now found primarily in contexts revolving around the stage.

15. See also Cooley, *Making Music*, 33–37; Timothy J. Cooley, "Folk Festival as Modern Ritual in the Polish Tatra Mountains," *World of Music* 41, no. 3 (1999): 31–55.

16. Górale performance practice historically assigned men to play instruments (as well as sing) and women to sing (only). During my fieldwork in Poland in 1985 and 1989, I never witnessed a woman playing an instrument—neither in public nor in more private performances. Notably, Timothy Cooley begins his book on the music of Podhale with a fieldwork account from 1992 in which a woman plays a prominent role as both singer and instrumentalist. *Making Music*, 49–57. Today numerous women play, both in traditional styles and performance contexts, and in styles and settings influenced by a globalized and commodified music market.

17. Anna Czekanowska, "Women in Contemporary Musical Life: Strengthening or Shattering the Traditional Structure? Artist-Manager-Ritual Person," in *Pathways of Ethnomusicology*, ed. Piotr Dahlig (Warszawa: Institute of Musicology of Warsaw, 2000), 189. In 2006 Czekanowska published an article devoted to Bronisława Konieczna-Dziadoń and her (female) pupil Stanisława Górkiewicz (see "Is Music Crucial").

18. A re-creation of this latter situation can be heard on band 8 of a 1995 recording, where some women's singing begins while the music is still playing for dancing. *Music of the Tatra Mountains: The Trebunia Family Band*, Monmouth, UK, Nimbus NI5137, 1995, compact disc. For a fuller discussion of gender within the context of the góralski dance, see Louise Wrazen, "Men and Women Dancing in the Remembered Past of Podhale Poland," *Anthropology of East Europe Review* 22, no. 1 (2004): 145–54.

19. Jan Sadownik, ed., *Pieśni Podhala: Antologia* (1957; repr., Krakow: Polskie Wydawnictwo Muzyczne, 1971), 5: Refleksyjne (75 texts), Społeczne (47), Żołnierskie (33), Zbójnickie (50), Myśliwskie (17), Pasterskie (114), Junackie (231), Zalotne (200), Miłosne (252), Rodzinne (149), Komiczne (528).

20. Górale man, personal communication, Chicago, May 1986.

21. Górale man, personal communication, Toronto, January 1985.

22. Louise Wrazen, "Privileging Narratives: Singing, the Polish Tatras, and Canada," *Intersections: Canadian Journal of Music* 27, no. 2 (2007): 60–80.

23. For other discussions related to emotion, see, for example, Catherine Lutz, "Emotion, Thought, and Estrangement: Emotion as a Cultural Category," *Cultural Anthropology* 1, no. 3 (1986): 287–309; Catherine Lutz and Geoffrey M. White, "The Anthropology of Emotions," *Annual Review of Anthropology* 15 (1986): 405–36; Judith Becker, "Anthropological Perspectives on Music and Emotion," in *Music and Emotion: Theory and Research*, ed. Patrik N. Juslin and John A. Sloboda (Oxford: Oxford University Press, 2001), 135–60; and Fiona Magowan, *Melodies of Mourning: Music and Emotion in Northern Australia* (Perth: University of Western Australia Press, 2007).

24. Though the sensual acoustic experience is decidedly different in this environment from that described by Steven Feld in Papua New Guinea, it is notable that the

acoustic experience remains so prominent despite the greater possibilities offered by the visual. "Waterfalls of Song: An Acoustemology of Place Resounding in Bosavi, Papua New Guinea," in Feld and Basso, *Senses of Place*, 91–135.

25. As sung for me in Biały Dunajec, June 1985. Compare this version with that given by Sadownik as number 830 (*Pieśni Podhala*, 128).

26. As sung by the ensemble from Poronin on *Polska Muzyka Ludowa* [Polish Folk Music], Podhale 2, Warsaw, Veriton SV-729, n.d., LP, and again by a more recent ensemble from Poronin on *Regle: Hej Poronin, Poronin*, Zakopane, Harnaś-audio 001, 2002, compact disc. Compare with number 784 in Sadownik (*Pieśni Podhala*, 123).

27. For the importance of place, see, for example, Frances Pine, "Incorporation and Exclusion in the Podhale," in *Lilies of the Field: Marginal People Who Live for the Moment*, ed. Sophie Day, Evthymios Papataxiarchis, and Michael Stewart (Boulder: Westview, 1999), 51; and Cooley, *Making Music*, 18. For a discussion of nuances, see Cooley, *Making Music*; Wrazen, "Men and Women Dancing"; and Wrazen, "Privileging Narratives."

28. Frances Pine, "Dealing with Money: Złotys, Dollars and Other Currencies in the Polish Highlands," in *Market and Moralities: Ethnographies of Postsocialism*, ed. Ruth Mandel and Caroline Humphrey (New York: Berg, 2002), 77.

29. Pine, "Incorporation and Exclusion," 55–59.

30. Wrazen, "Men and Women and Dancing."

31. Sadownik (*Pieśni Podhala*) lists the names of all singers (male and female), in relation to both texts and tunes. Where the sources for Kotoński's compilation derive from his own collecting, he provides the names of the individuals; see Włodzimierz Kotoński, *Piosenki z Podhala* (Kraków: Polskie Wydawnictwo Muzyczne, 1955). On the other hand, Stanisław Mierczyński, in *Pieśni Podhala na 2 i 3 równe głosy* (Warszawa: Wydawnictwo Związku Nauczycielstwa Polskiego, 1935); and Aleksandra Szurmiak-Bogucka, in *Górole, górole, góralsko muzyka: Śpiewki Podhala* (Kraków: Polskie Wydawnictwo Muzyczne, 1959) do not include this information.

32. For ensemble practices in Bulgaria during this period, see Donna Buchanan, *Performing Democracy* (Chicago: University of Chicago Press, 2006).

33. However, contrary to expectation, marriage did not necessarily prevent women from traveling with an ensemble. See Pine ("Incorporation and Exclusion") for a possible explanation.

34. Mazowsze was formed in 1948 under a decree by the Culture and Art Ministry and was initially led by composer Tadeusz Sygietynski and his wife Mira Zimińska-Sygietynski. Their repertoire focusing on the area of central Poland soon expanded to include virtually all regions of the country.

35. For consideration of nostalgia in Górale performance, see Cooley, *Making Music*, 222–26; and Louise Wrazen, "Diasporic Experiences: Mediating Time, Memory and Identity in Górale Performance," *Canadian Journal for Traditional Music* 32 (2005): 43–51.

36. Feld, "Waterfalls of Song," 91, 97.

37. For example, one of Aniela's photos of an ensemble trip pictures four women and eleven men.

38. Ellen Koskoff, "(Left Out in) Left (the Field): The Effects of Post-postmodern Scholarship on Feminist and Gender Studies in Musicology and Ethnomusicology, 1990–2000," *Women and Music* 9 (2005): 98.

Part Three
Nationalism and Indigeneity

Chapter Seven

Singing the Contentions of Place

Korean Singers of the Heart and Soul of Japan

Christine R. Yano

Performing emotions holds a particular niche in the field of intimate cultural production. Inasmuch as emotions occupy both private encounters and public disclosure, their performance on the commercial stage mixes these encounters and disclosures within processes of imaging and commodification. Performing emotions in particular ways can be a form of branding—and thus selling—a singer or a genre in East Asia, as elsewhere. Whole swaths of song may be noted for their sentimentality; within particular popular music genres in East Asia individual singers may be noted for their tears. Linking tears to women follows gendered expectations in East Asia of sentimentality and excess. Performing hyperemotions then takes on added meaning when the singer is a foreign woman. These conditions add issues of race, nation, and place to the already gendered performing stage.

In this chapter I examine performing emotions as part of branding the career and fandom in Japan of Korean female singer Kim Yonja. Kim sings a variety of songs, but specializes in *enka*, a sentimental genre appealing primarily to older audiences and known in Japan as expressive of the heart and soul of the nation. To understand the ironies embedded within the context of a Korean female singer performing enka more fully, one needs to further unpack the iconicity of this type of song. Enka comprises a genre of popular ballad known as *naki-bushi* (crying song), evoking tears through tropes of longing: departed lovers, rural hometowns, and memories of mothers. These textual elements combine with musical features that sound continually old: most notably, *yonanuki* ("without the fourth and seventh degrees of the scale"; pentatonic) scales, heard in folk songs and premodern popular tunes, and stylized vocal production with characteristically wide vibrato and *kobushi* (vocal ornamentation). This notion of music that "sounds old" adheres in spite of the incorporation of many elements that are new, particularly Western instrumentation (including electric guitar). What matters more in the placement of enka within the Japanese popular music pantheon is not parsing out what is new and what is old. Rather, what matters is the symbolic, nativized position of enka as the "song of Japan" and "the sound of tradition" that binds song, place, and emotion in overdetermined, multilayered ways.[1]

In drop-the-needle fashion, a listener in Japan need hear but the opening measures of an enka song to recognize it as the iconically linked sounds of bars, broken hearts, and the underside of Japan. This is Japan characterized through song as a nation of tears and longing. The genre lays claim as the "national song"—the industrially produced, nostalgized emblem of "Japan"— even though its active buying listenership is but a minute fraction of the market (e.g., just over 1 percent in 1998). Instead of high record sales, enka sustains itself symbolically and economically through replayings and repackagings, as well as through the media boost of Nihon Housou Kyokai (NHK; Japan National Broadcasting Corporation). In effect, enka maintains its reputation and status through constant cover versions of itself. The actual and symbolic sense of enka covering itself produces the genre's widespread sound of familiarity throughout the Japanese population. Even the many who profess not to like the music often know it and recognize it as "music overheard"—that is, songs that can be heard ubiquitously in public and private settings, even while not actively engaging listeners.[2] Enka may thus be characterized as sonic background to particular aspects of daily life in Japan.

Although most singers who perform enka in Japan are indeed Japanese, a small but significant number are not. In parallel with entertainment stages elsewhere, the commercial Japanese enka stage includes several minorities: Koreans, Taiwanese, *burakumin* (former outcastes), Japanese Brazilians, Japanese Americans, and even an African American.[3] Kim is thus not the only non-Japanese to populate the enka stage. However, in contrast to other Korean singers of enka who grew up in Japan as ethnic minority *zainichi Kankokujin* (living-in-Japan Koreans) and have hidden their ancestry due to long-standing discrimination, Kim arrived on the scene from Korea in 1988 specifically as a *Korean* singer.[4]

The fact that this particular genre may be sung successfully by Kim and other non-Japanese singers in Japan raises critical issues of the ironies of performance, emotion, and identity in a heterogeneous setting. This chapter asks what happens when the heart and soul of Japan is sung by a non-Japanese— that is, when a familiar national song is performed by unfamiliar nonnationals. How does Kim's performance refract the link between song, place, and emotion? And how does gender figure in this potentially disruptive, transnational moment? I base the bulk of my analysis on observations and interviews with Kim during my major period of fieldwork in Tokyo from 1991 to 1993, with subsequent updates through archival research. Ten years after 1993, the situation for Korean performers in Japan such as Kim changed dramatically with what has been dubbed the "Korean Wave"—that is, the intense popularity of

Korean television dramas in Japan and elsewhere in East Asia beginning in 2003. The Korean Wave brought young, attractive Korean nationals into the intimate televisual spaces of Japanese living rooms, providing a differently refracted spin on the foreignness of Korean things (and people) in Japan. I include commentary on Kim vis-à-vis the Korean Wave in the final section of this chapter as a postscript.

Framing Kim's Enka Stage

Kim's career trajectory in Japan has not been a smooth one. Although she had early success in Korea as a pop singer, she looked to Japan as the staging ground for a bigger, more lucrative career. Japan was well recognized as the primary source of fame and money in the popular music world of East Asia. Thus, Kim first attempted to break into the Japanese market in 1979. In spite of notable performances at the prestigious NHK Hall in Tokyo in 1983 and 1984, this first attempt at a Japanese career floundered. It was not until her energetic show-stopping performance of the theme song at the Olympics in Seoul in 1988, which I discuss later that she found success in Japan in a redebut. Her Olympics performance brought her the kind of limelight that she needed to break into the Japanese music world. Although the Olympics theme song was not enka, it provided sufficient impetus and prestige to dub Kim a noteworthy singer. The fact that she subsequently chose enka to build a Japanese career highlights what I call the many contentions of Kim's stage.

Several ironies frame this enka stage. The first of these situates her performances within a history of rancorous colonial relations between Korea and Japan. Beginning with Japan's annexation of Korea in 1910, its ill treatment of Koreans and exploitation of resources has left long and bitter animosity between the two countries. In colonial Korea the systematic attempt by the Japanese government to quash Korean language and culture included compulsory worship at Japanese Shinto shrines, elimination of Korean language and history in the education system, prohibition against publishing Korean-language newspapers, and the required adoption of Japanese names. These practices were instituted under the rubric of assimilation, with the aim of transforming Koreans into Japanese colonial subjects. During World War II the establishment of prostitution centers to service the Japanese military included the enslavement of Korean women—euphemistically labeled "comfort women."[5]

The ill treatment of Koreans extended overseas, as those brought to Japan as national subjects from 1910 to 1945 suffered severe discrimination. These zainichi Kankokujin constitute the largest foreign minority population in Japan. The 2005 statistics list 515,570 with permanent resident status and 284,840 naturalized Japanese citizens, a status available to those who legally adopt Japanese names.[6] However, the earlier denial of Japanese citizenship rights and continued discrimination in the workplace and at schools result in many Koreans choosing to live their lives "passing" as Japanese. Having grown up in Japan for generations, completely fluent in the language and knowledgeable of everyday life, these hidden Koreans take Japanese names and otherwise blend into Japanese society. In some instances parents have even hidden their Korean ancestry from their own children: one of the best known of these cases involves Miyako Harumi, a well-known enka singer who only found out her Korean background midcareer, as an adult. The extent to which these hidden Koreans choose to pass rather than face the public repercussions of their Korean ancestry in a Japanese society that celebrates its own constructed sense of homogeneity frames Kim's enka stage.

The conditions of Kim's song and performance in Japan embed her fully within these highly politicized issues of ethnic minority relations and ongoing international debates with Asian neighbors. These issues swirl around the emotionality of Kim's performance, provoking reactions of admiration and disdain amid the contentions of place. Kim confronts the issues head on, transcending genre by presenting herself not so much as an enka singer but as a more generalized "song stylist." She does so amid trademark tears, branding her own Korean self as gendered, racialized, and minoritized. Although tears are a familiar part of the enka stage, Kim's tears become branded as hers through their very copiousness, mixed with an intensity of performance style. Kim's tears heighten the emotional range of her stage because they seem to spill over the bounds of well-rehearsed pattern. This lends a vulnerability to her performance by which emotion, gender, and place intersect with the politics and poetics of Kim's tears.

As with minority populations elsewhere, a significant number of zainichi Koreans perform in the entertainment world, including enka. Thus in performances Kim appears as an "overt Korean," singing alongside other putative "covert Koreans," whose Japanese names, language, and song continue to shroud their identities in rumor. (Miyako Harumi, as a newly overt Korean, mentors Kim and even, at one point in her career when she temporarily retired, "handed over" her fans to Kim.)

The ironies also include the disputed history of enka itself, whose overlap with Korean popular song leaves its origins in question. Whereas Japanese scholars and public tie enka to other long-standing traditions of naki-bushi and other narrative laments, Korean adherents link enka to *pongchak*, a popular Korean ballad form that likewise focuses on sad melodies and lyrics. The link becomes all the more complicated with the period of Japanese colonization, during which now-famed Japanese enka composer Koga Masao (1904–78) lived in Korea as a young adult. Koga's place as a founding father of postwar enka raises the question of just which elements of his signature sound, known as *Koga merodii* (Koga melody)—guitar or mandolin tremolo, slow tempo, minor scale, dark mood—may have been influenced by his tenure in Korea and exposure to Korean folk songs, instruments, and popular melodies.[7]

Kim's performing stage must also be seen within the building rapprochement between Korea and Japan, achieved through international events from the late 1980s on, often focusing on sports. Scholars and media pundits point to the 1988 Seoul Olympics as a turning point in the image of Korea in Japan. Mori Yoshitaka explains, "It [Seoul Olympics] created a new representation of Korea, a more developed and urbanized one than was previously supposed in Japan." Notably, Kim Yonja played a significant role in this event, performing the official theme song, "Achim e nara eso" (later translated into Japanese as "Asa no Kuni kara," or From the morning country), which has since become a staple of her Japanese performing stage. Fourteen years later, the 2002 FIFA World Cup cohosted by Japan and Korea provided another turning point in relations between the two countries. Mori points out, "Although both countries had initially reluctantly accepted cohosting, it eventually resulted in creating unexpected mutual cheering for each national team and created a friendly atmosphere, particularly among young people."[8] Again, Kim was part of the event, releasing the single "Ai, Arigato" (Thank you for your love) as a song of support for the FIFA World Cup. Although bonding over sporting events may seem trivial within the realm of international politics, these two events paved the way for other forms of mutual cooperation, from government-sponsored events to coproductions of television dramas and other cultural exchanges.[9]

In the meantime, beginning in 1998 the Korean government incrementally lifted its decades-old ban on the importation of Japanese popular cultural products. Whereas the Korean government had banned these products from Japan (including the performance of any song in Japanese) since the end of the colonial period in 1945, the late 1990s witnessed the legal importation and performance of first children's songs, folk songs, and older melodies from Japan, then gradually other popular culture products from Japan. In a delicately crafted move, the Japanese embassy in Korea sponsored Japan Week in October 1998, during which Japanese popular singer Tomoe Sawa performed two Japanese songs preapproved by the Korean government. The choice of singer and songs demonstrates the cautious calculus of politics and performance for the event. Sawa herself is Japanese Korean from an elite family; the two songs she performed in Japanese were "Furusato" (Hometown), a children's song; and "Kokoro" (Heart), a musical rendition of a famous Korean poem written by Sawa's grandfather.[10]

Although this event represented the Korean government's first cautious forays into cultural rapprochement, and acceptance of Japanese cultural products has become widespread since then, the process of opening the gateways remains in recent memory. Tiptoeing through governmental regulations marks the contentions of Japan in Korea and thus the backdrop for Korea in Japan. In this arena, too, Kim has played an important role. Her concert in

Korea in 1999 marked a historic milestone as the first large-scale performance of Japanese popular songs following the lifting of the ban. That this breakthrough performance featured Kim as a Korean singer now popular in Japan, singing Japanese songs, demonstrates the carefully crafted steps of this pop cultural rapprochement. Kim's performance on the Japanese enka stage must be contextualized amid these newly forged flows and her central role within the maelstrom.

Kim's Translational Position: "More Japanese Than Japanese"

These contentious, often ironic, conditions shape Kim's career in ways that incorporate and extend the frame. Shu-mei Shih's discussion of multiple iterations of sinophone articulations is useful here. She writes, "The important point here is that the copy is never the original, but a form of translation. It may desire to be the original, or to compete with the original, but this desire always already predetermines its distance from the original as a separate, translated entity." On the enka stage Kim is this translated entity—inherently distanced, separate, othered—yet connected through song within the ironies and contentions of postcolonial relations. Translation itself raises critical issues: "Translation is not an act of one-to-one equivalence, but an event that happens among multiple agents, among multiple local and hegemonic cultures, registering an uncertainty and a complexity that require historically specific decodings."[11] The ironies and contentions of the enka stage form the backdrop of Kim as translation.

How do we decode Kim? I argue that she is Korea in Japan on Japanese terms, reproducing the colonial subject at one moment, manipulating the postcolonial position in another moment. Onstage she performs her Koreanness in various ways. Although enka is her mainstay, she includes Korean songs, sometimes in Korean dress, and references her Korean identity in her patter between numbers. Her usual costume onstage is an evening gown. However, in one portion of a 1993 concert I attended, Kim appeared onstage in kimono for the first time. When she first appeared thus dressed, the audience gasped slightly. Instead of downplaying the moment, she highlighted it as a noteworthy event, announcing this as a "kimono debut." The audience responded with warmhearted applause. Drawing out the moment further, Kim jokingly expressed her discomfort at wearing the constricting garment. She said she felt confined and trapped, hoping aloud that she would not trip in the floor-length, narrow robe. Standing stiffly, taking mincing steps, and otherwise looking extremely uncomfortable, she performed her anxiety broadly. In effect, she was debuting as an amateur Japanese. The audience giggled along with her, sharing her discomfort, enjoying the virginal moment. After her number, she looked around nervously and joked, "Can I really step forward in this?" In kimono, Kim thus becomes the translation—that is, the colonial subject, nervous and bound. But she is not gagged. Instead, she makes light of the postcolonial position, mocking her own discomfiture. In doing so, she makes light of the audience's own parallel discomfort—with kimono, with tradition, with the pressures of performance in everyday life, and with the constructed sense of "Japan." Their laughter acknowledges the complexities of a shared position.

That shared position is complex indeed. Kim's audience includes many zainichi Kankokujin, as well as Japanese. For the zainichi in the audience, Kim provides a platform to perform their own Koreanness. Thus, at a performance in 1993 zainichi members of the audience seated in the front row carried small Korean flags and waved them.[12] Theater goers who purchased a Kim CD were given a fan printed with the Korean flag. Kim has organized tours to Korea for her fans and has increasingly taken a politicized position as their spokesperson. At the same time, her Japanese audience consumes Kim as a Korean, not necessarily connecting her with the more problematic zainichi population in Japan. In mainstream enka fan magazine articles on Kim from 1999 to 2001, Kim is linked to Korea, but never to the Koreans long resident in Japan. Likewise, the fan magazines never mention the mixing in her audience. The mainstream enka world thus disentangles Kim's name from the whole minority issue of zainichi, even as she draws them to her concerts. In fact, Kim is not zainichi. But she is married to one; however, even that marriage is not part of many mainstream articles. Like much of the zainichi world, the marriage is public but not well publicized, occupying a parallel, shadow world. In many ways, Kim is and she isn't. It is exactly in these kinds of ambiguities that Kim so publicly straddles the national fence.

Language becomes an important and continuing site of that straddle, from pronunciation to vocabulary to general fluency. Early reviews of her performance scrutinized her pronunciation of Japanese. In 1992 one writer acknowledged, "It is easy enough to understand her, because she takes care in her pronunciation of Japanese lyrics with which she is not yet familiar."[13] The first test, then, for Japanese listeners is her understandability. They ask, "Does she sound like us?" and, more important, "*Can* she sound like us?" The first question focuses on the quality of her mimicry; the second question focuses on her effort and ability as translation. Both questions circumscribe her desirability. Industry watchdogs and listeners alike make Japanese language and its pronunciation the litmus test of acceptability. The irony of this public scrutiny lies in the many regional dialects within Japan amid the hegemony of *hyoujungo* (standard, official Tokyo-based speech) and the performance of many Japanese enka singers authenticating themselves as "rural folk" and the "voice of the people" specifically by way of their nonstandard dialect. In other words, Kim is placed under the kind of linguistic scrutiny to which other Japanese singers are not subject. Her variances from hyoujungo pronunciation become mistakes, whereas others are fully acceptable and even lauded as evidence of their Indigenous authenticity.

Language as a site of difference extends to vocabulary and general fluency as well. In the 1993 concert I attended, Kim joked about her early mistakes with Japanese language. She sheepishly admitted that she mistook the word *oshinko* (Japanese pickles) for *oshikko* (urine) in conversation—the kind of mistake that has become standard fodder of foreigner jokes in Japan. In this case, however, it is a self-deprecatory joke made by a foreigner to an older mixed audience of men and women, Japanese and zainichi, specifically about her own foreignness. The laughter comes at the foreigner's expense, but skillfully wrought to her own purposes. She is more than the colonial buffoon here. Rather, she manipulates her position, wringing empathy from the resident audience that can only enhance her career in Japan. In a televised interview in 1992, she slowed down at points in her speech, as if thinking through the more complicated Japanese language verb forms. By playing up her linguistic neediness as a foreign Korean, she elevates the audience's expertise as residents, whether Japanese or ethnic Koreans, and diminishes her own competence. She thus complies with both gendered and foreigner expectations of her mixed audience. For Japanese nationals she can be the helpless foreign Korean woman; for zainichi she can be the newcomer Korean, not yet fully assimilated linguistically or culturally, who needs their help. In another live performance I attended in 1993 at a midsize venue, the audience called out corrections to some of her linguistic mistakes, to which she responded with an embarrassed smile. These stumbling blocks of assimilation may be the highest form of compliment, but only when they stop well short of successful completion. In other words, Kim is always and ever the translation and never the exact copy. Even when her Japanese linguistic difficulties get smoothed out, she must find ways to continue performing herself as a foreign Korean.

The announcer to the 1993 concert introduced Kim by saying, "She is more Japanese than Japanese." This is an enunciative position attributed to adept foreigners not infrequently in Japan that bears analysis. The statement suggests both a codified state of "Japaneseness" as well as the recognition that there are varying degrees and ways of "being Japanese." In a kind of doublespeak, Japaneseness can be both ascribed (one born to the position, based in blood-based ideology) and achieved (accrued, learned, gained, or lost). Elements to this achieved Japaneseness include such external elements as language, music, food, and customs, such as bowing. However, more to the point are those internal elements, such as values exhibited through the externalized practices of manners, interpersonal relations, family interaction, and general demeanor. In a double move, calling someone "more Japanese than Japanese" first externalizes them to the ascribed position (i.e., makes them outsiders) and then internalizes them to the achieved state (i.e., makes them insiders of a sort). It is the specificities of the achieved insider state that is at issue. Within this achieved state, the phrase may be more explicitly reworked as "more like *past* Japanese than *present-day* Japanese," thus invoking both nostalgia for values and practices labeled "traditional," as well as a sense of loss in the contemporary world. The nostalgia is not only temporalized but also spatialized as the physical peripheries of Japan, putatively located at the margins of society.[14] These physical margins include rural areas of Japan, as well as more far-flung, older, diasporic settlements of Japanese migrants (e.g., Hawaii, Brazil) and selected former colonies of the Japanese empire (e.g., Micronesia). Indeed, calling Kim "more Japanese than Japanese" references her outsider status, overcome by the sincerity of her efforts to fit into the Japanese music world. But the statement also finds potential historical justification within the Japanese colony of Korea, in spite of the conflicts therein. In other words, even by her Korean nationality, she may be grasped as within reach of a colonial birthright to Japaneseness. She may not have grown up speaking Japanese, but her parents or grandparents may well have done so as subjects of Japanese rule. Performing enka, the song of Japan, as the child of colonial subjects of Japan clarifies Kim's position of translation.

The nostalgic position of performing as "more Japanese than Japanese" is gendered as well. One fan article states, "Kim Yonja epitomizes the shyness and modesty of Japanese women in the past."[15] As a nostalgized figure, she serves as a critique of contemporary Japanese women, who, by this argument, have forgotten the "shyness and modesty" of their past. Kim becomes the nostalgized Asian symbol vis-à-vis Japan. Her shyness and modesty is physicalized in her actions. Not only does she sing enka, the song of past women, she even dons kimono—occasionally, as a publicly marked moment—embracing the sartorial display of Japan's past. Whereas most Japanese enka singers appear onstage in kimono as a gendered emblem of Japanese tradition, few foreign female singers do.[16] Kim borrows the reference, trading on her ability to don Japaneseness as a poached idiom. That she does so with self-deprecating humor is part of her gendered star text of shyness and modesty that constitutes part of her appeal.

Performing Emotion as a Korean Woman

When Kim performs in Japan, she becomes racialized and gendered, not only in terms of language, dress, and comportment, but more specifically and importantly in terms of emotion. In fact, Japanese journalists focus on two intertwined aspects of performance when describing Kim: her voice and her emotional expressivity. One describes her as "a songstress . . . whose voice crosses national borders and oceans with its emotion."[17] Another gushes, "She sings with a voice from the depths of her heart and transmits a white-hot heat to us all."[18] Fans describe Kim's performances as "boiling over with true emotion" (*jikkan waku*), and one commented, "I think that people who have seen Kim Yonja onstage even once . . . cannot help but be overwhelmed by her intensity!"[19] It is exactly the "white-hot heat," "boiling over" with "intensity," that is Kim's trademark. In her hands emotion overflows as a barely contained force, a site of danger, and, importantly for our discussion, difference. Whereas certain emotional elements may be universal, on Kim's enka stage, they are culturalized, even racialized, as tied to fundamentals of place and person.

Stereotypically, fans and critics interpret Kim and other Korean singers as expressing emotion differently from Japanese, even while performing Japanese idioms of song. Korean expression of emotion, they say, is more heated, more intense; Korean tears fall uncontrollably. These characterizations exist primarily by contrast with Japan, whose tears reputedly fall not dangerously out of control, but as art. The difference can be interpreted both negatively and positively—that is, Korean emotional expression can be seen as maudlin melodrama or as natural, raw power. One journalist uses Kim and other Korean singers to critique Japanese performers, arguing, "Fans feel these ladies [Korean singers, including Kim] bring a more emotional rendition than their Japanese counterparts, who are at times more concerned with singing in the technical prescribed way with kobushi [vocal ornamentation] vibratto [*sic*]."[20]

As an example of Kim's "white-hot heat" in performance, let me describe one scene from a televised stage broadcast by NHK. The program billed itself as "The Japan-Korea Big Star Tottori [place-name] Concert," a bridge between Korea and Japan through popular song. The roster of Korean and Japanese singing stars included rumored, still "passing," zainichi as well as the true bridge, Kim Yonja. Kim performed solo and in duet, wearing glittery evening gowns, as was standard for this concert. But for the climax of her performance, a highly charged Korean enka-type song "Danchou no Miari Kouge" (Japanese title; Heartbreak of [Place-name]), she emerged resplendent in a billowy, bright pink Korean costume. She sang the first verse in Korean, the second in Japanese, and at the end, with a flourish of trumpets, she dropped dramatically to the ground as if overcome with emotion, fists punching the air for emphasis, tears flowing. And she remained there, head bowed, motionless save for occasional heaving sobs, throughout the audience's wild applause. The moment was electric.

This is not the first time that I had seen Kim cry onstage. In fact, I watched several times as she cried before, during, and after performances. Indeed, she was the only enka singer I have seen who has forgotten the lyrics to a song onstage, seemingly lost in the emotion of the moment. At one live radio broadcast I attended, she paused briefly midsong while the orchestra kept playing; a member of the audience hurriedly called out the lyrics to her, rescuing her from the moment. Critics decry this as unpolished and unprofessional. But her fans take this less as evidence of her failure and more as a virtue. That is, Kim is a performer in the moment, of the moment. To her fans' delight, she sometimes lets herself be overwhelmed by emotion in ways that other (Japanese) performers do not. However, being a performer in the moment may mean that if the moment overwhelms her, she needs her fans' assistance. They are more than willing to do so, creating what may in Japanese terms be considered a relationship built on dependency, here amplified by gendered and racialized assumptions.[21] What fans relish is the fact that Kim is an on-the-edge-of-your-seat performer, verging on the unpredictable in both her vulnerability and her brilliance. Danger, they say, becomes her, if that danger derives from the emotion of the performance. It is exactly the electricity of her tears, including the dangers therein, that draws fans to her and gets them to their feet, cheering her exquisite display of emotional abandon.

As might be expected, Kim garners her fair share of critique as well. When I showed a video clip of her Tottori performance to Japanese and Koreans, I got varying responses. One Japanese woman in her sixties commented, "She sings with too much passion! She's overdoing it. But that's because she's not really Japanese." A zainichi Korean woman in her thirties, likewise, agreed that Kim's performance was exaggerated, but her critique was slightly different: she faulted Kim for playing directly into the stereotype of Koreans as overly emotional. A Japanese enka composer commented that a singer such as Kim may have a powerful voice, but she does not possess the finesse and cultural knowledge to truly sing enka. According to him, true enka should be sung with characteristic kobushi and vibrato—both elements that Kim tends to ignore in favor of a less ornamented, more straightforward style. All three of these critics see in Kim a highly accomplished but specifically and always *Korean* display.

Kim becomes an exoticized and controversial site of gendered performance, her tears racialized by their copiousness. In singing within and between the contentious spaces of Korea and Japan, Kim has built a career on the idiosyncrasies of emotional expression understood through these highly racialized and gendered frames. She thus performs herself as a brand of emotion, gender, and race in a marketplace that trades on tears.

Kim Yonja's Star Text in the Context of the "Korean Wave" in Japan

A final word must be said about Kim given the context of her performance, newly reconfigured after my initial fieldwork of 1991–93. What has been called the "Korean Wave" (also known as Hallyu in Korean, Hanryuu in Japanese) hit Japan and other Asian countries with force in 2003, sparked by the extreme popularity of a Korean television drama, *Winter Sonata*. Originally a 2002 production of Korean Broadcasting Services (KBS), *Winter Sonata* told the melodramatic tale of lost teenage love regained in late adulthood. When NHK chose to broadcast the miniseries in 2003 (and subsequently three more times through 2004), it never anticipated the tremendous response, in particular from middle-aged housewives. One of the main attractions of the drama for its female fans was male star Bae Yung Jun (known affectionately as "Yon-sama"), whom women saw as a romantic alternative to Japanese men primarily because he is willing to express his feelings openly. Importantly, the drama generated Japanese public interest in things Korean, from language to food to culture to travel. As Mori Yoshitaka argues, *Winter Sonata* "played a crucial role in reconsidering the cultural relationship between Korea and Japan.... The mega hit ... changed a stereotypical image of Korean people and culture in Japan in an unprecedented way."[22] This change in attitude went well beyond the rapprochement effected by the Seoul Olympics of 1998 or FIFA cohosted games in 2002. Korea was not merely regarded in a more positive light; the country achieved cultlike status as the object of fans' desires.

However, this did not necessarily affect in situ stars, such as Kim Yonja, nor attitudes toward zainichi Kankokujin. For one, the Korean Wave was generated by and situated quite specifically in television dramas. Although it extended to other aspects of everyday consumption, such as food and travel, it did not include popular music.[23] This can be understood in terms of the central constituency for consumption of the Korean Wave—that is, middle-aged women. This age bracket is not usually the one listening to or purchasing more youth-oriented music, such as "K-Pop" (shorthand for Korean pop music).

Second, the Korean Wave traveled explicitly from Korea, not from the zainichi Korean community. Therefore, the feverish public interest in things Korean tended to disregard or denigrate those things Korean found within Japan's own shores, which had been there for generations. The distant, nostalgized novelty of *Winter Sonata* and its romantic lead drew fans who found little attraction to the much-maligned zainichi Korean minority living just next door. As Iwabuchi Koichi explains, "The impact of the Korean Wave still tends to be constrained by the dominant attention paid to inter-national relationships [Japan-Korea ties], which overpowers the concern with resident Koreans."[24] Thus, the Japanese government used the Korean Wave to initiate cultural exchange to improve relations with Korea, while ignoring discrimination against zainichi in areas of education and employment in Japan. According to Iwabuchi, the backhanded effect of the Korean Wave on zainichi is not merely that the phenomenon ignored them, but that it may have actively subverted further discussion of the structural complexities of their situation in Japan: "The positive image of South Korea that the Korean Wave promotes eventually works to newly marginalize and suppress postcolonial complexity and nuisances embodied in the historical subjectivity called 'resident Koreans.'" According to Iwabuchi, what results is "a postcolonialism without history."[25]

Post-Wave Kim: Performing Emotions, Gendering Places

The Korean Wave has been on the wane since 2005. Kim's performances—before, during, and after the wave—have been relatively unaffected by the vagaries of the fad. Although Koreanness may have become less culturally distant in many Japanese consumers' minds as a result of the wave, the "cultural odor" of difference remains.[26] It is a stubborn presence that links Koreans to high emotion, floods of tears, and the dangers therein. Kim resides amid that presence, tying her continually to Korea. In a sense, she must always perform her Koreanness, even as she deliberately builds her career by performing in Japan. Her translational performance of the heart and soul of Japan works best only through continual assertions of difference. Thus, she retains traces of her Korean accent, espouses her fondness for Korean comfort food, and sometimes dons Korean dress. Her official website is one shared by her zainichi husband and includes links to zainichi sites and news.[27] She is always and ever a Korean in Japan.

At the same time, she becomes a tribute to Japan: wearing kimono for the first time, learning Japanese, singing the song of Japan. She enacts colonial practices of assimilation on the Japanese stage. And she does so to the purpose of a more lucrative career than she could have ever had in Korea. According to Kim, her ultimate goal is to transcend both Korea and Japan and develop an international career. She sees Japan, then, as a critical stepping stone to the world. These aspirations reflect as much Japan's supremacy within Asia at the time of Kim's redebut in 1988, as well as its many multinational corporate ties to other parts of the world.

Inasmuch as this collection of essays focuses on attachments to place and to environments as generative of emotional expression, Kim Yonja provides an opportunity to extend these nascent ideas in provocative ways. Here, the place—Japan—is a geopolitical space rather than a natural environment, seen through the eyes, ears, and desires of a former colonial subject. In fact, Kim brings a postcolonial presence within her. Thus she can taste her new home of Japan as an old presence within her birthplace of Korea. The national-cultural "odor" of Korea both clings to her and responds to her manipulations.[28] Even as she retains the odor of Korea, she takes on a new charge, reaching out to zainichi, those remnants of the colonial period who missed repatriation. Emboldened by the Seoul Olympics, FIFA, and finally by the overwhelming phenomenon of the Korean Wave, Kim connects herself more and more publicly to zainichi. Indeed, they are a strong part of her fan base. They, too, form part of the "environment for Kim, whose sensory and social awareness of this backdrop strongly shape her emotional expression. Undeniably, she plays to them, even when it appears that she plays only to herself, so when she falls to her knees in tears or falters midsong groping for the word that got lost in the emotional shuffle, she affirms their place on her stage. They help her to her feet, supplying her with missing words.

Singing with high emotion is not all that Kim does. Like other entertainers, she involves herself with charity projects in Korea and Japan. Among the notable charity concerts she headlined in Japan were those for the victims of the Unzen volcanic eruption on Kyushu in 1993 that killed forty-three people and destroyed more than two thousand homes, and another for victims of the Hanshin earthquake in 1995 that killed more than six thousand people. These kinds of events tie her to Japan all the more as a model citizen and more specifically as a model daughter, her "shyness and modesty" intact.

I return to the question I posed at the beginning of this chapter: what happens when the heart and soul of Japan is sung by a non-Japanese? As audiences age, markets shrink, and globalization opens up new possibilities for recruitment into the enka roster of singers, it is a question that is being asked with increasing frequency. Under governmental espousal of multiculturalism, this kind of question is supposed to be moot. As an examination of Kim Yonja's enka stage tells us, however, the question is far from moot. Kim's case study demonstrates ways in which the divides and bridges between nations and cultures breed success. The divides of language and emotional expression ensure that Kim will always be a Korean, even when characterized as "more Japanese than Japanese." However, the bridges of gender, nostalgia, and "Asia" make the performance tenable. Kim's success rests in the ways she negotiates her colonial practices as postcolonial tribute. Singing about Japan as place is part and parcel of enka as a genre. For a Korean to do so does not extend Japan so much as reorganize place as an emotional space, denationalized and renaturalized. Kim transcends the disruptions of this transnational moment by her own expressive power, fists punching the air in defense of speechlessness.

Notes

1. For further discussion, see Christine Yano, *Tears of Longing: Nostalgia and the Nation in Japanese Popular Song* (Cambridge: Harvard Asia Center, Harvard University Press, 2002).

2. Ibid., 6, 7.

3. Notably, the most recent is Jero (née Jerome White Jr.), a twenty-six-year-old hip-hop-imaged African American male of part-Japanese ancestry from Pittsburgh, who debuted in 2008.

4. Kim is not the only overt Korean enka singer on the Japanese stage. Others include male singer Cho Yonpiru (debuted in 1982) and female singer Kye Unsook (debuted in 1985). I focus here, however, on Kim as the most successful of these three.

5. The military procured approximately two hundred thousand women as prostitutes from Japan and its colonies, including Korea, China, Philippines, and the Dutch East Indies. Of these, Korean "comfort women" have become emblematic of the wartime practice, in part because of their numbers, in part because of the media spectacle that has surrounded their plight.

6. Statistics found at: http://www.korea.net/korea/attach/D/03/123_en.pdf, accessed November 8, 2007. No longer available.

7. For teaching purposes the following YouTube resources may be useful for Kim Yonja performances: "Kawa no Nagare no You ni" (song originally made famous by Misora Hibari as her swan song), posted on YouTube by "KoreanNight2006," October 17, 2006,

http://www.youtube.com/watch?v=MxfQ3zigAvA&feature=autoplay&list=AVTGnpyrBl25zNZHdGieWlYAomffhTQ01G&lf=list_related&playnext=2; and "Midaregami" (song originally made famous by Misora Hibari), posted on YouTube by "KoreanNight2006," September 7, 2009, http://www.youtube.com/watch?v=Met7MFRcNQg&feature=bf_next&list=AVTGnpyrBl25zNZHdGieWlYAomffhTQ01G&lf=list_related.

8. Mori Yoshitaka, "*Winter Sonata* and Cultural Practices of Active Fans in Japan: Considering Middle-Aged Women as Cultural Agents," in *East Asian Pop Culture: Analysing the Korean Wave*, ed. Chua Beng Huat and Iwabuchi Koichi (Hong Kong: Hong Kong University Press, 2008), 129.

9. Iwabuchi Koichi, "When the Korean Wave Meets Resident Koreans in Japan: Intersections of the Transnational, the Postcolonial and the Multicultural," in Chua and Iwabuchi, *East Asian Pop Culture*, 251.

10. Note that *furusato* and *kokoro* (hometown and heart, respectively) are two of the most highly cited tropes of conservative values in Japanese popular culture. Representing old-fashioned virtues of family, countryside, and spirit, they can be seen as safe, apolitical topics of "universal" appeal, even if they may also be used as expressions of cultural nationalism. Yano, *Tears of Longing*, 17–21. Although Sawa was allowed to sing these songs, the government denied her request to perform an English version of the popular 1960s Japanese hit "Ue wo Muite Aruko" ("Walking while looking up"; known in the United States as "Sukiyaki," an iconic Japanese food dish). Japan Echo, "Breaking the Ice: South Korea Lifts Ban on Japanese Culture," *Trends in Japan*, December 7, 1998, http://web-japan.org/trends98/honbun/ntj981207.html.

11. Shu-mei Shih, *Visuality and Identity: Sinophone Articulations across the Pacific* (Berkeley: University of California Press, 2007), 5.

12. Although these audience members did not self-identify as zainichi, Kim's manager confirmed that they most likely were resident Koreans (personal communication).

13. Untitled review in *Karaoke Fuan* 9 (1992): 10–11.

14. Cf. Marilyn Ivy, *Discourse of the Vanishing: Modernity, Phantasm, Japan* (Chicago: University of Chicago Press, 1995).

15. Tajima Yoshio, "Kim Yonja," *Enka Jaanaru* 100, no. 4 (1997): 29.

16. Cf. Yano, *Tears of Longing*, 151.

17. Tajima, "Kim Yonja," 37.

18. Untitled review in *Karaoke Fuan* 9 (1992): 10.

19. Untitled review in *Karaoke Fuan* 6 (1993): 68.

20. Kim Yonja and Enka Stars from Across the Sea. *Eye-Ai*, July 2002.

21. Cf. Doi Takeo, *The Anatomy of Dependency* (Tokyo: Kodansha, 1971).

22. Mori, "*Winter Sonata*," 130–31.

23. Ibid., 129.

24. Iwabuchi Koichi, *Recentering Globalization: Popular Culture and Japanese Transnationalism* (Durham, NC: Duke University Press, 2002), 255.

25. Iwabuchi, "Korean Wave," 259–60.

26. cf. Iwabuchi, *Recentering Globalization*.

27. See Kim's website: http://www.senshu-kikaku.co.jp/, accessed November 1, 2007.

28. cf. Iwabuchi, *Recentering Globalization*.

Chapter Eight

"In Our Foremothers' Arms"

Goddesses, Feminism, and the Politics of Emotion in Sámi Songs

Tina K. Ramnarine

This chapter discusses how Sámi vocal genres can be interpreted in relation to traditional cosmologies, in particular to the goddesses. The Sámi are recognized as an indigenous people living in four countries (Norway, Sweden, Finland, and Russia). Such recognition is a result of the indigenous movement of the 1960s onward in which the revival of *joik* (a traditional Sámi vocal genre) was crucial in fostering a pan-Sámi indigenous sensibility. Although joik continues to play a defining role in representing a pan-Sámi political identity, it is not widespread across the region now known as Sápmi, the land of the Sámi (map 8.1). Among the Skolt Sámi in the eastern regions of Sápmi, the traditional vocal genre is the *leu'dd*—often a narrative about an individual, which can be understood as a form of oral history. Leu'dd is regarded as a disappearing vocal tradition, in contrast to joik, which continues to be preserved, transformed, and recreated for modern contexts.

Skolt Sámi have been forcibly relocated because of wars, Cold War military policy, and hydroelectric projects. Male singers have been killed by reindeer poachers, by alcohol abuse, or on military frontlines. The most recent recording project, undertaken in the mid-1990s, focuses, therefore, on female singers, for whom the life histories narrated in leu'dd often involve expressing distressing and overwhelming emotions.[1] In discussing both joik and leu'dd to explore gender, place, and constructions of pan-Sáminess, this chapter focuses on female singers, Sámi cosmologies, and Sámi feminist theorization. I refer to two singers in particular—Ulla Pirttijärvi and Tiina Sanila—to highlight the different ways in which singing evokes notions of Sáminess, the historical processes that have shaped women's vocal expressions, and the connections between traditional and modern musical practices. The emotional attachments

Map 8.1. Sápmi territories. Map by Angela Snieder.

to place and kinship bonds expressed in joik and leu'dd performance are analyzed in relation to the politics of identity and belonging.[2]

Introducing the Goddesses

In ancient Sámi cosmology the goddess Máttaráhkká (the ancestress) played a vital role in the creation of a human being. She received a human soul from Ráđđiáhkká, who was the wife of the ruling cosmic father, Ráđđiáhčči. Then Máttaráhkká created a body for the human soul. Her first daughter, Sáráhkká (the guardian goddess of women), looked after the growth of the human in the womb. She was the midwife who helped the human being enter the world. She lived in the central hearth of the *goahti* (the traditional dwelling of the nomadic

Sámi) and was also known as the mother of fire. After birth Máttaráhkká's daughter Uksáhkká protected the mother from illness and helped the child to grow. This goddess guarded the entrance to the goahti, looking over those entering and leaving. According to ancient beliefs, all humans were created to become female, but Máttaráhkká's third daughter, Juoksáhkká, was able to transform a fetus destined to be a female baby into a male one.

These beliefs about the goddesses were linked with shamanic practices, which included joik performance. Joik is a monophonic vocal genre featuring microtonal intervals and rich ornamentation, and it is described by the contemporary Norwegian Sámi performer Ánde Somby as being for people, animals, and land.[3] Christian missionaries regarded Sámi ancient beliefs as witchcraft. Joiking was punishable by death in the early 1600s. So, too, was playing the Sámi drum, the instrument that helped a shaman reach trance states. In the Swedish Kingdom, the death penalty for joiking and drumming was reinforced under the Criminal Act of 1734, but revoked in 1779.[4] Negative attitudes toward these beliefs and their associated musical practices persisted and were spread by Christian religious revival movements such as Laestadianism, which became widespread among the Sámi in the mid-nineteenth century. Even under these circumstances, joiks to the goddess Sáráhkká were remembered by Laestadians as late as 1912, as the Swedish researcher, Karl Tirén noted.[5]

In the first half of the twentieth century, joik researchers such as Tirén believed they were recording a dying tradition. With post–World War II processes of modernization, however, Sámi populations began to mobilize politically, asserting their own identities, languages, and cultural practices in fear of assimilation within majority populations. The Sámi ethnic political movement was linked with the global minority and revitalization movements of the 1960s and 1970s in which a new value was attached to traditional forms of cultural expression, beliefs, and modes of subsistence. This political movement gave rise to a new sense of pan-Sáminess and to the revival of joik as a traditional musical expression.

Notions of pan-Sáminess from which a place called Sápmi has emerged (and been politically recognized in some of the Nordic nation-states) contrast with the experiences of Sámi minorities within this minority population, thus pointing to the complexities of place. Several questions about place can be explored through the lenses of joik and leu'dd. What are the relationships between pan-Sámi mobilization and other kinds of Sámi political mobilizations? How is Sámi indigeneity performed across modern nation-state borders, and what do such performances tell us about emotional attachments to place? How do we analyze a transnational circulation of indigenous musical performances that also encompasses all the traditional homeland regions of the indigenous population? How are citizenship and kinship configured across shifting state borders? While responses to these questions highlight regionalism, shifting borders, and modern citizenship as contributing to complex geographic sensibilities, an attachment to place is also based on generations of belonging in particular homelands.

Stories about Máttaráhkká and her daughters are being revived in contemporary Sámi political discourses, particularly in feminist scholarship, as a way of understanding Sámi pasts and places as well as shaping a politics of intergenerational belonging for the future. Interwoven with the theme of place in this chapter, then, is an engagement with the theoretical work on gender in Sámi feminist scholarship to highlight the ways in which discourses on marginality (whether in terms of gender or indigeneity) are politically connected. The gendered dimensions of musical practice in my ethnographic examples can be understood as being only one aspect of music as a political practice and, moreover, as arising from particular historical processes rather than from essentialist concepts about, or social requirements for, gendered musical expressions.

Joik, Leu'dd, and Indigenous Politics in the Northern Fringes of Europe

The joik revival was crucial in the political representations of a cultural minority within modern nation-states, during which Sámi populations began to see themselves as having endured centuries of colonialism and to react against assimilation policies and negative cultural representations. Joik performers such as the Finnish Sámi singer and multimedia artist Nils-Aslak Valkeapää were also prominent indigenous political activists representing Sámi in the global indigenous movement.[6] In fact, it was through Valkeapää's joik performances that the Sámi were accepted as members of the World Council for Indigenous Peoples. Valkeapää also changed his citizenship from Finnish to Norwegian, a move commonly understood as a demonstration of arbitrary national belongings.

From Valkeapää onward, modern Sámi politics and music can be analyzed within the frameworks of relationships between minority populations and nation-states, global indigeneity, the pursuit of indigenous rights under international law, and alternative discourses on spirituality, reciprocity, and interdependence. Ethnographic descriptions of Sámi as traditionally nomadic reindeer people, together with modern transnational musical performances and the new travel technologies increasing Sámi mobility, have contributed toward an increasingly proactive ethnopolitical discourse, to a pan-Sámi consciousness, and to a global alignment with other indigenous peoples.[7] A pan-Sámi notion of belonging that stakes claims to a region that might be recharted as Sápmi holds the potential, in some political claims, to become the Sámi nation-state. Such notions of belonging reproduce the ideologies of nationalism (resting on the convergences of territory, culture, and ethnicity) rather than offer challenges that might lead toward a politics of postnationalism. Moreover, pan-Sáminess also rests on the emergence of North Sámi (as the largest Sámi population, most of whom live in the northern regions of the modern nation-state Norway) as a dominant cultural force within this political framework and on the joik as their traditional musical expression.

The success of the joik revival from the late 1960s has led to the increasing visibility of Sámi singers within and beyond Sápmi. Sámi singers enter music competitions—from the Sámi Grand Prix, which takes place during Easter in Kautokeino (Norway) and is focused on joik performance, to competitions determining the national entry for the Eurovision Song Contest (e.g., Ann-Mari Andersen's participation and runner-up performance in Norway's 2008 competition). Sámi singers also participate in collaborative projects with musicians within and beyond the Nordic region. One of the latest collaborations was a concert between the Sámi singer Mari Boine and the Norwegian Radio Orchestra, which took place in Kautokeino in March 2012. The World Indigenous Television Broadcasting Conference marketed the concert as "music history in the making." The leader of the orchestra, Rolf Lennart Stensø, noted that this was the orchestra's first collaboration with a Sámi artist and that it was important to perform in a Sámi region since the orchestra is an ensemble for the whole nation.[8]

The joik revival can be celebrated as the survival of this vocal genre as well as of social, cultural, and historical memories despite centuries of prohibition. Modern joikers have preserved different kinds of joiking styles, turning to older generations and to the archive, but they have also transformed traditional joik by interacting with a diverse range of musical styles and genres ranging from the symphony to rap.

While Sámi traditional homelands cut across four nation-states, the Sámi are in fact heterogeneous populations, speaking many Sámi languages (where these have persisted or have been reintroduced into education programs), dressing in a variety of place-related traditional clothing, and following different kinds of subsistence modes that are not limited to reindeer herding. In Sámi villages such as Kautokeino in Norway, prominent Sámi families trace their ancestors to migrants from central Finland. Also within the Norwegian areas of Sápmi are other minority populations such as the Finnish-speaking Kvens. Emphasizing the specificities of kinship and place is the traditional mode of Sámi social organization—the *siida* (village communities based around families and reindeer grazing lands). Ethnopolitical discourses and the ideology of pan-Sáminess, then, are fragile and have been forged through population movements, changing political agreements, and borders, and citizenship affiliations that have brought different siidas together or prompted their destruction through processes of assimilation and forced migrations. Sámi populations have also been refugees, even within Sápmi, relocating across nation-state borders in the wake of national independence movements and

World War II. The Skolt Sámi, for example, lived in the borderland areas of Finland, Norway, and Russia until World War II. There were seven Skolt siidas, and Skolt Sámi living in the three siidas in Petsamo that had become part of an independent Finland resettled as Finnish citizens when this region was ceded to the Soviet Union in 1947.[9]

The Skolt Sámi leu'dd was distinguished from other kinds of songs. This genre is now regarded as a dying tradition, though I shall discuss the beginnings of a revival process later on. Leu'dd could be either a composed or improvised form with musical motifs or melodies referencing particular families or places. A leu'dd would often begin with the names of the people being narrated. Thus, Markko Jouste, Elias Mosnikoff, and Seija Sivertsen suggest that this is "a form of narrative art which expresses the oral history of the Skolt Sámis." Interpreting a leu'dd text depends on cultural and historical knowledge as well as on knowledge of a sung language that differs from spoken language. Leu'dd researchers have noted the connections between this genre and other surrounding musical traditions. Skolt Sámi musical traditions are related to Finnish epic songs, Karelian laments, Russian laments, and ballads. These vocal genres are performed by unaccompanied singers and share a number of structural features such as sequential phrase structures and the use of epithets, parallel verses, and extra syllables to fill the meter.[10]

Given the musical connections across Sápmi, Finland, Russia, Karelia, and beyond, stories about goddesses and their sacred spaces lead into thinking about how Sámi song performances give expression to emotional attachments to place and how these attachments, formed across generations through bonds of kinship and belief, underpin contemporary indigenous and feminist politics in northern Europe. I turn now to two singers to discuss women's musical and political voices, the making of the region now called Sápmi, memory, loss, and the performance of belonging.

Máttaráhku askái: In Our Foremothers' Arms: Goddesses and Life Narratives in Ulla Pirttijärvi's Joiks

In an interview the joik performer Ulla Pirttijärvi told me, "Joik is not something you are taught. You hear and you try with your own voice. Joik is freer without any accompaniment—and you have to joik how you feel, joik your emotions."[11] Pirttijärvi is an example of a successful modern joik singer who has made CD recordings, undertaken international tours, and contributed to educational projects to promote the transmission of joik. At the Kautokeino Easter Festival in 2007, she was awarded the Aillohaš Prize for her work in promoting Sámi cultural practices.[12] She is a Finnish Sámi musician, a North Sámi. Born in 1971, when the Sámi ethnic mobilization movement was beginning to gather strength, she has been influenced by central musical figures in the indigenous movement (such as Nils-Aslak Valkeapää and the Norwegian Sámi singer Mari Boine). In contrast to Mari Boine (born 1956), who grew up in a Laestadian family and began to explore the Sámi shamanic heritage and joik once she had already begun her musical career, Ulla Pirrtijärvi has been engaged in joik practice since childhood. She grew up in the village of Angeli, near the Finnish-Norwegian border, and was a member of the group Riutulan Lapset (Riutula's Children), formed by a schoolteacher who wanted Sámi children to learn about joik. This group performed widely in the Sápmi region and also at the Finnish Folk Festival in Kaustinen (northern Finland) in 1982. From this ensemble, a music group called Angelin Tytöt (Girls of Angeli) was formed with Ulla Pirttijärvi and the two sisters Ursula and Tuuli Länsman.

As well as learning joiks in school music education projects, she learned from her family members. Her uncle was a traditional joik singer, who probably learned joik repertoires and techniques from migrations with his reindeer herd—traveling to relatives and other reindeer-herding families. He taught and guided Angelin Tytöt in their joik practice. As a teenager of fourteen or fifteen, she performed in joiking events in schools. A couple of years later, Mari Boine asked her to joik and to participate in some of the dance choreography for a piece ("Joik in the Lap of Space," 1988) produced for the Beaivváš Theatre in Kautokeino, Norway, and she learned a lot about musical experimentation and artistic presentation from this experience.[13] Pirttijärvi believes that in the past people learned about joik just from the musical ideas that came to them, but her own experiences demonstrate new joik learning contexts. With Angelin Tytöt she performed at a Sámi concert as part of a Sámi political delegation to Helsinki in 1992.[14] Pirttijärvi has been a guest teacher at the Sibelius Academy, produced joik teaching materials, and collaborated with researchers (for example, recording Sámi vocal music in Finland; see fig. 8.1).[15]

Máttaráhku askái: In Our Foremothers' Arms is the title of Pirttijärvi's 2002 CD recording, produced by Frode Fjellheim, a musician with whom she has collaborated on several musical projects since 1995. The imagery on the CD cover references Máttaráhkká's eldest daughter, Sáráhkká, as the goddess who dwells in the central fireplace of a traditional Sámi home. Pirttijärvi stands by the hearth, hands cupped as if holding flames from the fire in the foreground. The imagery evokes the creative and protective agency of the goddess and her daughters. The joiks in this recording provide perspectives on Sámi history, especially through reference to the experiences of Pirttijärvi's ancestors. The third track, for example, is about Pirttijärvi's great-great grandfather, who was said to be a shaman. This is noteworthy, for the album explicitly references maternal ancestors ("our foremothers' arms"), yet paternal ancestors are also evoked. Evoking both maternal and paternal ancestors accords them equal attention and challenges a contemporary discourse seeking to privilege the matriarchal past and conventional patriarchy. Ancestral sound worlds are also evoked, as the track begins with a recording of the joiker Niila Kitti from Inari,

Figure 8.1. Ulla Pirttijärvi in concert. Inari, Finland, August 22, 2009. Photograph by the author.

Finland, held in the archives of the Finnish Literature Society. The joik text to track 5, "Ládjogahpir" (The traditional Sámi hat) features the English translation: "We used to wear our traditional hat—until someone told us to burn it. They said it made us look like the devil." The text to "Áigi vássá" (Time doesn't stop) (track 11) reflects on the relation between past and present: "Time does not stop, and when the modern time arrives, the old one is forgotten. We wonder: which is the best?"

Questions about time are reflected in the soundworld of modern joik, which is rather different from joiks heard in archive recordings. Traditional joik techniques are combined with synthesized and acoustic accompaniments, countermelodies, and ambient textures in Pirttijärvi's recordings. Whereas Pirttijärvi's "Áigi vássá" text emphasizes the past as "forgotten," Mari Boine (2001) urges recognition of the continuity of the past into the future in her joik "Sáráhkká's Wine" (track 3).[16] This joik text invokes the god of thunder to roar, thereby forcing newborn children to look back on old Sámi paths while hurrying forward in life. (The invocation is made to help the children recognize that their life path is one rooted in a Sámi past.) This joik refers to the traditional practice of the midwife who drank wine in honor of Sáráhkká before the birth and who ate porridge (for divination purposes) after the birth.[17] "Áigi vássá" and

"Sáráhkká's Wine" offer reflections on Sámi histories, on remembering and forgetting, and on the moralities of cultural memory. Both singers reveal that joiks to or about the goddesses persist.

The theme of "in our foremothers' arms" is developed in Pirttijärvi's 2008 CD recording, *Áibbašeabmi* (Longing), which explores the emotional and intergenerational aspects of her own life story. Track 10, "Áhku báikkis" (Visiting grandmother), is an example. In the liner notes, the full joik text is given only in Sámi with a short English explanation ("all those small details I remember from visiting my grandmother's house on a nice relaxing afternoon"). What is clear, however, is that the "foremothers' arms" are places of care, safety, and nurture. Track 7, "Niila-Ánde," describes her son: "He is running easy and fast." The musicians who have helped to shape her musical practice—mentors, friends, and colleagues—are also referred to in this recording. Track 6, "Jearrat biekkas" (Questions in the wind) presents lyrics by Nils Aslak Valkeapää, and the last track, 13, is Frode Fjellheim's ("Frode's joik"). Friendship also takes a global dimension with a girl from Tanzania as the subject of the joik in track 4, "Prudenciana" (The Girl from Tanzania) ("In Bagamoyo, Tanzania, I met a girl called Prudenciana. This is her joik. Her friends are yoiking together with me"). And track 2, "Nieida" (The Sámi Girl), describes the Sámi girl: "beautiful as a mountain flower . . . a skilled reindeer herder, an expert in traditional handicrafts, almost supernatural."

These joik texts, in turning toward female ancestors and to goddesses who oversee human birth, seem to resonate with well-established conventions within the literature on music and gender focusing on women's musical practices in domestic spheres, especially in relation to their procreative capacity and nurturing roles. Whereas men occupy a public music stage, the performance arena of women is often a private one, sometimes a separate, all-female performance context.[18] However, these theoretical paradigms do not reflect the frameworks of Sámi women's performances. Even though Pirttijärvi's recordings refer to kinship, the inner spaces of the goahti, and Sámi stories about human birth, she performs on national and transnational public stages. Moreover, relying on the distinction between public and private is inappropriate because of the historical prohibitions against joik such that its survival depended on private performance, and we cannot interpret privacy as evidence of gendered musical roles. More fundamentally, traditional joiking was not a practice that required an audience. Nor was it necessarily performed in public spaces. Rather, it was an individual practice, a musical response to one's surroundings and circumstances, an expression of one's feelings. Joik performance thus draws our attention away from standard models of the gendering of musical practices and performance spaces.

What, then, can we learn about gendered musical performances by thinking about joik? In the discussion that follows, I indicate how Sámi discourses question constructions of gender. In contemporary performance there are no particular separate musical roles for women and men. However, external understandings of women's and men's roles in society may have had an impact on the survival, demise, and performance of joik in the past, such that it could have become a gendered practice. But the scholarship is contradictory, and gender equality is a contemporary concern. While Elin Margrethe Wersland and Gjert Rognli point out that Christian missionaries focused their attention on men's religious practices so that joik was more easily performed by women, Vuokko Hirvonen, by contrast, suggests that men could joik more freely as they worked in the fells, whereas women were at home taking care of children and elders, where they were surrounded by preachers and clergy.[19]

Despite the contradictions, questions about gendered musical practices are interlinked with thinking about a place called "Sápmi," which involves an indigenous political rejection of the former place-name, Lapland. Joik is a way of delving deeper into the Sámi past through reclaiming belonging to a place that precedes modern nation-states and also of recreating musical practices that persisted, despite negative perceptions, because church authorities did not regard men's and women's expressions equally. A joik album invoking the goddesses takes us into interconnected sacred and political spaces.

Máttaráhku askái: In Our Foremothers' Arms alerts listeners to the spiritual dimensions of Sámi musical practice, to a history traceable through the kinship links still in living memory and in archived recordings, and to an indigenous politics resting on surviving knowledge of ancient beliefs. The goddess is the foremother, and to be held in her arms—to be helped to enter the world by her daughter in the goahti's fireplace—is to be held also in the "lap of the universe." The hearth was sacred and so, too, was the landscape. For now, we can think about "Sápmi" as a political construct being many places, just like the many sacred sites and the many siidas, and not just as one place.[20] What kind of place does Sápmi appear to be from another of its locations?

Loss and Belonging in Tiina Sanila's Leu'dd Performances

Skolt Sámi came into increased contact with the Inari Sámi (another minority Sámi population living around Lake Inari in northern Finland) during the twentieth century. The Skolts, like the Inari, are eastern Sámi, closely related to the Akkala and Kildin Sámi (in the Russian Kola Peninsula). An ethnographic moment I would like to introduce took place in the traditional homeland of the Inari Sámi by the shores of Lake Inari in May 2007, as the last of the winter ice was melting and the sun did not set. This was at a new festival (launched in 2004) called Ijahis Idja (Nightless Nights). Sámi festivals, such as the Finnish Ijahis Idja, the Swedish Jokkmokk Winter Market, and the Norwegian Kautokeino Easter Festival, foster transnational joik performances with performers and audiences circulating between them in the wake of the

1960s joik revival. This festival, then, is situated within a broader context of live and mass mediated performances, including television, radio, CD recordings, and education projects—all of which work toward developing pan-Sámi sensibilities while simultaneously maintaining distinctly place-orientated Sámi performance traditions.

In 2007 different kinds of indigenous histories and song revivals were performed in Inari. There were concerts with performances by related indigenous people from Russia, by children and by some of the most well-known contemporary Sámi musicians such as the North Sámi (Finnish) joik singer Wimme Saari and the Skolt Sámi singer Tiina Sanila, who appeared onstage in Skolt Sámi dress. One of the guitarists in the band wore Inari Sámi dress. Another guitarist and a drummer appeared in jeans. In the audience young children wearing protective ear muffs were dancing at the front. The stage lighting changed colors and an artificial haze wafted around as different instrumental solos were presented between verses (see fig. 8.2).

Traditionally the Skolt Sámi did not sing joiks. Their traditional vocal genre is the leu'dd. While the postwar period marked the near extinction of traditional leu'dd expression, this song tradition is beginning to undergo a revival process. For example, the Skolt Sámi singer Jaakko Gauriloff wrote lyrics in Skolt Sámi for the 1991 album *Kuä'ckkem suäjai vuel'nn* (Under the wings of the Eagle).[21] He was a tango singer earlier in his musical career, and the album reflects the influences of Finnish tango style, though his live performances now present unaccompanied, dramatic, and ornamented songs.[22] Sanila's performances could be categorized as emerging from a rock rather than leu'dd genre. Indeed, she describes herself as "Rokki Koltta" (Rock Skolt) on her website.[23]

Nevertheless, performances such as these demonstrate the interests of young Skolt Sámi in wanting to learn the Skolt language (now spoken by only about three hundred people) and to wear traditional clothing. Skolt Sámi cherish their performances as being somewhat distinct from other Sámi ones. The emphasis on singing in a minority language is what allows Sanila's performances to be identified as Skolt Sámi. On Sanila's first recording, *Sää' mjânnam rocks!* (2005), only the last track is a leu'dd, and it is an unaccompanied piece about her reindeer. Reference to leu'dd appears in another song text: "Andy is animal. He was born to be a leu'dd machine. . . . He is the best leu'dd-master, the leu'dd machine in the world" (track 1, "Jååggarr lij jie' lli" [Andy is an animal]). Otherwise, the texts generally deal with love, loneliness, and betrayal, but following leu'dd models these themes are explored in relation to individual life stories. Sanila sings about Maaren, for example, who is going to be married to Saammâl, but from whom she receives a letter informing her that he has found another woman. Sanila's second album, *Kå' llkue'll še måttmešt talk* (Goldfish also get bored sometimes; 2007) tells stories about discovering one's partner has gambled away the house and savings; about the reindeer men who are wild, free, and captains of their lives; and about the "flirt machine."[24]

Figure 8.2. Tiina Sanila in performance. Inari, Finland, May 22, 2007. Photograph by the author.

Leu'dd texts are often about people. To hear a leu'dd is to remember the individuals it is about. As one singer, Maiya Prokop'evna Sergina, said in 1995, "Our leu'dds are always about somebody's life. They are not as pretty as the songs of the Russians. When I begin to remember, I start to cry." Leu'dds could make the performer pause in singing because of overwhelming emotion. To narrate the life histories in leu'dds is to perform a lament. To describe a leu'dd as being "difficult," therefore, does not refer to technical issues but to the difficulties in controlling one's emotions.[25]

Leu'dd texts are also about local social environments, which have changed substantially. In 1917 Finland became an independent nation-state, having previously been an autonomous grand duchy within Russia and, before that, a part of the Swedish Empire. In 1920 some of the Skolt Sámi became Finnish citizens and others Russian or Soviet citizens under the Tartu Peace Treaty signed between Finland and the Soviet Union. Redrawn borders affected traditional livelihoods, with the siidas split up and assimilated into Finnish, Norwegian, or Russian cultures. More Skolt Sámi fled Russia as wartime refugees and relocated to areas around Lake Inari in 1944, when Finland lost the Petsamo district to Russia and state borders were again redrawn. Their relatives on the Russian side of the border were resettled away from the border regions and farther into the Kola Peninsula. During this wartime period, a Skolt Sámi man called Nicolai "was called to the front. To fight a war against people he had never seen, or even less had anything against. To kill the 'enemy' as they called them. Some of the enemies were his cousins, according to his mother. . . . 'Nobody could have won,' he said to his father when he came home four years later. Everyone lost something."[26]

While traditional subsistence economies were based on reindeer, hunting, and fishing, organized by the siidas, the reindeer economy was collectivized in the 1930s under the Soviet system. In the postwar period the Soviet Kola landscape was heavily transformed by hydroelectric projects and dams that left villages under water. Skolt Sámi were forcibly removed from their homelands and transferred to reservations, as Cold War military policy dictated a hundred-kilometer border zone. In Finland, Skolt Sámi were perceived negatively in the postwar period. As one person commented, "If we wear our own traditional clothing we are seen as Gypsies or Russkies. . . . Other Sámi call us those names."[27] These experiences cut across panindigenous sensibilities.[28]

Sanila's leu'dd and leu'dd-inspired performances on record and at the Ijahis Idja Festival encourage thinking about borders, belonging, mobility, and citizenship. I have contrasted joik and leu'dd to reflect on the ideology of Sámi panindigeneity, but a caveat must now be introduced in noting similarities across this region in the intergenerational and spiritual references in both vocal forms. Joik and leu'dd are not disconnected vocal genres. In particular, I am interested in the persistence of the ancestral mothers or the goddesses. One of the leu'dds in the Ilpo Saastamoinen collection is "Two Tjahpan's Daughters," performed by Anfisa Ivanovna Gerasimova and recorded in 1994.[29] Saastamoinen notes the appellation *ääkka(ž)* in this leu'dd text, which means "grandmother" and is a term of respect applied to the landscape, including lakes, forests, and hills.

> *A Tuållâm u'cc lij siidâž a Tuållâm u'cc lij siidâž.*
> *Kue'htt Teäppan niõđe go le'jje joo.*
> *Sije pâi go va'zzače da Porjjâz-njaarg ääkka go mie'ldda joo.*
> *Porjjâz-ääkka mie'ldda go jo-oola.*

> Tuloma is a nice little village [siida; the line is repeated].
> There were two of Tjahpan's daughters. Gu lii-e [*go le'jje joo*].
> They keep walking along the Porjas-njargg [place-name, "sail cape"] grandmother [*ääkka*, used as a term of respect]
> The beauties used to walk.

The significance of the foremothers was already discussed with regard to the album *Máttaráhku askái: In Our Foremothers' Arms*. Saastamoinen comments that *ääkka(ž)* is also associated with "the personified, animistic power of the surrounding nature," an association that reminds us of the links between the foremothers, the sacred landscape, and the goddesses of ancient cosmologies.[30]

Sámi Feminist Scholarship and Political Activism

The Finnish folklorist Aili Nenola observes that becoming aware of traditions is connected with the assertion of rights and outlines four responses to tradition in the processes of emancipating women: (1) to question traditions and ask who has decided how to interpret sacred histories; (2) to return to traditions as a way of legitimizing demands for change in the present; (3) to reject oppressive traditions; and (4) to create new traditions.[31] Nenola's example for the second response—the quest by the women's movement for a matriarchal past or goddess religion—is relevant to my discussion. Recently, Sámi scholars have begun to consider female deities in traditional Sámi belief. Their reflections are important contributions to both feminist and indigenous political discourses.

Here I develop my political readings of *Máttaráhku askái: In Our Foremothers' Arms* and of the appellation *ääkka(ž)* in a leu'dd text by considering parallel voices in Sámi feminist scholarship. A common trope is that female deities indicate that Sámi women were traditionally powerful agents in Sámi society, revealing a matriarchal element in this society in the pre-Christian era. But division of labor seems to have been gendered along familiar patterns. While tasks like sewing provided clothing and ensured the survival of a woman's family (especially important in a harsh Arctic climate), the feminist, postcolonial scholar, and author of a study on Sámi women's writing, Vuokko Hirvonen, suggests that division of labor, following a classic model of men working outside and women inside in the domestic sphere, indicates gender dichotomies in traditional Sámi society.[32]

There is an interesting detail to add on ownership rights. Traditionally, women could also look after and own reindeer, and the inheritance of reindeer could be shared between women and men. In an anthropological study examining the lifestyle, demography, and local legal processes of the Skolt Sámi living in Petsamo in the 1920s, Väinö Tanner writes that inheritances were shared between boys and girls, although boys were given double amounts.[33] In the 1970s the Sámi feminist movement began when female reindeer herders asked for the same rights as their male counterparts. These rights are still under dispute. Rauna Kuokkanen writes that "government policies have made women invisible in the livelihood in which they have always played a central role," noting the case of a woman who lost her share of reindeer-herding subsidies when she divorced her husband in 2005, because the Reindeer Herding Act of 1978 in Norway protected only the rights of the (usually male) owner of the reindeer household.[34]

The claims presented by female reindeer herders since the 1970s reveal some of the ways in which the Sámi feminist and indigenous movements have been intertwined, highlighting that gender intersects with many other kinds of identity politics. Female reindeer herders have been concerned with drawing a distinction between indigenous and nonindigenous populations within the Nordic nation-states in which the traditional status of women emerges as one of the markers of difference. Their understanding of the lack of equal rights between Sámi men and women resulting from the imposition of external, nonindigenous views is confirmed by several contemporary scholars, highlighting the political implications of scholarship. The literary scholar Vuokko Hirvonen states that the Sámi are a marginal group despite the fact that they live in Europe, and that the Sámi woman has been marginalized as a Sámi, as a woman, and as a Sámi woman. From the spaces of marginality, however, the turn to the goddesses of the ancient Sámi religion in Sámi women's writing (and the point is applicable to Pirttijärvi's CD recordings) is an attempt to "return to the source of Sáminess." Hirvonen further suggests that "by making visible that which has been invisible and considered shameful for centuries, the authors are restoring to Sámi culture—and their own past—the value that it deserves among other cultures. Presenting fragments of the traditional religion of the Sámi can also be seen as a critique of patriarchal Christianity."[35]

Critiques of patriarchy (especially in relation to religious systems), postcolonial theorization (seeing Sámi as colonized people), and environmental thinking have shaped contemporary Sámi feminist scholarship. But the difficulties of tracing gender in the past are recognized. Rauna Kuokkanen notes, "Christianity and Laestadianism in particular have affected Sámi society for several generations. Contemporary perceptions of and attitudes toward women in Sámi society are, therefore, an entangled combination of influences of various origins and from different periods of time, making it rather difficult to trace back the traditional status and roles of Sámi women."[36]

Religious influences can be analyzed in contrasting ways. While the impact of Christianity on indigenous peoples has been a fundamental concern in indigenous politics, a postcolonial reading of Christianity as a space for indigenous resistance strategies can also be offered. Teemu Ryymin observes,

> The role of Laestadianism in the field of identity politics in Northern Norway is complicated. In addition to being an alternative to nationalist or ethnopolitical movements, it also contributed to uphold minority cultural traits, such as language. The use of Sámi and Finnish in the Laestadian movement as ceremonial languages functioned as a kind of resistance to the pressure of Norwegianisation, and probably contributed to the continuing survival of minority languages.[37]

Moreover, even when most Sámi had been converted to Christianity, newborn children were "christened" in the name of Sáráhkká, and children who were ill would be rechristened in her name. In fact, belief in Sáráhkká may have survived the changes introduced by Christian religious movements, as she was identified with the female Christian figure of the Virgin Mary.[38]

Postcolonial feminist interpretations of goddesses draw our attention to Sámi spirituality and the persistence of cultural memory, referring to the past as a way of promoting visions for the future. The political activism of writers such as Kuokkanen is apparent and promotes a view of women affected by colonialism and patriarchy and of feminist analysis as facilitating both decolonizing and gender equality strategies: "I strongly believe that our survival as a people is dependent on embarking on the path of transforming and decolonizing the colonial, patriarchal discourses reflected in every aspect of our society, hindering and distracting us from restoring and re-envisioning our communities and the future of our people." For Kuokkanen, the goddesses provide a way of thinking about social transformation so that the "myth" of strong women might be used in "a proactive strategy of healing and transformation. . . . We could start advocating and implementing our powerful female legacies found, for example, in the Sámi worldview and cosmic order that may well have centered around the female deity Máttáráhkká ('Ancestral Mother') and her three daughters Sáráhkká, Juksáhkká, and Uksáhkká, to advance and rebuild our communities."[39]

At stake in these contrasting views of powerful women versus women subject to male authority are the stories of both the past and the future. What is Sámi tradition? Which perspectives on traditional understandings should be reclaimed for current political projects? Feminist, postcolonial scholarship extends political debates and provides analytic tools through which certain kinds of histories can be told and indigenous rights can be asserted. But such analytic tools are themselves removed from the traditional worldviews and histories they hope to access—necessarily so, as they are part of a modern, politically engaged scholarship. History itself is a partial project. The terms of analysis, then, promote understandings of historical processes, Sámi indigenous sensibilities, and gender relations that are also based on current assumptions and concerns.

This scholarship emerges from the institutions of the Sámi women's movement, dating to 1910 with a women's association founded by Elsa Laula-Renberg, who expressed concerns about Sámi survival under assimilationist policies. Since then, Sámi women have held various seminars to discuss their social positions, employment, and representation in Sámi organizations. The goddess Sáráhkká lends her name to a women's organization established in 1988 aiming to raise women's awareness of their current roles, change social conditions, and promote gender equality.

Ecofeminism and Mother Earth

Environmentally conscious feminist approaches have regarded women and nature as subjugated by patriarchal systems of power, and the ecofeminist recuperation of goddesses and nature-based spiritualities resonates with the Sámi postcolonial feminist critique of patriarchal religion, as well as with a social turn toward romanticizing premodern beliefs. Ecofeminism maps onto indigenous discourses on nature, onto representations of indigenous communities as being in tune with nature, and onto indigenous critiques of the colonization of nature. Yet the notion of "goddess" itself is criticized in the ecofeminist perspectives of Jorunn Eikjok, who suggests that the term evokes ideas about "religion" that are not appropriate for describing a Sámi worldview in which *Mattaráhku* is the "mother" rather than the "goddess": "In Sámi, earth is '*eana*' and mother is '*eadni.*' There is a connection here, where the earth of old symbolized the motherly. Femininity had a symbolic status and meant growth, fertility, life-giving, and nourishing. In Sámi visions of the world, the animals and all that live have their own '*mattaráhkku*,' Indigenous mother." If the translation "goddess" is incorrect, ideas about feminine power, Mother Earth, and nature (*luondu*) nevertheless have a spiritual aspect, and "one can speak of humans, relatives, places, animals, and other living beings as having their own *luondu*." Ecofeminist theory is useful for Eikjok as a means of empowering Sámi women by recognizing their relationship to landscape and developing their ethnoecological knowledge. Her ecofeminist perspective enables my further interpretation of the imagery on Pirttijärvi's 2002 CD recording, *Máttaráhku askái: In Our Foremothers' Arms*, for fire was associated with feminine power among several Arctic indigenous communities and only women could touch fire.[40]

Eikjok comments on how the Mother Earth ideology is being used by indigenous communities simply to assert difference from Western ideas. This observation is relevant when thinking past the dichotomies of indigenous-nonindigenous in the Nordic context, which cannot account either for the histories of interactions among populations in this region or the shifting political structures of the modern Nordic nation-states now being represented as colonizing forces in indigenous politics. It is relevant, too, in thinking past the polarities of female-male musical spaces, practices, and opportunities. Eikjok suggests that the Mother Earth discourse of difference not only is essentialist but also obscures the variations of gender categories in indigenous societies, leaving us with "narrow" definitions of "woman."[41] If examples from the Sámi feminist literature surveyed here dwell on the theme of women as doubly oppressed by their gender and Sáminess and make political calls based on nationalist type aspirations toward the self-determination of decolonized populations in Sápmi, Eikjok's comment leaves us wondering what broader understandings of gender might be.

I would like to make two further points about goddesses and the boundaries between indigenous and nonindigenous populations in activist (postcolonial and ecofeminist) scholarship. First, rather than rendering the boundary between indigenous and nonindigenous problematic, the discourses outlined in this chapter reinforce and reinscribe indigenous identity politics in the complex scenarios of the Nordic world. Only Eikjok notes the politics of representing the Western as Other. As Thomas Hylland Eriksen highlights, such a politics of representation leads to the difficult ideological situation of the Sámi today. They are faced both with a number of cultural and political choices as minorities within modern states and with the dilemma of fighting for minority rights that must also be guaranteed by the state that threatens those rights.[42] Second, the return of goddesses can be understood as a modern phenomenon, and in this respect the boundaries between indigenous and nonindigenous are also rendered indistinct. In addition to the survival of cultural and spiritual ideas surrounding Máttaráhkká and her daughters, the social conditions for a contemporary turn to the goddesses have been fostered by representations of spirituality in the global indigeneity movement, neoshamanism movements in the Nordic world, and new media technologies and representations of the supernatural in popular culture. As Stig Hjarvard suggests (for examples such as *Harry Potter*, *Lord of the Rings*, and *The Da Vinci Code*), "The media have become the primary source of imagery and texts about magic, spiritualism, and religion, and as languages the media mould religious imagination in accordance with the genres of popular culture. The media as cultural environments have taken over many of the social functions of the institutionalized religions, providing both moral guidance and a sense of community."[43] These are the social and cultural environments that shape musical practice and scholarship alike. Recent trends in contemporary Finnish folk music have also included the exploration of incantations, magic spells, and the aesthetics of neoprimitivism, alongside musical collaborations in world-music scenes and experimental, improvisational approaches to reinterpret and to create new folk repertoires.[44]

Rethinking Gendered Musical Performance

In this chapter, I have focused on women as political agents giving expression to a politics of emotion with regard to place and past. Conceptual issues raised include how an emphasis on music and emotion as individual expression reconfigures discourses on gendered emotion in musical performance and how historical processes have created the social conditions for thinking about musical performance in gendered terms. A central point has been to understand the connections between gender and indigenous politics.

Indigeneity and citizenship across nation-state borders are also crucial in understanding musical performance and contemporary political identities. Both Pirttijärvi and Sanila are Sámi musicians, but their musical practices present different kinds of Sámi stories. While one is North Sámi and the other Skolt Sámi, they are both Finnish musicians. Their performances can be contextualized within Sámi politics, the intersecting musical and political expressions of Nordic nationalisms, Finno-Ugric sensibilities, and gendered musical experience in the Nordic area. Their performances are situated within a nexus of interconnected perspectives on memory, kinship, emotion, and authorship.

Points of comparison can be made with the globally successful group Värttinä, traditional Karelian ritual lamenters, and female composers such as Kaija Saariaho. I have considered their vocal music in parallel with feminist scholarship, which has been instrumental in pointing to structural inequalities and the lack of formal political representation. But these singers also point to different understandings of politics and gender, highlighting life narratives that contain historical insights, referencing places inhabited by the individuals who appear in joik and leu'dd texts, and providing instructive comments. Sámi women's social roles have changed dramatically over the past century, with shifts from traditional kinship systems and subsistence economies to a market economy. As Hirvonen notes,

> Very little is left of the traditional way of life and the social system in which people grew up in the early 1900s.... The family and kinship community have been replaced by a privatized community and services provided by institutions. Women work outside the home, and children go to kindergartens and schools. Thus the socialization of children is no longer the responsibility of the family and relatives alone: it is done by many different sectors.[45]

All of these shifts shape both Pirttijärvi's and Sanila's musical practices, the singers through whom I have pointed to the different ways in which singing evokes multiple notions of Sáminess and emphasized the historical processes that shape vocal expression in this region. Thinking about history is fundamental to analyzing gendered musical practices and helping to account for the recent prominence of women (rather than both women and men) in leu'dd recordings, for example.

Since this chapter begins with stories about goddesses and the life cycle, one might have expected that familiar tropes in the ethnographic and theoretical literature would be reiterated in the Sámi example regarding women's musical activities in domestic and private rather than public spaces, musical expression affecting a society's intergender relations, and constraints to and strategies adopted by women in forging professional musical careers.[46] Instead of interpreting the performances of Pirttijärvi and Sanila within these tropes, I have been concerned with the gendered dimensions of different but interconnecting places that connect Sámi populations: the hearth, the siida, Sápmi, the cosmos, and the ways in which these places are performed in song. Singers sing about their everyday environments, their families, and their reindeer. They joik their feelings. They cry as they remember people while performing leu'dd. They sing for themselves. They sing on public stages. The Norwegian Sámi singer Biret Ristin Sara told me that one opens oneself to joik. One joiks in sorrow, in love, in longing, and for strength. Joiks give advice; they teach children;

they mark places and spirits.[47] Singing, cultural memory, and sacred places have fostered contemporary indigenous sensibilities, revealing the politics of emotional attachment to place as being an aspect of identity politics. While my examples have been female singers, I have been careful to avoid labeling their practices as women's music. Such avoidance should not be read as disregard for modern gender politics; rather, it stems from an avoidance of seeing gender as circumscribed.

Sámi feminist scholarship has been connected with the political project of indigeneity since the 1970s, promoting the view that Sámi are colonized people so that struggles over gender emerge as being implicated in calls for decolonization, self-determination, and social transformation. But, as Joyce Green observes in the edited collection *Making Space for Indigenous Feminism*, women's agency is recognized in many indigenous contexts, making feminism seem irrelevant, and indigenous female scholars hesitant to claim the label "feminist." Indigenous critiques against feminism see this stance as "un-traditional, inauthentic, non-libratory."[48]

Nevertheless, some Sámi scholars have embraced this mode of theorization. Modern indigenous feminist thought provides valuable perspectives on the issue of gender, but I would like to highlight the ways in which theoretical discourses themselves (whether indigenous, feminist, or musicological) contribute to the gendering of musical practice. It might be valuable to think about Pirttijärvi's collaborations with Fjellheim, calling into question separate gendered musical practices. It might be valuable also to think about the ways in which understandings of gender have been externally imposed on indigenous populations and to consider what indigenous stories tell us about gender. The Sámi story about the goddess Juoksáhkká's ability to transform gender emphasizes current theoretical nuances to gender (as performed, socially constructed, changed, and examined in complex ways through looking at whole systems) that are overlooked in the polarities of gender discourses focusing only on women's and men's musical practices. Indeed, it was Juoksáhkká's role to transform a fetus into a male child and make boys good hunters. Both men and women perform joiks or leu'dds, and if not in the present (for leu'dd), at least in the past. There are no particular musical practices that can be identified as being female or male. Even when a joik is described as being "male" or "female" because of its stylistic features (low-pitched or lyrical, for example), both men and women can perform that joik.[49] What is important about joik and leu'dd performance is that individual expression is central.

The pitfalls in thinking about gender within the polarized confines of matriarchal or patriarchal power are that theoretical tropes and orthodox views of gender and intergender relations are perpetuated. Instead, serious thought could be given to what these stories about goddesses might tell us about our notions of gender. While gender has become implicated in Sámi indigenous politics through political activism and feminist theorization, my main concerns in thinking about the politics and performance of emotion and place have followed rather different trajectories—tracing the story of Máttaráhkká and her daughters to raise issues about memory and kinship, the spiritual discourses in indigenous politics, the musical turn to ancient beliefs, the impact of gendered social experience on musical performance, and emotional attachments to places as performed in song. These are the modern musical expressions of belonging "in our foremothers' arms."

Notes

1. Ilpo Saastamoinen, *Son Vuäinn: Hän Näkee; Kolttasaamelaisten leuddeja Kuolasta Helsinki: Maailman Musiikin Keskus* (Helsinki: Maailman Musiikin Keskus, 2007).

2. I am grateful for funds from the Leverhulme Trust and the British Academy, which enabled field research in the Nordic countries, undertaken in several short trips over the period 2006 to 2010.

3. Ánde Somby, "Joik and the Theory of Knowledge," available at http://www.stavacademy.co.uk/mimir/joik.htm (accessed April 24, 2013). Orig. pub. in *Kunnskap og utvikling*, ed. Magnus Haavelsrud (Tromsø: Universitetet i Tromsø, 1995).

4. Vuokko Hirvonen, *Voices from Sápmi: Sámi Women's Path to Authorship* (Guovdageaidnu [Kautokeino]: DAT, 2008), 129.

5. Karl Tirén, *Die Lappische Volksmusik: Aufzeichnungen von Joikos-Melodien bei den schwedischen Lappen* (Uppsala: Nordic Museum, Hugo Gebers Förlag, 1942), 54.

6. See Harold Gaski, "Voice in the Margin: A Suitable Place for a Minority Literature?," in *Sami Culture in a New Era*, ed. Harald Gaski (Kárášjohka: Davvi Girji OS, 1997), 199–220; and Tina K. Ramnarine, "Acoustemology, Indigeneity and Joik in Valkeapää's Symphonic Activism: Views from Europe's Arctic Fringes for Environmental Ethnomusicology," *Ethnomusicology* 53, no. 2 (2009): 187–217.

7. Sámi mobility has been shaped by travel technologies such as snowmobiles and cars, which have changed traditional herding and social practices. Sámi mobility has included migration to and settlement in Alaska, when Sámi reindeer herders were asked to share their herding skills with Alaskan communities, as well as migration to major Nordic urban centers such as Oslo.

8. See "Music History in the Making," http://www.nrk.no/witbc2012/1.7971927 (accessed March 21, 2012).

9. Markko Jouste, Elias Mosnikoff, and Seija Sivertsen, *Maaddârää'jji Leeu'd: Esivanhempien Leuddit, the Leu'dds of the Ancestors* (Kaustinen: Folk Music Institute/Inari: Sámi Museum Siida, 2007), 13.

10. Ibid., 13, 14.

11. Ulla Pirttijärvi, interview by the author, Inari, Finland, May 23, 2007 (my translation).

12. Ailloha š is the name by which Nils-Aslak Valkeapää is commonly known by many Sámi.

13. Biographical details based on the interview with Pirttijärvi.

14. See Tina K. Ramnarine, *Ilmatar's Inspirations: Nationalism, Globalization, and the Changing Soundscapes of Finnish Folk Music* (Chicago: Chicago University Press, 2003), 181–84.

15. Ulla Pirttijärvi, *Honkon Dohkká* (Guovdageaidnu [Kautokeino]: DAT, 1996), compact disc; Pirttijärvi, *Honkon Dohkká* (Kautokeino: DAT, 1996), compact disc.

16. Mari Boine, Sáráhkká's Wine," on *Eight Seasons, Gávcci Jahkejuogu*, Oslo: Universal Music, LC 00699-017019-2, 2001, compact disc.

17. Elin Margrethe Wersland and Gjert Rognli, *Joik i den gamle samiske religionen (Yoik in the Old Sami Religion)* (Nesbru: Vett and Viten AS, 2006), 78.

18. See Ellen Koskoff, ed., *Women and Music in Cross-Cultural Perspective* (Urbana: University of Illinois Press, 1987).

19. Wersland and Rognli, *Joik*, 11; Hirvonen, *Voices from Sápmi*, 137.

20. In Sámi mythology the *sieidi*—natural stones, mountains, or even islands—were sites of worship that recycle the earth's energy. Offerings were made to honor the powers of nature. The sieidi were doorways to other worlds, where people could meet spirits. They were also linked with specific siidas.

21. Jaakko Gauriloff, *Kuä'ckkem suäjai vuel'nn* [Under the wings of an eagle] (Nummi-Pusula Finland GAU CD1, 1991), compact disc.

22. Jaakko Gauriloff, personal communication, Inari, Finland, May 25, 2007. Ethnographic recordings made by Finnish researchers enable us to gain some ideas about the leu'dd tradition in the past (including recordings made by Itkonen in 1913, Launis in 1922, Väisänen in 1926, and Ala-Könni in 1961). A recent compilation of Ala-Könni's historical recordings from the archive was made by Jouste, Mosnikoff, and Sivertsen (*Maaddârää'jji Leeu'd*). As soon as the borders to the Russian Kola Peninsula were opened, the Norwegian researcher Ola Graff began a collaborative recording project (from 1994 to 1997) with the Finnish researcher (and a folk revival performer in the 1970s) Ilpo Saastamoinen. They reported that they found no male Skolt singers in the 1990s. Men had been sent to frontlines or had turned to alcohol, and women had been left to bring up their children alone in the Soviet era, sometimes hunting elks in secret from Soviet authorities. Saastamoinen, *Son Vuäinn*, 18.

23. Tiina Sanila's website (www.tiinasanila.com), accessed August 2009. No longer available.

24. Tiina Sanila, *Kå' llkue'll še måttmešt talkk*, Finland, Tuupa Records Oy TREC-010, 2007, compact disc.

25. Maiya Prokop'evna Sergina, cited in Saastamoinen, *Son Vuäinn*, 22.

26. Sunna Kuoljok and Johan E. Utsi, *The Sámi: People of the Sun and Wind* (Luleå: Ájtte, Swedish Mountain and Sámi Museum, 2000), 44–46.

27. Quoted in Veli-Pekka Lehtola, *The Sámi People: Traditions in Transition* (Inari: Kustannus-Puntsi, 2004), 67.

28. On the case of Inari Sámi rap, see Tina K. Ramnarine, "Musical Creativity and the Politics of Utterance: Cultural Ownership and Sustainability in Amoc's Inari Sámi Raps," in *L'Image du Sápmi*, vol. 2, ed. Kajsa Andersson (Göteburg: Örebro University, forthcoming).

29. Saastamoinen, *Son Vuäinn*.

30. In Skolt Sámi, Saastamoinen, *Son Vuäinn*, 32 (English translation on page 73).

31. Aili Nenola, "Problems of Emancipation and Tradition Awareness," in *Folklore Processed: In Honor of Lauri Honko on His 60th Birthday*, ed. Reimund Kvideland (Helsinki: Finnish Literature Society 1992), 185–88. Gender issues became prominent in Finnish academic circles in the 1980s and 1990s (as in other geographic contexts), and folklorists pointed out that views of Finnish folklore may be distorted by an incomplete picture of gender in the first European country to have given women the right to vote. See Satu

Apo, Aili Nenola, and Laura Stark-Arola, eds., *Gender and Folklore: Perspectives on Finnish and Karelian Culture* (Helsinki: Finnish Literature Society, 1998).

32. Hirvonen, *Voices from Sápmi*, 162.

33. Väinö Tanner, *Ihmismaantieteellisiä Tutkimuksia Petsamon Seudulta*, vol. 1, *Kolttalappalaiset*, ed. Paulo Susiluoto, trans. (from French) Pirjo Hyvärinen (Helsinki: Suomalaisen Kirjallisuuden Seura, 2000), 95.

34. Rauna Kuokkanen, "Myths and Realities of Sámi Women: A Post-colonial Feminist Analysis for the Decolonization and Transformation of Sámi Society," in *Making Space for Indigenous Feminism*, ed. Joyce Green (London: Zed Books, 2007), 79.

35. Hirvonen, *Voices from Sápmi*, 36, 233–34.

36. Kuokkanen, "Myths and Realities," 75.

37. Teemu Ryymin, "The Rise of Nationalism and Development of Northern Norway," in *The North Calotte: Perspectives on the Histories and Cultures of Northernmost Europe*, ed. Maria Lähteenmäki and Päivi Maria Pihjala (Helsinki University: Puntsi, 2005), 65.

38. Wersland and Rognli, *Joik*, 77. These entangled religious ideas find a contemporary musical expression in Fjellheim's composition, *Aejlies Gaaltije: The Sacred Source; An Arctic Mass* (1995). This work is based on the South Sámi liturgy, and the various movements include "Kyjrie" (*kyrie*), "Jupmelen laampe" (*agnus dei*), "Jupmelen vuelie" (yoik of God), "Laavloen heevehtibie" (Benedictus), "Kun tieni avian [ahdas on]" (when my road [is] very [narrow]; a Finnish hymn), "Biejjiem jih askem" (a South Sámi hymn), all of which point to the interwoven strands of Sámi spiritual and religious musical experience. Ulla Pirttijärvi is one of the joikers in the recorded performance (Norway: Vuelie, VUCD801, 2004) compact disc.

39. Kuokkanen, "Myths and Realities," 85, 87.

40. Jorunn Eikjok, "Gender, Essentialism and Feminism in Samiland," in Green, *Making Space*, 117, 120, 117.

41. Ibid., 118.

42. Thomas Hylland Eriksen, "Ethnicity versus Nationalism," *Journal of Peace Research* 28, no. 3 (1991): 272.

43. Stig Hjarvard, "The Mediatization of Religion: A Theory of the Media as Agents of Religious Change," *Northern Lights* 6 (2008): 24.

44. See also Ramnarine, *Ilmatar's Inspirations*.

45. Hirvonen, *Voices from Sápmi*, 213.

46. For women's musical activities in private spaces, see Susan C. Cook and Judy S. Tsou, eds., *Cecilia Reclaimed: Feminist Perspectives on Gender and Music* (Urbana: University of Illinois Press, 1994); for musical expression, see Koskoff, *Women and Music*; and for women's professional musical careers, see Marcia Citron, *Gender and the Musical Canon* (Urbana: University of Illinois Press, 1993.

47. Biret Ristin Sara, personal communication, Inari, Finland, May 24, 2007.

48. Joyce Green, "Taking Account of Aboriginal Feminism," in Green, *Making Space*, 21, 20.

49. Per-Niila Stålka, personal communication, Jokkmokk, Sweden, September 2006.

Afterword

Beverley Diamond

The triple themes of *Performing Gender, Place, and Emotion in Music* demonstrate how important it is to see the connectedness of different concepts of embodiment. These culturally variable terms of physicality and spirituality reach both inwardly toward the most intimate of human sensations or emotion and outwardly to larger environments of place and space. These studies demonstrate how social mediation occurs in relation to each of the three concepts, shaping behaviors and expectations of how music, among other things, both represents and constitutes the ways that we are embodied, emplaced, and "emotioned."

These chapters evoked memories and stories from my own work. In Canadian studies, I had at one point become interested in assertions about the gender of the nation-state as well as its provinces or regions. I thought of various contested but evocative images, including a number of nineteenth-century political cartoons depicting Canada as the demure maiden next to a matronly woman representing Britain, for instance (unlike the masculinist Uncle Sam imagery of the United States).[1] I recalled Elspeth Probyn's argument that Quebec's mode of "outside belonging" positions it as gay within Canadian identity constructs, an argument that challenges the heterosexist "broken marriage" imagery that she saw in the prereferendum period of the early 1990s.[2] Ian McKay's contention that Nova Scotia was imaged in the mid-twentieth century as a region of hardy males whose realm was the sea also came to mind.[3] These images and interpretations are arguably strategic and intentional assertions—not necessarily discursive formations that are culturally reinscribed and shared by large numbers of people.

Closer to socially shared discursive formations, however, are the many instances of song that imagine the importance of place. While the masculine gendering of mid-twentieth-century Nova Scotia might have been strategic for folklorists, broadcasters, and a nascent tourist industry, it would be hard to deny that the sea shapes the musical imaginary of many Nova Scotians, as it does in my home province of Newfoundland.[4] The wide range of shipwreck songs in the traditional repertoire (or an occasional rescue tale) or songs composed after the devastating 1992 cod-fishing moratorium come readily to mind. I think also of music that evokes nostalgia for places left behind when Newfoundland and Labrador communities were resettled, particularly since the 1950s and 1960s, or songs that helped families cope with local disasters. The distinctions between strategic assertions and deeper socially shared discursive formations are significant in evoking and shaping emotional responses.

In indigenous studies I thought of the evocative mappings of the body, the physical world, and emotion within both Sámi and First Nations teaching practices. Sámi artisans, for example, often depict a layered universe on the membranes of drums. Various Anishnabe teachings similarly use images of bodies (human and other species) as maps of the universe, while others regard the body of a two- or four-legged being or other sensate objects (including some musical instruments) as "lodges" through which humans travel in the course of their life. Such images and teachings sometimes have gendered dimensions. The dance drum that has been adapted to become the powwow drum may embrace male and female qualities or elements, particularly if animals of both sexes "gave" themselves to be part of the instrument. For the Anishnabe, musical instruments may have kinship terms, as in the case of the tall "grandfather" water drum and its spiritual counterpart, the "little boy." In every case, these are quick points of resonance that have emerged in my studies over the years, but ones that confirmed to me the ways in which the themes of the anthology extend to other cultural realms.

Perhaps more relevant is a question that these personal memories and moments of learning imply. Is this desire to add one's memories to the conversation an emotion, I wonder. It doesn't fit comfortably within a specific label for any emotion that I recognize. Is it pleasure? Is it excitement? Arguably, the intense desire to interact in a conversation is not conventionally an emotion at all in the cultural spaces in which I move. But it is intensely feelingful. Having a conversation with one's colleagues over intellectual issues is certainly engagement. Just what is engagement in terms of the constructs that the authors of this anthology explore? Among other things, it is embodied and feelingful as well as emplaced.

Cross-Cultural Ranges of Meaning: Gender, Place, and Emotion

As an afterward to such a powerful body of work, I decided first to reread the conceptual range of each of the central concepts as revealed by the studies in this anthology (although the introduction to the volume does an exceptional job of this). Then I offer a few comments on aspects that thread through the chapters that are arguably marginalized here but worthy of becoming the central foci of future work. Third, I think briefly about the implications of this anthology for understanding and dealing with radical change (increasingly our experience of place in a time of globalization and rapid environmental shifts) but also for comprehending our experience of embodiment and emotion in the twenty-first century.

Of the three concepts, "emotion" is for me the most daunting. As I have revealed, the ambiguity within my own thought process about the distinction between engagement and emotion—and hence my own struggle to know the boundaries of what an emotion *is*—is in itself a challenge. The enormity of the literature on emotion as well as its psychological depth, psychology being a field outside my training, make it still more challenging to venture well-informed thoughts about this construct. Jerome Kagan suggests that there are four distinct domains within the study of emotion: (1) changes in brain activity, (2) changes in feeling that have sensory qualities, (3) cognitive interpretations of those changes in feeling using words, and (4) preparedness for or display of a behavioral response. Ethnomusicologists might contest the separation but agree that we deal with the last three of the four. I am heartened by Kagan's advice to "turn our attention to the cascade of observations to which the abstract concept refers."[5]

There are certain points that this anthology emphasizes and that I believe most ethnomusicologists would agree on, namely, that emotion is defined differently in different historical and cultural circumstances and that cultural performance plays a key role in both teaching and articulating what emotion is. The anthology scholars go beyond this, however, to illustrate how cultural expectations also constrain the performance of emotion in various ways and how anomalous performers, such as Kim Yonja in Japan (discussed by Christine R. Yano) find effective ways to negotiate those constraints.[6] Some contributors, such as Jonathan McIntosh, in his discussion of the Barong dance in Bali, also demonstrate the capacity for inverting expectations in ritualized circumstances. Several chapters demonstrate ways in which the language for emplacing emotion maps onto the body itself. Barley Norton describes how Vietnamese performers use metaphors that refer to the heart, stomach, and mind; Fiona Magowan references Yolngu concepts that situate emotion in the stomach, but she also refers to "mind names." While many chapters in this anthology focus on culturally constructed *performances* of emotions (e.g., Norton, Magowan, McIntosh, Wrazen, Yano) and some also deal with individual *feelings* of emotion (see, e.g., Norton, Magowan, Walmsley-Pledl), the emphasis is on the former, on the relationality of emotion, reflecting the etymology of e-motion as moving outward.

Place is, of course, a particularly charged and complex notion in an age of unprecedented human mobility, as many theorists of globalization have argued eloquently. Arjun Appadurai writes that "the landscapes of group identity—the ethnoscapes—around the world are no longer familiar anthropological objects, insofar as groups are no longer tightly territorialized, spatially bounded, historically unselfconscious, or culturally homogeneous. . . . The ethnoscapes of today's world are profoundly interactive."[7] In this anthology the framing of place is necessarily varied in different contexts; places are at times a sort of scape on which human music making takes place and at others a sort of sonic extension of the body itself. In some community contexts (north Vietnamese mountains and rivers described by Norton, the kinship-defined lands of the Yolngu where Magowan works, or the mountains of the Górale studied by Wrazen), place is first and foremost the natural environment. While the vastness of mountains and rivers seem closer to region or settings, it is clear that the authors of this anthology explore them as socially inscribed in multiple ways.[8] Each case study adds a rich layer of information about how different sorts of culturally constructed meanings are mapped onto these natural environments. As Norton describes, the gendering of these places is explicit in north Vietnam, for instance, where male and female spirits are variously associated with mountains and forests and with lowlands and rivers. Mountains near the Górale communities of Poland, on the other hand, are spaces that female singers use to extend their voices. Mountains become a technology of the self, in Michel Foucault's terms.[9] All these authors take into consideration the technologies by which modern existence has been mediated. As Louise Wrazen ably demonstrates, Aniela's rural background did not preclude her becoming an early recording artist in the late 1950s; she continues to be sought by ensembles for indoor performances even if they evoke the outdoors. Tina K. Ramnarine writes powerfully of nature as gendered in the Sámi world, explaining associations between fire and feminine power but also reflecting on a feminist critique of the Mother Earth imaginary that is often a stereotype of indigenous culture. This anthology adds, then, to the growing literature on natural places as sensate in themselves.

Many of the studies in the anthology, on the other hand, focus on localized places as sites of memory. Here the personal stories of individuals reveal how the memory of place, together with the memory of song, vitalizes all the senses and evokes the memories of significant events or human encounters. Those memories are especially intense in the case of lost places or people. Some cultural communities, such as those of the Yolngu, have developed the potential of song to mediate loss so that as Magowan writes, repeated performances build on the "multiple layers of love, concern, guilt, or remorse about relatives who have died or left the community." Loss of the freedom to see places and people dear to them was also mediated by song for the male Guugu Yimithirr inmates of the correctional institute where Muriel Swijghuisen Reigersberg's women's choir performed. In both cases song effectively transformed both performers and listeners. Other ethnomusicologists have drawn attention to similar phenomena. David Samuels has explored how the San Carlos Apache embed complex memories, stories, and moral judgments in topographies. Keith Basso described how his Apache elders taught him that "wisdom sits in places" and that the very mention of a place-name recalls floods of events, stories, or expressive creations. Steven Feld has extended the interpretive connections that we make between place and cultural knowledge under the rubric of "acoustemology," which he defines as sonic knowledge and sensibility.[10]

Other studies emphasize the historically constituted nature of politically recognized places, especially nation-states. Ramnarine outlines how the struggle for Sámi sovereignty was paralleled by a burst of cultural production since the 1980s, but she emphasizes the regional differences among the Sámi, particularly the Skolte Sámi, who suffered dislocation during the Soviet regime. She sees the turn of several female recording artists to subjects that reflect a common mythological past as a solidarity strategy that affirms the power of women but also contests Western models of feminism. Yano explores the challenges and ironies of Korean-born residents in Japan, a country with a history of discriminating against Koreans, through the high profile career of Korean-born Kim Yonja. Yano's exploration of the ways in which Kim negotiates acceptance as a singer of enka, a genre often identified as the emotional soul of Japan, is multilayered.

Finally, gender and its musical expression are associated here in relation to place and emotion. As a dimension of embodiment that is socially and discursively constructed, gender has more often been studied in relation to the power-laden social constructs of class, ethnicity, and race. While earlier anthologies have included chapters that unpack the intersections of these cross-culturally variable social hierarchies, none to date have focused on the relationships to place and emotion.[11] The case studies in this volume (like those in virtually every anthology produced thus far) emphasize that music may reproduce or reinforce heterosexist difference, discursively, economically, and culturally. But they also demonstrate how music may challenge binaries of male and female and even cross boundaries between humans and other species. Of particular interest to me were ways in which apparent anomalies actually were not particularly anomalous. Sara R. Walmsley-Pledl's interviewee Gabriela might sing in a tenor voice, setting her apart from most of the women in the Bavarian choir in which she sings, but might express a love of being in the middle, surrounded by other voices, hence emphasizing the emotion she associates with belonging. While the women of Podhale do not sing for the male-dominated dance tradition of the Górale and must, as dancers, be led onto the floor by a man, their individual repertoires offer them space for asserting a different kind of power. Aniela, with whom Wrazen has worked, finds a way to extend the reach of her voice by singing outdoors, using the natural resonance of the mountains to carry her voice far, but she accepts the social constraints on being a woman in other circumstances. Similarly, as Yano describes, Korean enka singer Kim Yonja gains acceptance in Japan by becoming the Other while simultaneously daring to assert postcolonial messages through her use of the Japanese language, her shifts in costume, and her means of invoking fan support. As Yano succinctly puts it, the "relationship [is] built on dependency" but individual musicians creatively find ways to trouble those dependencies.

Contingencies That Merit Focused Attention in Future Research

I turn now to two other issues that also thread through this volume. They are not identified as central issues here, but these contingencies clearly merit focused attention in future music research. The first of these is ability; the second is age.

Ability is a factor that societies generally validate in culturally specific ways, and such forms of cultural validation implicate gender, place, and emotion. Musical ability may indeed allow individuals to transcend norms of behavior. The Podhale singer Aniela illustrates this, as Wrazen demonstrates. So too do two of the Bavarian choir members interviewed by Walmsley-Pledl, as well as the Korean star Kim Yonja in Japan, studied by Yano. But expectations of who is capable have much deeper implications, of course. Colonial hierarchies are hard to eradicate and create lasting scars, as in the case of the men and women with whom Swijghuisen Reigersberg works. While the Aboriginal men of the community might well have risen to the occasion, they were not trusted with responsibilities in colonial contexts such as the Lutheran church and turned to self-destructive behaviors. The women of the community had more liberty to feel part of the Christian institutions that were introduced and now have the strangely configured opportunity to use Lutheran hymns in their own language to evoke powerful memories of home for the men who have been incarcerated in alien spaces. The very ability to sing is, of course, a poignant memory for those whose skill has been questioned in their early years. The case of Andreas, one of the Bavarian choir members interviewed by Walmsley-Pledl, is a case in point. His youthful hopes to play an instrument dashed, he turned to a choir to consolidate his sense of belonging and his expectations of Heimat (the complex concept of homeland that operates in German-speaking nations with regionally differentiated spaces, including Bavaria).

A second contingency in the anthology is age, generation, and age-related social roles. In recent decades, we have most often regarded gender and sexuality as performative effects; that is, by reiterating certain behaviors or ways of interacting so often that these behaviors become naturalized or at least normalized, certain ideas of gender and sexuality are produced and entrenched in specific social contexts.[12] The emphasis on reiterated behaviors and ways of being, however, may obscure the fact that we change these patterns in relation both to physical aging and to the various roles ascribed to us as we age. Hence, while constructs of gender and sexuality are undoubtedly among the most powerful shapers of social norms and behavior, the chapters in this anthology demonstrate that age and generation are also powerfully intertwined with both emotion and place and persuasively rearticulated through musical performance. While McIntosh is the only one to focus specifically on children and the way they learn to perceive gendered emotional behavior in relation to Balinese Barong performances, many of the authors observe generational differences. Magowan, for instance, writes of the ancestral lineages that give elder Yolngu clan members the right to know, tell, sing, and dance. She discusses the important mother–child dyad that defines interclan relationships and explains the crying-song style expected of older women, since younger women should not sing in public. While young and old both know the histories of dislocation embodied in the communal history of the Guugu Yimithirr about which Swijghuisen Reigersberg writes, the older people know versions of the non-Christian stories that existed prior to missionary contact.

This points to an issue of central importance to these chapters: how loss and absence of both people and places can be reconstituted through performance. These are powerful referents of events that evoke tears and song, but often such emotions are available only for those whose lives have been long enough to feel loss and absence. This is not to suggest that children do not have these experiences, and, indeed, children who feel loss are particularly vulnerable. Music scholars have not yet studied the strategies that people of different ages employ when dealing with loss and absence. This anthology, however, provides some valuable clues suggesting occasions where music brings the comforting memory of a place or person back into the lived experience of an individual. Walmsley-Pledl's account of the Bavarian construction of Heimat in song is one persuasive example. In many cases we describe such expression as nostalgic. As Svetlana Boym has demonstrated, nostalgia may be both reflective and productive in times and spaces of social rupture.[13] It often seems to be a hope-filled attempt to recreate idealized pasts, and yet it also speaks about the unrealized visions that may inform the future. Yano's work is illustrative, demonstrating that music may play a complex role in idealizations of the past. Song may articulate nostalgia for enka as the "heart and soul of Japan" while also maintaining very current social divisions between "real" Japanese and outsiders and offering implicit comments on place as emotionally charged through its denationalization and denaturalization.

Gender, Place, and Emotion in the Context of Massive Environmental Change

Environmental change reinflects any idea that place is stable or definable by means of a stable set of cultural and emotional responses. Increasingly in the twenty-first century, the rivers that were life-giving may become life-threatening; the habitats that sustained a secure food supply may now destroy that security. Clearly, music cannot solve problems of such magnitude. The studies in this chapter, however, point to two roles that expressive culture plays when place is destabilized. One is the role of mediation and social transformation. Song becomes a significant means of enabling humans to cope with the crises that rapid change invariably causes. A second is the role of offering alternative models for relating to the environment. It is not surprising that many of the chapters in this anthology are situated in indigenous cultures where harmony and balance among all sensate beings is a value that informs traditional lifeways. The ecological knowledge of such cultures may rapidly become more central in the context of changes that are global in scope. They will not be easily dismissed as anachronistic but rather relevant to a sustainable future. As Julie Cruikshank has eloquently demonstrated, a dialogue between indigenous knowledge and Western science is urgently needed.[14] It is increasingly clear that alternative models of sustainability will be essential components in ecology and that such models are often interwoven with forms of expressive culture such as song. This anthology helps readers begin to think about such urgently current issues in the early twenty-first century.

Notes

1. Many early examples by Canadian illustrator John Wilson Bengough that were originally published by Grip Publishing or Diogenes are reproduced in Bengough's *A Caricature History of Canadian Politics: Events from the Union of 1841, as Illustrated by Cartoons from "Grip," and Various Other Sources* (Toronto: Grip, 1886; Toronto: Martin Associates, 1974).

2. See Elspeth Probyn, "'Love in a Cold Climate': Queer Belongings in Quebec," in *Outside Belongings* (New York: Routledge, 1996), 63–92.

3. Ian McKay, *The Quest of the Folk* (Montreal: McGill-Queen's University Press, 1994), 92.

4. Of course, as McKay notes, for some segments of the population, the forests or the mines may be more central parts of their daily activities and imaginations (ibid.).

5. Jerome Kagan, *What Is Emotion? History, Measures, and Meanings* (New Haven: Yale University Press, 2007), 19, xi.

6. John Burrows, *Drawing Out Law: A Spirit's Guide* (Toronto: University of Toronto Press, 2010). He records his dream worlds in drawings inspired by Anishnabe pictographs as a means of stimulating reflection on the part of his readers. The drawings generally have a sphere inside a rectangle, most often with a double line running horizontally through the middle.

7. Arjun Appadurai, *Modernity at Large: Cultural Dimensions of Globalization* (Minneapolis: University of Minnesota Press, 1996), 48.

8. Compare, for instance, Margaret Rodman's persuasive argument that multilocality is as significant as multivocality. "Empowering Place: Multilocality and Multivocality," *American Anthropologist*, n.s., 94, no. 3 (1992): 640–56.

9. Michel Foucault "Technologies of the Self," in *Technologies of the Self*, ed. Luther H. Martin, Huck Guttman, and Patricia Hutton (Amherst: University of Massachusetts Press, 1998).

10. David Samuels, *Putting a Song on Top of It* (Tucson: University of Arizona Press, 2004); Keith Basso, *Wisdom Sits in Places* (Albuquerque: University of New Mexico Press, 1996). Steven Feld, "Waterfalls of Song: An Acoustemology of Place Resounding in Bosavi, Papua New Guinea," in *Senses of Place*, ed. Steven Feld and Keith H. Basso (Santa Fe, NM: School of American Research Press, 1996).

11. Ellen Koskoff, ed., *Women and Music in Cross-Cultural Perspective* (Urbana: University of Illinois Press, 1987); Marcia Herndon and Susanne Ziegler, eds., *Music, Gender, and Culture* (Wilhelmshaven: Florian Noetzel Verlag, 1990); Pirkko Moisala and Beverley Diamond, eds., *Music and Gender* (Urbana: University of Illinois Press, 2000); Tullia Magrini, ed., *Music and Gender: Perspectives from the Mediterranean* (Chicago: University of Chicago Press, 2003).

12. See especially Judith Butler, *Gender Trouble: Feminism and the Subversion of Identity* (New York: Routledge, 1990).

13. Svetlana Boym, *The Future of Nostalgia* (New York: Basic Books, 2001), xvi.

14. Julie Cruikshank, *Do Glaciers Listen? Local Knowledge, Colonial Encounters and Social Imagination* (Vancouver: University of British Columbia Press, 2005).

Selected Bibliography

Bakan, Michael B. *Music of Death and New Creation: Experiences in the World of Balinese Gamelan Beleganjur*. Chicago: University of Chicago Press, 1999.

Bandem, I. Madé, and Fredrik de Boer. *Kaja and Kelod: Balinese Dance in Transition*. Kuala Lumpur: Oxford University Press, 1981.

Barkin, Elaine, and Lydia Hamessley, eds. *Audible Traces: Gender, Identity, and Music*. Zurich: Carciogoli Verlagshaus, 1999.

Becker, Judith. *Deep Listeners: Music, Emotion, and Trancing*. Bloomington: Indiana University Press, 2004.

Blickle, Peter. *Heimat: A Critical Theory of the German Idea of Homeland*. Rochester, NY: Camden House, 2002.

Brett, Philip, Elizabeth Wood, and Gary C. Thomas, eds. *Queering the Pitch: The New Gay and Lesbian Musicology*. New York: Routledge, 1994.

Bruner, Edward M. "Introduction: Experience and Its Expressions." In *The Anthropology of Experience*, edited by Victor W. Turner and Edward M. Bruner, 3–20. Urbana: University of Illinois Press, 1986.

Buchanan, Donna. *Performing Democracy*. Chicago: University of Chicago Press, 2006.

Citron, Marcia. *Gender and the Musical Canon*. Urbana: University of Illinois Press, 1993.

Connell, John, and Chris Gibson. *Sound Tracks: Popular Music, Identity, and Place*. New York: Routledge, 2003.

Cook, Susan C., and Judy S. Tsou, eds. *Cecilia Reclaimed: Feminist Perspectives on Gender and Music*. Urbana: University of Illinois Press, 1994.

Cooley, Timothy, J. *Making Music in the Polish Tatras: Tourists, Ethnographers, and Mountain Musicians*. Bloomington: Indiana University Press, 2005.

Corn, Aaron. "Ancestral, Corporeal, Corporate: Traditional Yolngu Understandings of the Body Explored." *Borderlands* 7, no. 2 (2008): 1–17.

Dunn, Leslie C., and Nancy A. Jones, eds. *Embodied Voices: Representing Female Vocality in Western Culture*. Cambridge: Cambridge University Press, 1994.

Endres, Kirsten W. *Performing the Divine: Mediums, Markets and Modernity in Vietnam*. Copenhagen: NIAS Press, 2011.

Feld, Steven. *Sound and Sentiment: Birds, Weeping, Poetics, and Song in Kaluli Expression*. Philadelphia: University of Pennsylvania Press, 1990.

Feld, Steven, and Keith H. Basso, eds. *Senses of Place*. Santa Fe, NM: School of American Research Press, 1996.

Finnegan, Ruth. *Communicating: The Multiple Modes of Human Interconnection*. London: Routledge, 2002.

———. "Music, Experience, and the Anthropology of Emotion." In *The Cultural Study of Music: A Critical Introduction*, edited by Martin Clayton, Trevor Herbert, and Richard Middleton, 181–92. New York: Routledge, 2003.

Garnett, Liz. "Choral Singing as Bodily Regime." *International Review of the Aesthetics and Sociology of Music* 36, no. 2 (2005): 249–69.

Gold, Lisa. *Music in Bali: Expressing Music, Expressing Culture.* New York: Oxford University Press, 2005.

Grau, Andrée. "On the Acquisition of Knowledge: Teaching Kinship through the Body among Tiwi of Northern Australia." In *Common Worlds and Single Lives*, edited by Verena Keck, 71–93. Oxford: Berg, 1998.

Hallam, Elizabeth, Ian Cross, and Michael Thaut, eds. *The Oxford Handbook of Music Psychology.* Oxford: Oxford University Press, 2009.

Hayes, Eileen M., and Linda F. Williams, eds. *Black Women and Music: More Than the Blues.* Urbana: University of Illinois Press, 2007.

Herndon, Marcia, and Susanne Ziegler, eds. *Music, Gender and Culture.* Wilhelmshaven, Germany: Florian Noetzel Verlag, 1990.

Hobart, Angela. *Healing Performances of Bali: Between Darkness and Light.* New York: Berghahn, 2003.

Hochschild, Arlie. *The Managed Heart: Commercialization of Human Feelings.* Berkeley: University of California Press, 1983.

Ingold, Tim. *The Perception of the Environment: Essays in Livelihood, Dwelling and Skill.* London: Routledge, 2000.

Ivy, Marilyn. *Discourse of the Vanishing: Modernity, Phantasm, Japan.* Chicago: University of Chicago Press, 1995.

Iwabuchi Koichi. *Recentering Globalization: Popular Culture and Japanese Transnationalism.* Durham, NC: Duke University Press, 2002.

Jackson, Michael. *The Politics of Storytelling, Violence, Transgression and Intersubjectivity.* Copenhagen: University of Copenhagen, Museum Tusculanum Press, 2006. First published 2002.

Juslin, Patrik N., and John A. Sloboda, eds. *Music and Emotion: Theory and Research.* Oxford: Oxford University Press, 2001.

Kaplan, Steven, ed. *Indigenous Responses to Western Christianity.* New York: New York University Press, 1995.

Keen, Ian. *Knowledge and Secrecy in an Aboriginal Religion.* New York: Oxford University Press, 1994.

Knopoff, Steven. "Value in Yolngu Ceremonial Song Performance: Continuity and Change." In *Beyond Price: Value in Culture, Economics, and the Arts*, edited by Michael Hutter, 127–40. Cambridge: Cambridge University Press, 2008.

Koskoff, Ellen. "(Left Out in) Left (the Field): The Effects of Post-postmodern Scholarship on Feminist and Gender Studies in Musicology and Ethnomusicology, 1990–2000." *Women and Music* 9 (2005): 90–98.

———, ed. *Women and Music in Cross-Cultural Perspective.* Urbana: University of Illinois Press, 1987.

Kreutz, Gunter, Stephan Bongard, Sonja Rohrmann, Volker Hodapp, and Dorothee Grebe. "Effects of Choir Singing or Listening on Secretory Immunoglobulin A, Cortisol, and Emotional State." *Journal of Behavioral Medicine* 27 (2004): 623–35.

Kuokkanen, Rauna. "Myths and Realities of Sámi Women: A Post-colonial Feminist Analysis for the Decolonization and Transformation of Sámi Society." In *Making Space for Indigenous Feminism*, edited by Joyce Green, 72–92. London: Zed Books, 2007.
Kuoljok, Sunna, and Johan E. Utsi. *The Sámi: People of the Sun and Wind*. Luleå: Ájtte, Swedish Mountain and Sámi Museum, 2000.
Leavitt, John. "Meaning and Feeling in the Anthropology of Emotions." *American Ethnologist* 23, no. 3 (1996): 514–39.
Lehtola, Veli-Pekka. *The Sámi People: Traditions in Transition*. Inari: Kustannus-Puntsi, 2004.
Le Tuan Hung. *Dan Tranh Music in Vietnam: Traditions and Innovations*. Melbourne: Australian Asia Foundation, 1998.
Levin, Theodore. *Where Rivers and Mountains Sing: Sound, Music and Nomadism in Tuva and Beyond*. With Valentina Süzükei. Bloomington: University of Indiana Press, 2006.
Lutz, Catherine. "Emotion, Thought, and Estrangement: Emotion as a Cultural Category." *Cultural Anthropology* 1, no. 3 (1986): 287–309.
Lutz, Catherine, and Geoffrey M. White. "The Anthropology of Emotions." *Annual Review of Anthropology* 15 (1986): 406–36.
MacKinlay, Elizabeth. "Maintaining Grandmother's Law: Female Song Partners in Yanuyuwa Culture." *Musicology Australia* 23 (2000): 76–98.
Magowan, Fiona. "Globalisation and Indigenous Christianity: Translocal Sentiments in Australian Aboriginal Christian Songs." *Identities: Global Studies in Culture and Power* 14, no. 4 (2007): 459–83.
Magrini, Tullia, ed. *Music and Gender: Perspectives from the Mediterranean*. Chicago: University of Chicago Press, 2003.
Massey, Doreen. *Space, Place and Gender*. Cambridge: Polity, 1994.
McClary, Susan. *Feminine Endings: Music, Gender and Sexuality*. Minneapolis: University of Minnesota Press, 1991.
McIntosh, Jonathan. "Preparation, Presentation and Power: Children's Performances in a Balinese Dance Studio." In *Dancing Cultures: Globalization, Tourism and Identity in the Anthropology of Dance*, edited by Hélène Neveu-Kringelbach and Jonathan Skinner, 194–210. New York and Oxford: Berghahn, 2012.
McPhee, Colin. *Music in Bali: A Study in Form and Instrumental Organization in Balinese Orchestral Music*. New Haven: Yale University Press, 1966.
Mead, Margaret. "Strolling Players in the Mountains of Bali." In *Traditional Balinese Culture*, edited by Jane Belo, 137–45. New York: Columbia University Press, 1970. First published 1940.
Milton, Kay. *Loving Nature: Towards an Ecology of Emotion*. London: Routledge, 2002.
Moisala, Pirkko, and Beverley Diamond, eds. *Music and Gender*. Urbana: University of Illinois Press, 2000.
Morphy, Frances. "Performing the Law: The Yolngu of Blue Mud Bay Meet the Native Title Process." In *The Social Effects of Native Title: Recognition, Translation, Coexistence*, edited by Benjamin R. Smith and Frances Morphy, 31–57. Canberra: ANU ePress, 2007.
Norton, Barley. *Songs for the Spirits: Music and Mediums in Modern Vietnam*. Urbana: University of Illinois Press, 2009.

Parker, Lyn. *From Subjects to Citizens: Balinese Villagers in the Indonesian Nation-State.* Copenhagen: Nordic Institute of Asian Studies, 2003.

Parkinson, Brian, Agneta H. Fischer, and Antony S. R. Manstead. *Emotion in Social Relations: Cultural, Group, and Interpersonal Processes.* New York: Psychology Press, 2005.

Pine, Frances. "Incorporation and Exclusion in the Podhale." In *Lilies of the Field: Marginal People Who Live for the Moment*, edited by Sophie Day, Evthymios Papataxiarchis, and Michael Stewart, 45–60. Boulder: Westview, 1999.

Probyn, Elspeth. *Outside Belongings.* New York: Routledge, 1996.

Ramnarine, Tina K. "Acoustemology, Indigeneity and Joik in Valkeapää's Symphonic Activism: Views from Europe's Arctic Fringes for Environmental Ethnomusicology." *Ethnomusicology* 53, no. 2 (2009): 187–217.

———. *Ilmatar's Inspirations: Nationalism, Globalization, and the Changing Soundscapes of Finnish Folk Music.* Chicago: Chicago University Press, 2003.

Rapport, Nigel. *Transcendent Individual: Towards a Literary and Liberal Anthropology.* London: Routledge, 1997.

Rapport, Nigel, and Andrew Dawson, eds. *Migrants of Identity: Perceptions of Home in a World of Movement.* Oxford: Berg, 1998.

Rice, Timothy. *May It Fill Your Soul: Experiencing Bulgarian Music.* Chicago: University of Chicago Press, 1994.

Rodman, Margaret. "Empowering Place: Multilocality and Multivocality." *American Anthropologist*, n.s., 94, no. 3 (1992): 640–56.

Rosaldo, Michelle. "Toward an Anthropology of Self and Feeling." In *Culture Theory: Essays on Mind, Self, and Emotion*, edited by Richard A. Shweder and Robert A. LeVine, 137–58. Cambridge: Cambridge University Press, 1984.

Ryymin, Teemu. "The Rise of Nationalism and Development of Northern Norway." In *The North Calotte: Perspectives on the Histories and Cultures of Northernmost Europe*, edited by Maria Lähteenmäki and Päivi Maria Pihjala, 54–66. Helsinki: Puntsi, 2005.

Samuels, David. *Putting a Song on Top of It.* Tucson: University of Arizona Press, 2004.

Sandgren, Maria. "Evidence for Strong Immediate Well-Being Effects of Choral Singing: With More Enjoyment for Women than Men." *Proceedings of the Seventh Triennial Conference of European Society for the Cognitive Sciences of Music*, edited by Jukka Louhivuori, Tuomas Eerola, Suvi Saarikallio, Tommi Himberg, and Päivi-Sisko Eerola, 475–79. Finland: Department of Music, University of Jyväskylä ESCOM, 2009.

Schafer, R. Murray. *The Tuning of the World.* Rochester, VT: Destiny Books, 1977.

Scott, Joan W. "Experience." In *Feminists Theorize the Political*, edited by Judith Butler and Joan W. Scott, 22–39. New York: Routledge, 1992.

Sheets-Johnstone, Vivienne. "Emotion and Movement: Analysing Their Relationship." In *Reclaiming Cognition: The Primacy of Action, Intention and Emotion*, edited by Rafael Núñez and Walter J. Freeman, 259–77. Thorverton: Imprint Academic, 1999.

Shore, Bradd. *Culture in Mind: Cognition, Culture, and the Problem of Meaning.* New York: Oxford University Press, 1996.

Stobart, Henry. "Bodies of Sound and Landscapes of Music: A View from the Bolivian Andes." In *Musical Healing in Cultural Contexts*, edited by Penelope Gouk, 26–45. Aldershot: Ashgate, 2000.

Stokes, Martin, ed. *Ethnicity, Identity and Music: The Musical Construction of Place*. Oxford: Berg, 1994.

Stoller, Paul. *The Taste of Ethnographic Things: The Senses in Anthropology*. Philadelphia: University of Pennsylvania Press, 1989.

Stubington, Jill. *Singing the Land: The Power of Performance in Aboriginal Life*. Strawberry Hills, New South Wales: Currency House Press, 2007.

Sugarman, Jane C. *Engendering Song: Singing and Subjectivity at Prespa Albanian Weddings*. Chicago: University of Chicago Press, 1997.

Swain, Tony, and Deborah Bird-Rose. *Aboriginal Australians and Christian Missions: Ethnographic and Historical Studies*. Bedford Park, South Australia: Australian Association for the Study of Religions, 1988.

Swijghuisen Reigersberg, Muriel E. "Research Ethics, Positive and Negative Impact, and Working in an Indigenous Australian Context." *Ethnomusicology Forum* 20, no. 2 (2011): 255–62.

Tamisari, Franca. "Names and Naming: Speaking Forms into Place." In *The Land Is a Map: Placenames of Indigenous Origin in Australia*, edited by Luise Hercus, Flavia Hodges, and Jane Simpson, 87–102. Canberra: Australian National University, 2002.

Titon, Jeff Todd, ed. *Worlds of Music*. 4th ed. New York: Schirmer, 2002.

Toner, Peter. "Melody and Musical Articulations of Yolngu Identities." *Yearbook for Traditional Music* 35 (2003): 69–95.

Tuan, Yi-Fu. *Space and Place: The Perspective of Experience*. Minneapolis: University of Minnesota Press, 1977.

Wolf, Richard, ed. *Theorizing the Local: Music, Practice, and Experience in South Asia and Beyond*. Oxford: Oxford University Press, 2009.

Wong, Deborah. "Taiko and the Asian/American Body: Drums, Rising Sun and the Question of Gender." *World of Music* 42, no. 3 (2000): 67–78.

Wrazen, Louise. "Relocating the Tatras: Place and Music in Górale Identity and Imagination." *Ethnomusicology* 51, no. 2 (2007): 185–204.

Yano, Christine. *Tears of Longing: Nostalgia and the Nation in Japanese Popular Song*. Cambridge: Harvard Asia Center, Harvard University Press, 2002.

———. "Torching the Stage: Korean Singers in a Japanese Popular Music World." *Hybridity* 1, no. 2 (2001): 45–63.

Contributors

BEVERLEY DIAMOND is the Canada research chair in ethnomusicology at Memorial University of Newfoundland, where she established and directs the Research Centre for the Study of Music, Media, and Place (MMaP). Her research has spanned Canadian historiography, feminist ethnomusicology, the social meaning of music technology, and indigenous modernities (Native American and Sámi). Among her publications are *Native American Music in Eastern North America* (Oxford University Press, 2008) and *Music and Gender* (coedited with Pirkko Moisala; University of Illinois Press, 2000). She was elected to the Royal Society of Canada in 2008 and named a Trudeau Fellow in 2009.

FIONA MAGOWAN is a professor of anthropology at Queen's University, Belfast. Her publications focus on Yolngu music and dance in northeast Arnhem Land, Northern Territory, Australia. Her books include *Anthropology of Sex* (Berg, 2010); and *Melodies of Mourning: Music and Emotion in Northern Australia* (James Currey, School of American Research Press, 2007); and three coedited books: *Trangressive Sex* (Berghahn, 2009); *Landscapes of Performance* (Aboriginal Studies Press, 2005); and *Telling Stories* (Allen and Unwin, 2001).

JONATHAN MCINTOSH is an assistant professor of ethnomusicology at the University of Western Australia, where he teaches classes on ethnomusicology, popular music, and music of southeast Asia. His 2006 PhD dissertation focused on children's practice and performance of dance, music, and song in Bali, Indonesia.

BARLEY NORTON is a senior lecturer in ethnomusicology at Goldsmiths College, University of London. He specializes in the music of Vietnam, and his publications include a monograph, *Songs for the Spirits: Music and Mediums in Modern Vietnam* (University of Illinois Press, 2009), an edited book, *Music and Protest in 1968* (Cambridge University Press, 2013), and an ethnomusicological film, *Hanoi Eclipse: The Music of Dai Lam Linh* (Documentary Educational Resources, 2010).

TINA K. RAMNARINE is a professor of music at Royal Holloway University of London. She is the author of various studies on music, politics, and the environment, including *Ilmatar's Inspirations: Nationalism, Globalization, and the Changing Soundscapes of Finnish Folk Music* (University of Chicago Press, 2003) and *Beautiful Cosmos: Performance and Belonging in the Caribbean Diaspora* (Pluto Press, 2007).

MURIEL SWIJGHUISEN REIGERSBERG obtained her PhD in 2009 at Roehampton University. Her applied PhD research focused on the influence of Christian choral singing on the construction of Australian Aboriginal identities in Hopevale, northern Queensland. Her research interests include applied and medical ethnomusicology, spirituality, postcolonialism (community and culture-centered) music therapy, and education.

SARA R. WALMSLEY-PLEDL, an independent scholar, received her PhD in 2007 from Queen's University, Belfast. She is an applied ethnomusicologist, facilitator, and creative practitioner. Through her research interests in community music making and applied community art projects, she founded SoundMór, a creative business that actively links communities and those external agencies wishing to engage with them through sound and music to produce unique pieces. Her work on social art and music explores sound through digital media and narrative performance in response to project specific themes. To date she has worked at community level within the voluntary sector and public sectors of education, health, and cultural heritage.

LOUISE WRAZEN is an associate professor in the Department of Music at York University, Toronto, Canada. Her studies on music, identity, and displacement have focused on the music and dance of the Górale of southern Poland and have appeared in the journals *Ethnomusicology*, *Intersection*, and *Yearbook for Traditional Music*, among others.

CHRISTINE R. YANO is a professor of anthropology at the University of Hawaii. Her books include *Tears of Longing: Nostalgia and the Nation in Japanese Popular Song* (Harvard University Asia Center, 2002), *Crowning the Nice Girl: Gender, Ethnicity, and Culture in Hawai`i's Cherry Blossom Festival* (University of Hawaii Press, 2006), and *Airborne Dreams: "Nisei" Stewardesses and Pan American World Airways* (Duke University Press, 2011).

Index

An italicized page number indicates a figure or table.

Aboriginals Protection and Restriction of the Sale of Opium Act (1897), 89. *See also* Australian Aborigines
"acoustemology," 5, 13n30, 139–41, 143n24, 189
"affective system," 21–28
Agung, Mount, 44
alcoholism, 96, 97, 162
American Indians, 8, 88, 188–89
ancester veneration, 63–64, 66–74, 78–79, 188
Andersen, Ann-Mari, 166
Anishnabe pictographs, 186, 192n6
Appadurai, Arjun, 187–88
Arja dance-dramas, 43, 46, 48, 52, 53, 58
Arnhem Land, 63–79, *64*, 87, 92, 93, 102
Australian Aborigines, 7–8, 63–79, 187; assimilationist policies for, 90, 95–96; choral singing among, 85–88, *87*, 90–104, *97*, 190; cosmology of, 64, 71–72, 78–79; English of, 89, 92; initiation rituals of, 95, 105n8; land rights of, 65, 86–87, 95, 106n21; marriage among, 66, 94; missionaries of, 88, 89, 94–95; relocation of, 86, 89, 91, 102; substance abuse among, 96, 97

Bae Yung Jun, 157–58
Bakan, Michael, 47
Bali, 7–8, 38–58, *39*, 187, 191
Ballinger, Rucina, 39, 40, 60n15
Bambie, Myrtle, 99, 106n17
Bandem, I Madé, 40, 60n15
Bao, Nguyen Vinh, 33, 37n30

Barong performances, 38–58, *51*, *53*, *54*, *57*, 187; children's reactions to, 43–46, 191; improvisation in, 51, 54; landscape and, 38, 40, 44–45, 60n29; masks in, 41–42, 46, 49–52; "sonic landscape" of, 48–49, *49*
Barwick, Linda, 94
Basso, Keith H., 7, 77, 188–89
batel cycle, 47–49, *49*, 52
Bateson, Gregory, 45, 57, 61n34
Bauman, Zygmunt, 5
Bavarian singers, 8–9, 109–23, 189–91
Becker, Judith, 31, 32, 102
Behrendorf, Frank, 91
Bell, Diane, 94
Belo, Jane, 56, 57, 61n34
Bengough, John Wilson, 192n1
bhuta kala (spirits of chaos), 43
bilma manikay (unaccompanied Yolngu men's songs), 67
Blickle, Peter, 109, 111
Boine, Mari, 168, 169
Bourdieu, Pierre, 32, 111
Bowen, George, 92
Bowen, Matthew, 96
Bowen, Walter, 91–93
Boym, Svetlana, 191
Brazil, 148, 155
BRECVEM model, 4
bunggulmirri manikay ("dance-having songs"), 67–68
"burn time ceremony," 95
Burrows, John, 192n6
Buyu-Djarrakmirr, Murukun, 70–71

Calonarang dance-dramas, 39–40, 43, 59n9

Cameron, Alick, 95
Cao, Le Ba, 33–34, 37n32
Casey, Edward L., 4, 8
Certeau, Michel de, 111
chau van music, 18–20, *20*, 24, 28, 30–35
Cho Yonpiru, 160n4
Chor Kreis Deggendorf, 109–23, 189–91; emotional states and, 118–22; gendered notions and, 109, 113–23; *Heimat* narratives and, 110–12; music-making experiences in, 114–18; repertoire of, 110; sonic memories of place and, 112–14
Christianity: Bavaria and, 109, 110, 114; Hopevale Community Choir and, 85–88, *87*, 93–104, *97*, 190; Sámi people and, 164, 168, 171, 176; Yolngu and, 75, 92, 93. *See also* missionaries
Christie, Michael, 73
clapsticks, 19, 67
Cobus, Violet, 98, 100
colotomic structures, of gamelan ensembles, 48–50, *49*
Con songs, 25
Cooley, Timothy, 143n16
Corn, Aaron, 67, 72–74
cosmology: of Australian Aborigines, 64, 71–72, 78–79; of Barong performances, 42–43, 46, 53–54; of Sámi people, 163–65, 168, 177; of Vietnamese rituals, 18–26, *22*
Costello, Shirley, 104
"Country": Hopevale notion of, 86–88; Yolngu notion of, 63, 66, 71–78, 79n2, 86. *See also Heimat*
Cruikshank, Julie, 192
Czekanowska, Anna, 131

dance: Arja, 43, 46, 48, 52, 53, 58; *bunggulmirri manikay*, 67–68; Calonarang, 39–40, 43, 59n9; Górale, 130–32, 135; Topeng, 48, 52, 53, 58; Yolngu, 65–67, 77–79; *zbójnicki*, 130
Daugherty, James, 115–16
de Certeau, Michel, 111

Deeral, Gertie, 98–100
Deeral, Henry, 99, 100
Deggendorf choir. *See* Chor Kreis Deggendorf
Dharrpa, Dora, 92
Diamond, Beverley, 2, 10–11, 185–92, 201
Dibia, I Wayan, 39, 40, 60n15
didjeridoo, 66, 67, 81n25
Distler, Hugo, 116, 124n27
don ca tai tu music, 18, 33
Durga (deity), 42
Dussart, Françoise, 94
Dutton, Denis, 4

Eikjok, Jorunn, 178–79
Ekholm, Elizabeth, 115
emotion, 3–8, 147–48; "affective system" of, 21–28; Chor Kreis Deggendorf and, 118–22; commodification of, 10, 150; empathy and, 32; Hopevale Community Choir and, 96–102, *100*, *101*; Japanese *enka* songs and, 150, 155–57; Sámi songs and, 162–63; "sentimental relations" and, 32–34; Vietnamese rituals and, 17–31, 35
"emotion-talk," 4
"emotional texture," 27–28
enka songs, 10, 147–48, 150–53, 155–57, 160, 191
environmentalism, 187, 191–92; feminism and, 177–79
Eriksen, Thomas Hylland, 179
Eurovision Song Contest, 166

Feld, Steven, 4, 13n18, 77; on acoustemology, 5, 13n30, 139–41, 143n24, 189
FIFA World Cup, 151, 158, 159
Finnegan, Ruth, 3–4, 6, 128, 133
Finnish Folk Festival, 168
Fiust, Aniela, 136–41, *140*
Fjellheim, Frode, 168, 170, 181
Fjelstad, Karen, 36n17
Flierl, Johann, 89
Foucault, Michel, 122, 188

Four Palace religion (Dao Tu Phu), 18, 22–24, *23*
Friedrich, Paul, 80n25
funeral customs: Vietnamese, 32; Yolngu, 68–69, 75–76, 79n10, 102

gamba gamba (women elders), 94, 96
gamelan ensemble, 38, 41, 43, 46, 55, 60n25, 61n45; colotomic structures of, 48–50, *49*; instruments in, 47
Gammeltoft, Tine, 29, 32
Ganambarr, Manydjarri, 69–70
Garma Festival of Traditional Culture, 65
Garnett, Liz, 121–22
Garnggulkpuy, Joanne, 73
Gauriloff, Jaakko, 172
gender, 2–8, 40, 179–82, 189–90; Barong performances and, 38, 42, 45–46, 55–58, *57*; choral singing and, 93–96, 103, 109, 113–23; gamelan ensembles and, 46–47, 55; Japanese songs and, 152–53, 158; Polish mountain songs and, 127–42, *140*; Sámi singers and, 162–63, 175–82; Tyrolean notions of, 113; Vietnamese rituals and, 17–20, 25, 28–29, 34–35, 36n20, 188; Yolngu songs and, 67–71, 102, 107n40
"gendered absence," 93–96, 103
General Tran Hung Dao (spirit), 18
Gerasimova, Anfisa Ivanovna, 174
Gibson, James, 71
globalization, 187
Gold, Lisa, 47, 48
Górale people (Poland), 9, 127–42, 188, 189; during communist era, 137–39; dances of, 130–32, 135; earliest folk ensembles of, 136–38; marriage among, 133, 135–36, 141
Graff, Ola, 183n22
Green, Joyce, 181
Gumbula, Joe, 67
Guugu Yimithirr, 88–104, 188, 190, 191

"habitus" (Bourdieu), 32, 111
Hamlot, Daisy, 98, 104n2, 106n17
Hanshin earthquake (1995), 160

Hawaii, 155
Heidegger, Martin, 58, 62n65
Heimat, 109, 190, 191; musical narratives about, 110–12; sonic memories of, 112–14. *See also* "Country"
Herndon, Marcia, 2
Hinduism, on Bali, 38, 40–42, 44, 46, 55
Hirvonen, Vuokko, 171, 175–76, 180
Hjarvard, Stig, 179
Hobart, Angela, 42, 55, 56
Hopevale, Australia, 85–104, *86, 87*

identity, 9–11; gender, 8, 17–18; Górale, 127, 130, 135; Japanese, 148–50, 153–55, 160; Korean, 153–54; Quebecois, 185; Sámi, 164, 165, 174, 176, 180–82; Vietnamese, 17, 22, 25
Ijahis Idja Festival, 171–72, 174
improvisation: during during Barong performances, 51, 54; in Bavarian choir, 116, 117; in Sámi songs, 167, 179; during Vietnamese rituals, 33; in Yolngu songs, 68
Ingold, Tim, 71, 78, 114
initiation rituals: of Australian Aborigines, 95, 105n8; of Vietnamese mediums, 27–29
"interanimation," 7
Isaacs, Jennifer, 74
Iwabuchi Koichi, 158

James, Wendy, 75
Janosik songs, 130, 133
Japan, 10; annexation of Korea by, 149; dialects of, 153; emigrants from, 148, 155; enka songs of, 191; immigration policies of, 149–50; Korean rapprochement with, 151–52, 158; Korean singers in, 147–60, 187–90
Jensen, Gordon D., 61n34
joiks (Sámi vocal genre), 162–67, 171–72, 180, 181; of Pirttijärvi, 167–71, *169*
Jouste, Markko, 167
Juslin, Patrik N., 4

Kagan, Jerome, 187

Kautokeino Easter Festival, 167, 171–72
Kemp, Pamela, 98–100
Khe, Tran Van, 33
Killick, Andrew, 124n23
Kim Yonja, 10, 147–60, 187–90; early career of, 149; "kimono debut" of, 152–53, 155; vocal style of, 156–57; YouTube performances of, 160n7
kinship groups: among Sámi, 171; of Yolngu, 66–74, 78–79, 188
Kitti, Niila, 168–69
kobushi (vocal ornamentation), 147
Koga Masao, 150–51
Konieczna-Dziadoń, Bronisława, 131
Korea, 10, 148; ballads of, 150–51; emigrants from, 147–60, 187–90; Japanese annexation of, 149; Japanese rapprochement with, 151–52, 158; melodramas of, 157–58; Olympic Games in, 149, 151, 158, 159
"Korean Wave," 148–49, 157–59
Koskoff, Ellen, 2, 5, 141
Kuokkanen, Rauna, 175–77
Kvens peopls, 166
Kye Unsook, 160n4

Laestadianism, 164, 168, 176
land rights, of Australian Aborigines, 65, 71, 78, 86–87, 95, 106n21
landscape, 6–9, 25–26; Barong performances and, 38, 40, 44–45, 48–49, *49*, 60n29; emotions and, 7–8; Japanese *enka* songs and, 147–48, 159–60; Polish Górale songs and, 133–35, 139–41; Vietnamese rituals and, 24–26, 34; Yolngu songs and, 63–65, 67–79
Länsman sisters, 168
Laula-Renberg, Elsa, 177
Le Ba Cao, 33–34, 37n32
Leavitt, John, 21
len dong (spirit possession rituals), 7, 17–35, *19, 20, 22,* 187
leu'dds (Sámi vocal genre), 162, 163, 167, 171–75, 180, 181, 183n22
Lohmar, Dieter, 4

Lotus Glen Correctional Centre (Australia), 85, *97,* 97–102, *100, 101*

Magowan, Fiona, 1–11, 63–79, 92, 94, 102, 187, 201
Maiffret, Lisa, 36n17
Maori culture, 88
Marawili, Djambawa, 63
Mareeba, Australia, 85, *97*
Marienlieder (May songs), 114
marriage, 185; among Australian Aborigines, 66, 94; in Górale communities, 133, 135–36, 141
matrikin alliances, 66
Mawul Rom Mediation Project, 65
Mazowsze ensemble, 138
McIntosh, Jonathan, 7, 38–58, 187, 191, 201
McKay, Ian, 185
McPhee, Colin, 39, 46, 47
Mead, Margaret, 39, 45, 46, 57, 61n34
Meeker, Lauren, 33
melismatic style, 124n27
Milton, Kay, 114
missionaries: of Australian Aborigines, 87–89, 94–95; of Sámi people, 164, 171. *See also* Christianity
Miyako Hirumi, 150
Moisala, Pirkko, 2
Mori Yoshitaka, 151, 158
Morphy, Frances, 65
Morphy, Howard, 66, 75–76
Mosnikoff, Elias, 167
Munn, Nancy, 68
Myers, Fred, 78

naki-bushi (crying song), 147
Naylor, Phylomena, 99
Nenola, Aili, 175
Newfoundland, 185–86
ngäthi manikay (Yolngu women's "crying songs"), 67–71, 102, 107n40
ngelawang. *See* Barong performances
Ngurruwutthun, Dula, 76
Nguyen Vinh Bao, 33, 37n30
Nihon Housou Kyokai (NHK), 148, 149, 156–57

Norton, Barley, 7, 17–35, 82n40, 187, 188, 201
Noszlopy, Laura, 56
Nova Scotia, 185
Nowy Targ (Poland), *129*, *140*
Ntaria Ladies Choir of Hermannsburg (Australia), 94

Olympic Games (Seoul), 149, 151, 158, 159
omang cycle, 48–50, *49*

Palmer River Gold Rush (Australia), 89
Papua New Guinea, 143n24
Pearson, June, 90, 101
Pearson, Noel, 96
Pelinski, Ramon, 4
Phu Giay festival, 35n4
Phu songs, 25, 33–34
Picard, Michel, 39
Pine, Frances, 135
Pintupi people, 68, 78
Pirttijärvi, Ulla, 10, 162–63, 167–71, *169*, 176, 178–81
Podhale region (Poland), *129*, 130–42
Pohlner, Howard J., 90
Poland, 9, 127–42, *128*, *129*, *140*, 188, 189
Poland, Wilhelm, 91, 95, 106n16
pongchak (Korean ballad), 150
Probyn, Elspeth, 185

Quebecois, 185

Rainbow Spirit Theology, 103–4, 105n7
Ramnarine, Tina K., 10, 162–82, 188, 189, 201–2
Rangda (deity), 39–46
rap music, 166, 183n28
Rapport, Nigel, 111–12
Rodman, Margaret, 192n8
Rognli, Gjert, 171
Rosendale, George, 95, 103–4
Roth, Walter E., 105n8
Ruhland, Konrad, 118
Ryymin, Teemu, 176

Saari, Wimme, 172
Saariaho, Kaija, 180
Saastamoinen, Ilpo, 174–75, 183n22
Sadownik, Jan, 133, 143n19, 144n31
sakti (spiritual power), 40–41
Sámi people, 10, 162, *163*; cosmology of, 163–65, 168, 177; languages of, 166; religions of, 164, 168, 171, 176; songs of, 162–82, 188, 189; during World War II, 166–67, 173–74
Samuels, David, 188
Sandgren, Maria, 119
Sanger, Annette, 39
Sanila, Tiina, 10, 162–63, 171–75, *173*, 179–80, 183n23
Sápmi territories, *163*, 166, 167, 171, 180
Sara, Biret Ristin, 180–81
Sawa, Tomoe, 151
Schafer, R. Murray, 5
Schultz, Andrew, 107n32
Schwarz, George Heinrich, 89, 91, 94, 95, 105n10, 106n16
Scott, Joan W., 142nn6–7
Seeger, Charles, 13n18
Sergina, Maiya Prokop'evna, 173
shamanism, 164, 168
Shih, Shu-mei, 152
Shore, Bradd, 120
Sivertsen, Seija, 167
Siwa (deity), 42
Slovakia, *129*, 130
soccer, World Cup of, 151, 158, 159
Solarzowa, Zofia, 137
somatic expressions: of Bavarian singers, 115–18; in Górale songs, 134, 137, 139–41; in Vietnamese rituals, 29–31, 35; in Yolngu songs, 72, 75
Somby, Ánde, 164
"songscapes," 19–20, 31–32; of Barong performances, 48–49, *49*; of *enka*, 148
Stensø, Rolf Lennart, 166
Stobart, Henry, 8–9
Suarta, I Wayan, 62n53, 62n60
substance abuse: among Australian Aborigines, 96, 97; among Sámi, 162

Suryani, Luh K., 61n34
Sutton, R. Anderson, 41
Swijghuisen Reigersberg, Muriel, 79n2, 85–104, 188, 190, 191, 202
Sygietyński, Tadeusz, 144n34

Taiwan, 148
Tamisari, Franca, 77
Tanner, Väinö, 175
Tanzania, 170
Tartu Peace Treaty, 173
Tatra Mountains (Poland), 127–42, *128, 129*
tinh cam ("sentimental relations"), 32–34
Tirén, Karl, 164
Toner, Peter, 72, 80n25
Topeng dance-dramas, 48, 52, 53, 58
Trainor, Paul, 33, 37n30
Tran Van Khe, 33
Trenner, Stefan, 110, 118
Tytöt, Angelin, 168

Uduk people (Sudan), 75
Unzen volcanic eruption (Japan), 160

Valkeapää, Nils-Aslak, 165, 168, 170, 182n12
Verein (club or society), 110, 122
Vietnamese spirit possession rituals, 7, 17–35, *19, 20, 22*, 187
Vinh Bao Nguyen, 33

Walmsley-Pledl, Sara R., 8, 109–23, 189–91, 202
Wenke, Vic, 91
Wersland, Elin Margrethe, 171
White, Jerome, Jr., 160n3
William, Gordon Kalton, 107n32
Williams, Nancy, 67

Winter Sonata (Korean melodrama), 157–58
Woibo, Ella, 98
Wolf, Margery, 127–28
Wolf, Richard, 27–28
Woorabinda, Australia, *86*, 90–91, 95, 102
World Council for Indigenous Peoples, 165
World Indigenous Television Broadcasting Conference, 166
World War II: Australian Aborigines during, 89, 91, 102; Koreans during, 10, 149; Sámi during, 166–67, 173–74
Wrazen, Louise, 1–11, 127–42, 188–90, 202

Xa songs, 24, 25

Yalu' Marrngithinyaraw Group, 73
Yano, Christine R., 10, 147–60, 187–90, 202
yiḏaki (didjeridoo), 66, 67, 81n25
yin/yang, 22–24, *23*, 26, 28
Yolngu, 7–8, 63–79, 87, 187; Christianity among, 75, 92, 93; cosmology of, 64, 71–72, 78–79; dances of, 65–67, 77–79; funeral customs of, 68–69, 75–76, 79n10, 102; kinship groups of, 64–74, 78–79, 188; land rights of, *64*, 65; marriage among, 66; notion of "Country" among, 63, 66, 71–78, 79n2; paintings of, 65–66, 75–76, 79
Yoren, Mavis, 98, 99
Yunupingu, Mandawuy, 73–74

Zakopane (Poland), *129*
zbójnicki dance, 130
Zimińska-Sygietyńska, Mira, 144n34

www.ingramcontent.com/pod-product-compliance
Lightning Source LLC
Chambersburg PA
CBHW020332240426
43665CB00043B/445